Jeremy Brett

Jeremy Brett

The Man Who Became Sherlock Holmes

Terry Manners

Virgin

First published in Great Britain in 1997 by
Virgin Books
an imprint of Virgin Publishing Ltd
332 Ladbroke Grove
London W10 5AH

A catalogue record for this book is available from the British Library.

ISBN 1 85227 616 9

Typeset by TW Typesetting, Plymouth, Devon

Printed and bound by
Mackays of Chatham, Lordswood, Chatham, Kent

Contents

Acknowledgements

So many people have helped me to write this book. But to those who, for reasons best known to themselves, did not contribute to remembering Jeremy, I say thank you. You made me even more determined to tell his true story.

A special thanks, however, to Linda Pritchard.

Illustrations

At the famous Baker Street residence (*Ronald Grant*)
The obsessive Holmes (*Aquarius Library*)
Holmes takes a quiet moment with his pipe (*Aquarius Library*)
The Final Problem (*Ronald Grant*)
On the set of *The Secret of Sherlock Holmes* in 1988 (*Universal Pictorial Press*)
Jeremy rehearses through recurring bouts of ill health in 1991 (*Universal Pictorial Press*)
With Linda, early in their friendship
Mad Dogs and Englishmen, 1994 (*Kobal*)
'If God has a theatre in heaven, Jeremy will have auditioned by now' (*Universal Pictorial Press*)

Prologue

Jeremy closed his eyes. Was *he* coming – or was *he* already here? Did *he* exist? The thoughts sped through his mind like blinding flashes of light. The common was filled with ghosts that night. Jeremy could see them . . . the ghosts of Zeus and God and Holmes and the coal boy.

The common, his favourite common, was dark, very dark, as dark as the life of St Joan before the flames. The flames that took her life were as hot as the burning thoughts that sped through his mind like fleeting arrows. Where were his arrows? Ah, he could see them now . . . Zeus was flying through the air on one. It could be Zeus, or it could be *him*, that cunning, deeply black, shadowy master of disguise.

'Are you friend or foe?' Jeremy shouted to the man speeding by on the arrow. 'Are you Arthur Ignatius Conan Doyle? Answer me!' He rolled over on to his back and laughed. 'If music be the food of love, play on!'

His mind was telling the voices to go away. He would buy them champagne so that they would go away. They were speaking and shouting. Someone grabbed his arm. Was it *him*?

'His feet, God, look at his feet, they're bleeding, he's not wearing any shoes! For Christ's sake let's get him out of here!' a voice said.

They seemed to drag him up and carry him out, or was he just floating away? Where was Bunny, darling Bunny? She would rescue him in a minute. These must be her friends, these hands around him. Or were they *his* hands? Why was the sodding world pink and white?

'Dear hearts, what are you doing? Bob, where are you?' Questions, always questions, all his life questions.

Slowly, carefully, they carried the man who became Sherlock Holmes off Clapham Common to sanctuary.

Introduction

JEREMY BRETT WAS A MAN who did everything too much ... loved too much, drank too much, smoked too much, spent too much and worked too much. In the end, he suffered too much. Those who were close to him suffered too.

He will always be remembered for his television role as The Man Who Never Was – Sherlock Holmes. Just like the fictional Victorian supersleuth of Sir Arthur Conan Doyle's imagination, he too had dark, haunting secrets and a split personality. Holmes needed his Watson to steady him, care for him, and Jeremy needed his friends and family to do the same. But in the end he didn't have as many friends as he thought, for some found the illness that plagued him difficult to cope with.

Jeremy battled against the agony of manic depression and found in the brooding, fictional Holmes a friend. Holmes was a shell in which he began to live. The dark, cerebral detective sometimes took him over, and the actor and the part he played for ten years eventually became one.

It took a long time for Jeremy to realise that he was a manic depressive. It was only at the height of his fame as Holmes that the truth manifested itself. Slowly and painfully he fought his way out of the pit of despair and began to learn about the demon within him.

Strangely, Jeremy, one of Britain's finest actors, always doubted himself and believed he was The Actor Who Never Was. At the heart of his story is an illness characterised by extreme mood swings, veering from wild elation to the blackest caves of the mind, from clarity to confusion. Its victims may talk rapidly and loudly or make incessant conversation with complete strangers. Sometimes they become over-confident and launch themselves into meaningless arguments, delivering their point of view with great force. They cannot sleep and suffer disturbed eating patterns; they recklessly overspend, have grandiose plans, uninhibited sexual behaviour, become irritable and refuse to acknowledge any attempts at reason. They hallucinate, have a rapid flow of ideas – often penetrating, imaginative and perceptive. Their movements become fast, energetic and exaggerated and they have an inflated view of their own self-importance.

When a person suffers a manic depressive attack, life for those around them is like a bad dream. Friends, colleagues and family are embarrassed as the person becomes high, excitable, and talks all the time without making much sense. They often don't realise that this is a sign of illness, and the manic depressive's isolation is increased by the fact that friends can't bear to be near them when they are manic, and when they are depressed they never see anyone. After hospitalisation the victim feels uncertain about relationships, worrying that those same friends, colleagues and relatives are looking for signs of madness. That is the time when the victim discovers who his or her true friends are. And that is the time when they are most vulnerable. They may have been told that they have suffered grandiose fantasies . . . seeing themselves as Jesus, the Virgin Mary or even Superman. They may have had conversations with God. They feel guilty, ashamed of the past. This is the moment when they are at their lowest ebb . . . and this is the moment when they need the most care. Such care can only come from real carers, people who deeply love the victims of this terrible, sometimes soul-destroying illness. But the carers must safeguard their own sanity and in the end they may need counselling themselves.

Research into manic depression has found no definite cause for the illness. The victim may have inherited a genetic predisposition to the condition which is often triggered by major stress events such as bereavement or bankruptcy or hormonal changes during adolescence or childbirth. When that happens there is a chemical imbalance affecting the area of the brain responsible for moods which causes changes in feelings and behaviour. A strong yet depressive mother and a weak father can sometimes increase the risk factor. While the energy of mania can be exulting, inspirational and euphoric, the depression is like drowning. Maintaining relationships and jobs can be difficult. As Kay Jamieson says in her autobiography, *An Unquiet Mind*, 'If you have had stars at your feet and rings of planets through your hands,' then normality is rather flat. 'I am a hard act for me to follow.'

But with treatment, the majority of manic depressives live fulfilling, creative and productive lives. That was the message Jeremy Brett wanted to give to the world.

1 From the Very Beginning . . .

The childhood shows the man,
As morning shows the day

Milton, *Paradise Regained*

PETER JEREMY WILLIAM HUGGINS was born on 3 November 1933, at Berkswell near Coventry, one of four sons of distinguished army officer Lieutenant-Colonel Henry William Huggins, who was also Lord Lieutenant of Warwickshire, and his wife Elizabeth Edith Cadbury, known to her family and friends as Bunny.

Jeremy's patriotic father, Bill to his intimates, was awarded one of the first DSOs of World War I and twice won the Military Cross. He always believed that a man had responsibilities and should not shirk them. An Irish Quaker from Kilcanny, he was educated at Rugby School and Trinity College, Cambridge. He joined the Warwickshire Royal Horse Artillery and was commissioned with the rank of second lieutenant in 1912. During the war he was mentioned in despatches five times. When he left the army in 1920 he joined the family's successful brass and iron tube manufacturing business, later becoming managing director.

It was then that he met Jeremy's mother Elizabeth, a member of the Birmingham Cadbury family, heirs to the chocolate empire. Her grandmother was Miss Edith Cadbury and her grandfather the benevolent George Cadbury, the man mainly responsible for establishing the world-famous company. The moment he saw her, the war hero was swept off his feet. The dazzling young socialite with long black hair had a warmth he had never found in a woman before. He fell in love that first night at a Quaker meeting house in Birmingham. Over the next few months their courtship was conducted in a manner appropriate to the circles they moved in. Both of them were strong, independent people but both of them had a deep capacity for kindness. They became friends and then lovers. In some ways it was a strange relationship – a professional soldier courting a woman from a family with pacifist principles whose only battle was social reform.

Elizabeth's grandfather George was the son of the Quaker John Cadbury, a tea and coffee merchant based in Bull Street, Birmingham. George and his brother John took over the business and went on to establish Bournville, the model 'company' village centred around the factory. Bourn was a local name and 'ville' was taken from the French – in the late nineteenth century most good chocolate came from France, so the name was a marketing device. Twice-married George had eleven children, and for a while the business empire was something of a dynasty.

George was also well known for his work in political and philanthropic causes. The Quakers had a lot going for them. But what always irritated Jeremy later in life was the fact that many people did not seem to realise the significance of the movement's place in the growing pains of their country. They may have read that William Penn founded a new community in America and remembered that Elizabeth Fry and William Tuke were prison and mental health reformers, or that Joseph Sturge agitated against slavery, but even as a young boy Jeremy would often have to remind people of other Quakers who transformed Britain into an industrial society in the eighteenth and nineteenth centuries . . . the Darbys of Coalbrookdale, fathers of the iron industry; Sampson Lloyd of Birmingham who founded Lloyds Bank; the Hanburys who made tinplate in Wales; and the Pease family who created Middlesbrough.

Bill and Elizabeth had a good start. On their marriage they moved into Holly Lodge, Duggins Lane, Berkswell, a sprawling mansion that was a gift from the groom's family.

They lived an active life. Bill, a keen horseman, rode with the local hunt and served as president of the Balsall and Berkswell Institute. Elizabeth, a fine archer, became president of the Berkswell Women's Institute and was a passionate believer in the Red Cross.

In 1929, having produced their first three sons, John,

Michael and Patrick, Bill and Elizabeth moved to Berkswell Grange, a seventeenth-century timber and brick manor house in nearby Truggist Lane, with plans for an even bigger family. The two-storey house, once owned by a brickmaker, covered with flowering wisteria and surrounded by rolling green lawns, was a child's dream. There were the lawns to play on, out-houses to hide in and trees to climb.

When Jeremy was born, Bill had a huge nursery built on the west side of the house. It was later to become a snooker room where the boys would spend hours on the green baize. Over the years their parents made many more additions to their home – tennis and squash courts, new stables, a dovecote and even an air-raid shelter as World War II loomed. It was a world of horses and dogs, dinner parties and fun. When Jeremy was three his father had a drawing-room extension built, and while the builders were there he pressed his toddler son's podgy little hand into the still-wet cement of the outer brickwork. The imprint is there to this day.

Jeremy was an energetic little boy, always on the move. He hardly seemed to sleep and always wanted to be the centre of attention. He was into everything and anything, sticking his fingers into Cook's cake mix, emptying his mother's cupboards and dressing up in his brothers' clothes.

Jeremy's mother created a beautiful terraced garden at the Grange, which was the envy of all her neighbours. She was everyone's friend – even tramps and gypsies. She was outgoing and generous and the door of her home was always open. In the early years Jeremy's father was quite taken with her freedom of spirit and generosity, but as the years went on he became frustrated with it. His gentle reprimands were to no avail. Bunny simply couldn't help herself. She had a deep and genuine interest in people, with a bottomless capacity for friendship and seemingly a bottomless purse. For her, people always came first. Tramps would leave secret signs to tell their fellow travellers that the Grange was a friendly and generous home. Elizabeth would welcome them, feed them, and let them bathe, wash and dry their clothes. Sometimes the 'Lady of the Manor' would even give them new ones . . . or her husband's cast-offs. Bill was forever rummaging around looking for an old pair of trousers or shirt he was sure he had in the wardrobe. Often he would arrive home to find a gypsy encampment with a huge steaming cauldron in the walled courtyard. When he walked off in a huff to the saddle room he would be confronted with a sea of washing lines where the travellers had hung their shirts, frocks and underwear to dry. Elizabeth would tell him that her travelling friends would pay their way by doing some gardening . . . but the truth was they did little. Most of the time they just sat around enthralling Jeremy with their wonderful tales of the road. Michael, later to become a painter, would sketch them as they arrived.

Bunny was incapable of being unkind and her kindness was never forgotten. One middle-aged traveller, John Dixon, always wanted to repay the beautiful mistress of Berkswell Grange – but knew in his heart he would never be able to. When he died after being hit by a car, police found a note in his pocket bequeathing all his worldly goods to her, a little bag with his keepsakes – an old watch, a scarf and a picture or two. Elizabeth was deeply touched, and distressed by his death. It was only then that Jeremy's brothers discovered from the police that their mother had made an arrangement with the bank so that John could collect half a crown whenever he was hungry.

This was a sign of the caring Cadburys. Bunny's kindness was instilled in her from the Quaker family line, and that streak in her character was passed on to Jeremy, as time would prove. Bunny seemed to understand her youngest son's passions and would never try to limit his dreams. She had a wonderfully sensitive knack of being able to tell the difference between a phase he was going through and a more serious commitment. But even the phases were tolerated with kindness and imagination. Jeremy had strong and absolute passions. If he needed a pony he would have to have one. If he had to go to the tuck shop, nothing would stop him. If he wanted to sit up all night nursing a sick rabbit, he would.

As a boy Jeremy was spellbound by the wonderfully elegant parties his parents hosted at the Grange. He would peep into the ballroom and watch the women glide about in satin or peacock-blue breeches and white wigs. His uncle, Dr Leslie Huggins, director of music at Stowe School, was master of ceremonies and used to play the grand piano at the far end of the hall. Forty people would arrive for dinner and dancing. No one got any sleep because the dancing finished so late that breakfast was served to the guests before they left.

One of Jeremy's favourite haunts at this time was the local bakery run by Mr Elson. The smell of hot buns and freshly baked bread was irresistible and Jeremy would spend hours in the kitchen. His most memorable moment was when Mr Elson allowed him to put a well-fingered, grubby piece of dough into the oven to cook. The result – a hot but uneatable bread roll!

In the dark days of 1939, as the war clouds gathered over Europe, Jeremy's father was asked by the War Office to raise a regiment. Bunny and the boys were worried but threw themselves into supporting him. Bill had left the army in 1920 with the rank of major but was now promoted to lieutenant-colonel. Early that spring he placed advertisements in local newspapers and an information kiosk was manned near the town hall in Birmingham. In two days more than 600 volunteers, from every walk of life, had been recruited. They met twice a week, on Mondays and Thursdays, at the rear of the British Legion headquarters in Solihull. At first, until they were issued with proper uniforms and weapons, they had to parade and drill with brooms. Five-year-old Jeremy was taken along one day and watched them stamp up and down outside the Nissen huts, bumping into each other and dropping their sticks as they tried to execute an 'about-turn'.

By early summer the 120th Field Regiment, Royal Artillery, was officially formed. The adjutant was Arthur Chamberlain, nephew of Prime Minister Neville Chamberlain. The colonel's brother, Dr Leslie Huggins, from Stowe School, was Officer Commanding 270 Battery.

Jeremy's father was liked by his men and respected as an officer who never asked anyone to do anything he wouldn't do himself. Once he charged up a steep hill on a motor-cycle. When he returned he announced: 'There you are, if I can do it, you bloody well can!'

In August that year the regiment went to the territorial army camp at Dalditch, near Budleigh Salterton, Devon, and when war was declared they were incorporated into the regular army.

They were the victims of abject military poverty. The new regiment had merely a few obsolete guns from some earlier British Army conflict and they were mobile only because they had managed to borrow some lorries from a brewery. By stealth and cunning they later miraculously acquired a fleet of ex-taxi cabs – battered Ford V8s. But their greatest coup was getting their hands on 150 Hercules bicycles.

Colonel Huggins commanded the 120th Field Regiment from 1939 until 1942 when he was posted to the 35th Signal Training Regiment, Royal Artillery, at Rhyl, North Wales. The men of the 120th were then dispersed and served their country with honour on three continents.

Jeremy would always have fond memories of the Grange during the war years – throwing wet mud at cloth-capped gardener Tom Houghton; sneaking into the kitchen to spirit away cook Lily Knight's pies; bouncing on the trampoline in the circus tent set up on nearby Balsall Common and listening to bedtime stories from his much-loved nanny, Ellen Clifford, who was to be with the family for 53 years.

There were nursery teas inside the Grange and on the lawns, and riding afternoons on his beloved donkeys from Ireland – Betsy and Mahal. Later came his first pony . . . Babs. Jeremy became so skilled on her that he rode her up the stairs to his bedroom just to annoy Nanny Clifford. She would chase them out of the house, scooping up behind Babs who would be fertilising the carpet. On other occasions he would ride over neighbours' lawns until he was shouted at. These were the early beginnings of the outrageous streak that was to be the hallmark of the boy who would one day become Sherlock Holmes. Everything Jeremy did was to extremes, right down to cutting his short trousers with a pair of Cook's scissors one morning because he thought they were too long.

Jeremy was taught to ride by Frank Horn, a favourite 'uncle' to all the local children. Skinner Horn was one of the North Warwickshire Hunt's most ardent supporters and instilled in

Jeremy a love for the chase. He had a stables at nearby Honiley where Jeremy would spend hours galloping across the fields. One morning Jeremy and a friend raced their ponies to a hedge near the railway line and waited for hours to catch a glimpse of the King and Queen on the royal train.

Jeremy's love of animals was obvious to everyone. His passion for them was absolute and he would treat them like humans, getting down on all fours to speak to dogs, whispering in the ears of horses and tenderly stroking the tiniest frog held in the palm of his hand. He always felt at one with the animal kingdom and was soon known in the county as a fine horseman, entering gymkhanas and winning prizes.

Jeremy always believed that his affinity with animals evolved out of his loneliness. His brothers were off doing their own thing, Bunny was always busy helping others, and his father was with the army, winning the war. He also suffered a speech impediment which some of the children he played with laughed at. He found it difficult to sound his Rs and Ss and embarrassment often made him withdraw into himself.

Jeremy would always bounce back, even if he did sometimes feel isolated, for he was filled with a powerful feeling of well-being. Whenever he had money he would treat others to something in the village tuck shop. It comforted him. A bar of Cadbury's chocolate, a gob-stopper, chewing gum – anything he had enough pocket money to buy he would give away. Hours afterwards he would feel embarrassed and strangely guilty about it, as if he were buying friendship. His father would lecture him about the value of money time and again. But then his mother would tell him to leave the boy alone.

Jeremy listened to the roar of the planes overhead as Bunny went to check the blackout curtains. It was 14 November 1940, a date that would stay firmly entrenched in the family's memory forever.

His mother peeped out at the night sky for a moment, watching the endless sweeps of the searchlights. They could just hear the sirens and the dull thudding of bombs.

'It's Coventry again,' she said. 'Those poor people.'

Jeremy was a little scared but he thought it was exciting. Then Cook came in and broke the news to them.

'They've been dropping incendiary bombs so that even the firemen are forced to take shelter,' she said. 'Harold Tomkins from the Civil Defence is in the kitchen. He says there are hundreds of fires all over the city. The Rover factory is burning and so is the Midland Bank in the High Street. He's heard that the Central Fire Station has been hit too, even the cathedral.'

'Stay there with Jeremy for a moment,' said Bunny.

She went out into the night air and on to the drive looking towards Coventry. The heavens were ablaze. The city was ringed with parachute flares and spotlights and flames roared skyward, adding to the glare which was spreading a crimson dome over the whole area. The constant drone of heavy bombers and the banging of anti-aircraft guns told her this was no ordinary raid. She went back inside, feeling guilty that she was escaping the mayhem. 'I wonder how many people will die this evening?' she said to Cook.

All night she and Jeremy lay awake side by side in her bedroom, listening to the relentless drone of the Luftwaffe's bombers, wondering when they would go. Bunny prayed for daylight, when the city would surely be reprieved.

When dawn broke, it was quiet and drizzling and Jeremy was asleep. But Bunny was gone, weaving her way in her little Austin car through the heavy armour and lorries pouring into the devastated city.

What she saw when she finally arrived profoundly affected her. She walked the streets in the damp, fine rain, and was always to remember the thick, smoky-grey mist that seemed to cling to her. Men and women were crawling out of their shelters, looking for their friends. Bunny couldn't believe her eyes as she surveyed the ruins. Hardly a building remained intact and it was impossible to see where the central streets she knew so well had been. Fires were still raging in every direction and from time to time she heard the crash of a falling window or wall. She was dismayed to see the cathedral without pillars or a roof. It was impossible to think of it as the building she had often sung in. None the less, the long, heaped-up piles of rubble seemed to retain a degree of beauty all of their own, as though God were trying to save something from the devastation for people to believe in, a sort of symbol of hope.

The bombing of Coventry touched the hearts of the nation. The smouldering cathedral was a constant reminder to the proud city of the evil that had blown their way. But dignitaries were never to forget the wonderful arrangement of flowers they found on the altar the next day as they walked through the rubble. Many remarked on it, but it was not until after Bunny's death that Jeremy and his brothers discovered that the beautiful bouquet had been placed at the foot of the cross by their own mother.

She had vowed then to do even more to help others.

The sound of a spluttering engine grew louder. Jeremy looked out of the bedroom window down at the drive. A family were arriving on a motor-bike and sidecar. The Westons had fled Coventry and were looking for somewhere to stay. As always, the Florence Nightingale of Berkswell was standing at the door with a smile. Bunny welcomed them in and introduced them to her youngest son. Within a week, 42 members of the extended family had arrived, taking over the staff sitting room. The women and children slept in the ballroom and the men slept in the stable and saddle room. For Jeremy, now seven, it was a fantastic adventure. At last he had lots of children to play with and they all wanted to live at the Grange, although he didn't really understand why. Weren't all children happy, living in their houses with their fathers and mothers? Luckily the Grange had a large kitchen and its own electricity supply and water pump, so it was self-contained and could accommodate the army of guests with ease. Jeremy romped in the hay with his new friends and showed them the quickest way to climb the old oak tree at the end of the drive.

The Westons weren't the only people to benefit from Bunny's good nature. The Women's Institute members were able to use the specially extended kitchen to make jams and other foods for the war effort and Jeremy was never short of sausages – filled with gristle, jam and bread. But most of all he loved to sneak out with a jar of Cook's home-made plum jam and scoop out the contents with his fingers.

Jeremy's school life started at home under the guidance of a stern but fair lady named Miss Kenderdine. She was a Coventry evacuee who moved her school to the nursery at the Grange, then later to a house at Balsall Common, home of the visiting circuses and village fêtes. It was here that Jeremy began to display the first painful signs of dyslexia. He couldn't keep up with the other children in the class and so became mischievous and inattentive. His hyperactive nature was difficult to handle. Miss Kenderdine noticed that he was transposing letters in his written work and found it difficult, sometimes even impossible, to spell words aloud. His memory skills in his English lessons were often appalling. Things just did not seem to sink in. Dyslexia was almost unheard of at this time and some teachers believed that children who had difficulty in understanding speech were unintelligent or slow. At first it was thought that Jeremy was deaf – but tests showed that his hearing was perfect. When the condition was finally diagnosed his mother read to him at home alone in his bedroom and he began to pick up, even though he would still struggle to write words such as 'necessary', labouring over where the Es and Ss should go. The problem would remain with him all his life.

Even at this time he was aware of his prettiness and the fact that some of the other boys stared at him a lot. He felt strangely drawn towards them and he didn't know why. The innocence of his childhood was shattered one morning by the clattering wheels of a coal barrow.

When Jeremy heard the noise for the first time, he wondered what it was. He threw back the blankets on his bed and ran to the window in his pyjamas. Below was a young coal boy making his way across the drive. Without another thought Jeremy rushed down the stairs and out of the house, finally catching up with the lad. They were inextricably bonded from that moment on. Each week, Jeremy would run out of the house to the coal shed, shouting excitedly to his new friend, who would lift him up and sit him in the barrow, managing somehow to keep the gritty black dust off the little Huggins.

Jeremy would ride all the way to the shed, shrieking with joy. It was a marvellous game. The shed was an old horse stall, with two panelled wooden doors. The coal boy's job was to shovel the coal into the barrow and cart it to the coal hole at the house. But one morning he closed one of the doors and invented a new game, undoing the top button of Jeremy's shorts under his fancy little top. He asked the innocent three-year-old if he would like to play with his 'lighthouse'. Jeremy wasn't frightened. It was an adventure in his innocent mind. He didn't know any better. But the once-a-week game was to haunt his conscience . . . and his relationships forever. The damage was done.

Jeremy's robust, sometimes hot-tempered father had given him a love for the outdoor life . . . archery, swimming, tennis and riding to hounds. Archery was his favourite sport and he admired his mother for her strength and bowmanship. He was blooded at eight – subjected to the custom of initiating a child into the hunt by smearing his face with the blood- and excrement-stained severed tail of a fox. But Jeremy had a softer side. He loved village life and was always ready to volunteer for the local plays, mostly organised by Mrs Hadley, who ran the local café. One year he appeared in a nativity play and later found himself standing in the audience as the collection plate came round. As he never carried any money, Jeremy gave his best cap to baby Jesus on the spur of the moment.

The lawns of the Grange in the summer were a marvellous venue for the little theatre productions and Jeremy was always anxious to get a part in them. One blistering hot summer's day he was desperate to be included in a production featuring the four and twenty blackbirds baked in a pie. He was crestfallen to discover, however, that there were not enough blackbird costumes to go around, but was still determined to get on stage. He finally appeared before his mother and father, who were sitting gamely in the audience, as a gnome. It didn't bother him; he didn't feel shy. He felt like a star among the blackbirds in a part he had made all his own. That same year he made his cabaret debut as Little Boy Blue in a concert at Bournville.

George Cadbury had been deeply moved by the ill-health and suffering of the children in the poor areas of Birmingham. As in most large towns and cities in Victorian times, the slum areas were made up of back-to-back houses with small living/kitchen areas opening directly on to the street. They had just one bedroom where most of the family slept and an attic with a low ceiling. Such houses, built in double rows, had poor ventilation and limited daylight. There was also a complete lack of washing and sanitary facilities. The houses were often behind shops, with factories and slaughterhouses crowded amongst them. The atmosphere was heavily polluted and the gutters in a putrid state, reeking with the contents of water closets. Such deprivation led to crime and other social problems. Nearly one quarter of Birmingham's population lived in undrained streets, many of which were unpaved and turned into quagmires when it rained. Most of the city's water supply came from wells or water carts and was sold by the gallon. But it was often so dirty that it could only be used for washing and scouring. In this environment children died fast. There were more bugs than babies. George and his brother Richard felt strongly that the industrial worker should enjoy the good clean air of the country without being separated from the workplace. Their business, in Bridge Street, Birmingham, had expanded, and with 2,000 workers they needed more space.

On 18 June 1878 they bought fourteen acres of land between the villages of Stirchley, King's Norton and Selly Oak, about four miles south of the city. Bournville was born on sloping meadowland with a trout stream and a solitary building, Bournbrook Cottage, which was pulled down. The only thing left was an old pear tree which grew in the garden and still stands outside the company's reception area. Jeremy always wanted to climb it, but of course was never allowed.

By 1899 the original area of the factory buildings had trebled, and over the following years the results of the Cadburys' vision were plain to see. The company was the first in Britain to introduce the five-and-a-half-day working week and pioneered shutdowns on bank holidays. A swimming pool was opened, young employees were encouraged to play games, there were works outings and education schemes, bonuses for punctuality, medical and dental departments – and a pension fund started with a capital gift from the chocolate brothers. Trade unions were encouraged – but had limited appeal because of the excellent working conditions.

Jeremy's great-grandfather George was a housing reformer deeply interested in improving people's lives by providing a community of decent homes for working men and their families. The housing estate was open to anyone who wanted to live there – not just to Cadbury employees. His homes featured a parlour, living room, scullery with WC and a coal house on the ground floor, with three bedrooms on the first. Some people argued that his rows of houses were dreary and monotonous – but there was no doubt that living standards were greatly improved and people flocked to live in them.

By the time Jeremy arrived to star as Little Boy Blue, Bournville covered more than 1,000 acres. As they drove through the streets his mother would point out various places of interest and talk about some of the local families she had known as a little girl. That afternoon his cabaret debut was seen by Cadburys and workers alike.

Every Boxing Day as many as 100 Cadburys assembled at Winds Point in the Malvern Hills, a house sold to George Cadbury by the singer Jenny Lind, affectionately nicknamed 'The Swedish Nightingale'. But there was little talk of chocolate or cocoa. Instead it was a time for Christmas celebration and fun. Elizabeth took Jeremy once, and he was always to remember the giant Christmas tree in the hallway with its coloured bells and candles – and of course the endless supplies of Cadbury's milk chocolate.

When the war was finally over, Jeremy's father returned home and the Grange was full of noise and laughter again. Jeremy, now eleven, would join his mother on her missions of mercy. Taxi drivers would pick them up and drive them to a local squatters' camp where Bunny would collect all the children and take them home for a bath. Then they would all be dressed and fed before being driven back spick and span. Jeremy wondered how anyone could be as kind as his mother.

When a neighbour told her that her soldier son was somewhere in Germany suffering from polio, Bunny used all her charm and army connections to get a telephone call through to his commander so that mother and son could be reunited.

Jeremy was forever a dreamer . . . and the dream that now consumed him was Hollywood. He loved going to 'the pictures'. Four times a week he would cycle to the little Cameo Cinema in Berkswell Road near his home, paying one shilling for a seat. The film that moved him most was *Wuthering Heights*, starring Laurence Olivier. The romance between Heathcliff and Cathy left him in tears and he sobbed all the way home. He imagined himself as Olivier, the poor young stable lad who was being eaten away by love. Jeremy desperately wanted to have that effect on people, that 'on-screen' power to touch people's hearts. He was sure that one day he would. From that moment on he would sit up at night telling Bunny over and over again how he would one day be a star.

Bunny was his confidante – the one person he would always take notice of. She would assure him: 'I don't want you to do anything until you absolutely can't help it, or you are sure you want to do it.'

Often in those years his father would return home and shout at her: 'For God's sake, get these boys going!'

'I told you before, Bill, not until they know what they want!' she would shout back.

By now the rows between them were growing more frequent and Jeremy began to wonder if his parents' marriage would last. His father was becoming increasingly frustrated with Bunny's generous ways. She was always off doing 'good works' somewhere and he never seemed to see her. She hated arguments and began to suffer from depression, disappearing in the car for whole days.

Jeremy mostly enjoyed life at his smart and strict Worcestershire prep school Abberley Hall, but he didn't show much academic promise. His mother took heart in the fact that he often shone at history, however, while his father was comforted to learn that he was something of a sporting fanatic. They both noticed that girls didn't really interest him, but then he was too young for such things.

Jeremy left Abberley Hall to follow his three brothers to Eton, where he shone as a boy soprano in the choir. He didn't really know what he was doing at this most revered of British institutions as he never really believed his father had any real money to speak of. He always seemed to think of his father on a horse and not behind his desk at Tube Investments.

He never forgot his first night at Eton. The four walls of his room seemed so close after the huge, airy spaces of the Grange, and the nylon sheets felt sticky and unpleasant. He was used to the starched crispness of laundered cotton. He found it even more difficult than usual to fall comfortably asleep. On the few occasions his eyes did close those first few nights, he found himself back at home, riding Babs, romping with his dog Mr Binks or cycling to the pictures. Often he would wake up in a pool of sweat the sheets had failed to absorb. He knew then that he would never like Eton.

It didn't take Jeremy's tutors long to realise that he was not a great academic achiever, and he became legendary for his histrionics. His dyslexia was a drawback, and although he took comfort in the fact that Albert Einstein, Leonardo da Vinci and Franklin Roosevelt had suffered from the same condition, he just couldn't be bothered to work twice as hard as the other boys to catch up. For a long time he felt terribly adrift. He found Eton a culture shock. Twenty-eight houses, nearly 1,200 boys, 80 or 90 masters – it was a huge community for the boy from the Black Country, a boy whose favourite pastime was talking to horses and dogs. Eton seemed to have a social world all of its own, full of compartments – the comfortable life of the library and the tea table; boys sauntering arm in arm; the Pop rooms; the Ascham Society; the masters' boathouse; the dinner parties; sponge-bag trousers; coloured waistcoats; rolled umbrellas; black braid on blue coats; top hats and fancy shirts. Jeremy found it a strain to be dressed constantly in the uniform of striped trousers and black coat, and told his mother that he felt lost in the quagmire of little black people. On the face of it, Eton didn't seem a tough world but it was, and he realised that he was rather wet and spoilt. He was saved from bullying only by his strong physique and because he was an excellent listener – concerned, calm, fun, sincere, unshockable. He liked the other boys to feel he took them seriously in their hour of need. He truly cared about them as people and not just as social products on the upper-class conveyor belt to success. But there were many who still hurt him to the core by teasing him for his speech impediment, which grew worse when he was nervous. It was so bad that when he became upset he had to struggle to form a sentence. Much to his despair, because of this he was never asked to take part in any of the school drama productions. But he never abandoned his dream of being the new Laurence Olivier, even though he felt crushed at being called Jewemy or Buggins, Juggins and, more frequently, Muggins. But what hurt him most was the nickname 'The Tart of Eton', bestowed because he sang like a girl and had pretty-boy looks.

It was at this time that he suddenly became aware that he was giving out the wrong signals to some of the other boys. Jeremy loved flattery and assumed that most of the looks and smiles were because of his singing voice. He received lots of fan mail and even had a photograph taken for one boy who requested it. But then it dawned on him that his friends' admiration went further than mere friendship. He began to experiment sexually with one or two of the other boys but then Jeremy began to worry that he was unnatural. He felt guilty. He desperately wanted to be a real man. The dark days of the sexual abuse he had suffered in the coal shed were closing in on him.

To make himself feel better he developed an imaginary love affair with the actress Jean Simmons, whom he saw one afternoon in the David Lean film *Great Expectations*. He even wrote to her confessing his love – and she sent him back a card which he was to cherish all his life.

Jeremy adored the Lower Chapel at Eton, with its simple stonework, fine glass and war memorial tapestries. When he was in a muddle with his work and the outlook appeared bleak, the 20 minutes of service in the morning were a comfort. He imagined that he left all his worries behind in the antechapel along with his hat. He loved the potent magic of Sunday service. The vicar was to him a romantic figure, like a sorcerer, to be feared and respected. He felt somehow secure there, loved in a pure way. He belonged to God or some kind of deity who was watching over him. The music master, Dr Sydney Watson, had picked him out to sing the solos.

One afternoon thirteen-year-old Jeremy stood staring at the stained-glass windows and the ornate wood carvings of the altar. He felt a sort of inner peace standing there like an angel in his ruff. It was an overwhelming feeling of contentment that he hadn't felt for a long time, not since the first morning he was allowed to ride alone across the fields near his Warwickshire home on Babs, the pony his father had bought him. He remembered a feeling of complete euphoria as he sat in the saddle, watching the sun go down.

Today the dying sunlight flicked at the altar and little specks of white burst on the sombre brown wood. Choirmaster Watson ushered the 32 saintly looking boys nearer the window for evensong in front of an audience of 500 other boys. He eyed the histrionic young man with the beautiful voice and hoped he wouldn't try to be too clever. Jeremy Huggins was so unpredictable. His saving grace was that he could sing like an angel.

Jeremy loved music. His awareness of the sounds of the organ was intense. It was as if each individual note was exquisitely poignant. The music would be of such piercing beauty and clarity that even at such a young age he was sometimes moved to tears by it.

He suddenly caught choirmaster Watson's gaze and looked away. His mind wandered to the diving competition the next day which had been bulletined on Spottiswoode's Window, the noticeboard that heralded everything from a lost pocket-book to a water polo match. He wondered which of the older boys would win it. Perhaps Evans or Kent-Lemon. One day, though, he would take the title. There was no doubt about it. He had an overwhelming feeling of destiny about it. He was one hell of a good swimmer, agile, athletic. He was the best. And when that day finally came they would never call him Jewemy, Muggins or Buggins again, even if he still had a lisp.

The shaft of sunlight suddenly lit up a spot in front of him a few feet away and he quickly moved into it, believing it was meant for him. It was a sign, a message from on high. He felt honoured as, quietly and with a smile, he began to sing. 'And ye now therefore have sorrow, but I will see you again, and your heart shall rejoice . . .'

One morning, a few years later, no longer a soprano, Jeremy found himself in a field overlooking the muddy waters of the Thames in the shadow of the Eton spires. There was no one around because Sunday was a day of rest at the school; no games were played and the river was out of bounds. That was good; he wanted to be alone. The afternoon had brought a horde of visitors – parents and old boys from Oxford or Sandhurst, others in charabancs as if on a seaside outing. Some of the boys amused themselves by showing foreigners around the school and receiving sixpence for their trouble. But now it was quiet. The early signs of summer were all around him . . . meadow buttercups and daisies, new, shiny, fresh green leaves, and warm yet fading orange sunlight. There was a feeling of freshness and purpose in him as he marched on down to the riverbank, imagining he was the only person alive on planet Earth, kicking at the tufts of grass and spinning around and around with his hands in his pockets. He stood for a moment staring at the murky waters that none the less seemed to sparkle in the sun's rays. Soon he and the water would be one. No one could beat him in the diving competition, he felt sure of that, as sure as he had been three years ago when God's finger of sunlight had pointed at him in the chapel at Evensong. His lean, well-muscled body would pierce the river like a dart. He would be a legend. But then he always knew he would be famous; he had told his mother that at the age of three.

He lit a Woodbine cigarette and inhaled the smoke deeply. It made him feel good as he looked over his shoulder to see if anyone was watching. If a master saw him he would be 'busted' again, for law-breaking. If only his mother could see him now. Bunny, his dear, kind mother. He had started smoking at around the same time as he had first told her he would be famous. She had given him a cigarette in the hope that it would put him off the habit, but it had had the opposite effect. There was a kind of release in sucking down the thick, white smoke, and it made him feel good. Just opening up the packet, lighting the tobacco stick and inhaling was a ritual as rich in relaxation and spiritual awareness as the Chinese tea ceremony. He liked rituals. Lighting a cigarette was sophistication personified, something rebellious, and he wanted to be rebellious, he wanted to be noticed. The world would notice him soon, he knew that. Perhaps secretly he wanted to be caught smoking. Drinking was the same, although he never really liked beer with his beef at the school's traditional Sunday lunch. He vowed to himself that he would always be a fine-wine man. Or champagne. Why not? He would always be able to afford such little luxuries, he was sure of it.

Jeremy blew smoke rings into the air and looked down at the water. There was something different about it that evening. A green mass of flotsam floated by the crumbling jetty and he turned away, not wanting to think about jumping into it. Still, ducks lived in the nearby reeds and he had caught fish there in little nets suspended from the ends of bamboo canes, so the river couldn't be poisonous, he reasoned. His heart was gladdened to see several perch hugging the riverbank a little further along. Anyway, his body was just an instrument. It was strong and healthy and he was in control of his destiny. The only thing he cared about was winning. How he wished he could just dive into the clean water of his swimming pool at home. But the only water to plunge into at Eton was the murky Thames, where many a lower boy or wet-bob oarsman had died throughout the school's history.

The sun seemed to die on him and he felt the need to bring it back. He looked around to see if anyone was watching and then launched himself into a ritual ballet, waving his arms at the sky in a sort of gymnastic dance. It worked and the sun seemed to hold its glow for a moment. He threw himself on to the ground, lying on his back, staring at the universe and all its mysteries. Someone out there was watching him, guiding him, he felt that. He could feel himself gliding, flying, now and again lurching through cloud banks, past stars and across fields of ice crystals. He could see the plains of Mars in his mind's eye, and the hot, huge fireballs of the sun.

The day was fading to dusk and he glided back to earth for forthcoming fame. He sighed, eased himself up and walked back towards his rooms. But he was in no hurry. He hated Eton, the regimentation of it, always had. One master had told him he was excessively dramatic about everything. But didn't they realise he was different? His schedule at school was demanding but he managed to juggle it, bullshit his way through. He particularly disliked studying the term's set book, a collection of Sherlock Holmes stories. He had no interest in the great detective and had come to the conclusion that since Sir Arthur Conan Doyle's creation was a terrible know-all, Doyle probably was too. He much preferred Dr Watson. In any case, the stories did nothing for him. What was the point of studying Holmes? Shakespeare he could understand, but not Doyle. Shakespeare recreated history – Richard III, Henry V and others – not fictional, boring detectives in funny hats. Ah well, Jane Austen was next, perhaps she would be more interesting. He hoped so. But no one could be as interesting as his fictional hero Biggles.

As he grew weary he wandered back across the field into the old cemetery, reading the names and wording on the fading, weather-beaten gravestones. He wanted to dance on them and bring the bodies back to life but he couldn't be bothered. He didn't want to party with the world any more. He felt strangely dark and he didn't know why. He strolled slowly around Cloisters, stopping here and there to take in the memorial tablets of those killed in the war – men of the Grenadier Guards and the Rifle Brigade. His father would have been proud of him, remembering war heroes, paying his respects to young soldiers. Jeremy's own favourite was the American boy 'of infinite daring' who was killed because he 'returned to fight for the love of Eton'. One day he would fall in love with an American boy who would remind him of that inscription. But then he would love an American woman too, and she would capture his heart more fully than any other person in his life.

Jeremy felt a sense of unease wash over him as he shut the door to his rooms. The feeling of isolation and love of solitude that were to haunt him later in life perhaps began at Eton. The aim of the school was to instil in its boys independence and self-confidence. From the moment a boy walked through its doors he found himself suddenly grown up, with a room of his own. This was not just to ensure physical privacy, but privacy of mind as well – a mental room to himself, where his tastes, thoughts and interests were free to develop along their own lines. Jeremy's thoughts were focused on the feeling that he had been chosen, chosen to stand in the spotlight.

They stood watching him. He liked that. There must have been about 100 boys on the riverbank. The greasy Thames slapped against the wooden jetty. He pledged to himself that he would show them now. They could stuff their academically qualified minds . . . he would be a sporting hero. He threw his perfectly formed sixteen-year-old body into the air and kept it muscularly straight as he hit the water, squeezing his eyes tight as he felt the muddiness surround him and rush into his ears. He prayed he would hold his breath long enough to come to the surface and breathe in the clean Windsor air. When he did emerge he could hear the cheering from the bank and he waved his hand, swallowing some of the gritty water swilling around in his mouth. He had won their votes and the first heat . . . and he knew that he would win every other.

Time and again he threw himself into the murky water and time and again he came up the winner in the opinion of the small panel of voters on the riverbank. Each time he coughed louder, spitting the mud out of his mouth and wiping it from his ears. It was all worth it. Even the defeated challengers from an hour ago were cheering him on. He had more energy than any of them. Of course he knew that, but they had to know that too.

Hours later he was standing in the spotlight of the last dying rays of the early evening sun as people slapped him on his wet and aching back. Jeremy was Eton's champion diver . . . but as his life was always to prove, it would be a hollow defeat.

A few days later his feet swelled up, boils appeared on his ears and his forehead began to pour with sweat. In one blinding moment, his legs went from under him and he passed out.

* * *

The room was floating. No, not floating, sinking. There were shapes, moving about. Pink and red and white and blue shapes. Then there was an archer's bow and a horse and a swaying tree. And his dog Mr Binks.

Something touched his brow. It was soft, a soft pink hand that wouldn't go away. He thought he saw his mother's face for a moment, then he closed his eyes and suddenly saw water, grey muddy water. He felt it splashing over him. His hair was dripping wet and he was shouting, laughing, choking. There was pain – in his ear, or was it in his head?

'For God's sake, can't we do anything?' his mother shouted at the doctor standing beside her, mopping her son's brow with a wet flannel.

'We've done all we can, Bunny, it is up to the Almighty now, but he's a strong boy, agile and fit. At sixteen he has age on his side.'

She kept stroking her son's forehead, pushing the sweat back into his hair. The boils in his ears made her wince. 'He must be in so much pain,' she said.

The doctor didn't answer, just nodded as he watched Jeremy toss and turn, the sweat trickling down his inflamed cheeks. The X-ray machine had shown that his heart was twice the normal size. He went to the window and looked down at the tennis court. The large figure of the boy's war hero father was puffing and blowing as he played against one of his other three sons. Mr Binks, Jeremy's little Jack Russell, was barking in the background. They were lucky, all four of the boys. They were spoilt rotten. They had gardens to run in, horses to ride, real bows and arrows to shoot with, a pool to swim in, squash and tennis courts, freedom, everything that a boy could possibly want when growing up. The doctor sighed and looked back at his patient. In his heart he knew that the lad would pull through, but the legacy of rheumatic fever would probably haunt him for the rest of his life. He knew that recurrences of the acute illness could occur over a period of years. Jeremy would probably suffer long-term consequences, including damage to his heart valves, maybe even a deforming arthritis or persistent neurological problems such as St Vitus's dance later in life.

Jeremy kept floating in and out of consciousness, shivering one minute and fighting to get out of bed the next, as the fever gripped his young body. He could hear the voices around him as he lay there, not caring if he drifted away. He wondered if he was going to die, was about to be taken off somewhere by a greater being. It would surely be a kind release. He would, of course, be forever remembered and loved. He would be a star in their hearts forever and achieve immortality.

'Will he die, Doctor?'

'He is very ill. We must pray for him.'

Bunny stroked the swelling on her son's knee. His wrists seemed to be inflamed too, and more rashes were appearing all over his body. In those dark days Bunny and Bill thought they would lose the beloved younger son they had nicknamed Benjamin. But slowly, over the following few weeks, the family's prayers were answered. Sadly, however, the doctor's fears would prove true.

A few months later, Jeremy woke up to find his father standing at the bottom of his bed.

'A surprise for you, my boy!' he said, and suddenly stood back to reveal a gleaming motor-bike at the end of the room. His three brothers had struggled up the staircase with it and put it at the foot of the bed. Days later Jeremy was speeding around the estate. He opened up the throttle, spun out of control, hit a tree and broke his leg.

'Well, Benjamin, now you're back in bed,' said his father, staring down at the plaster cast.

Jeremy's leg was broken, but his spirit wasn't.

As he grew stronger the summer seemed to grow longer. It frustrated him to hear his brothers shouting in the garden and the sounds of laughter from his parents' guests.

But true to his family's imaginative style, his mother, who alone understood Jeremy's love of nature, had thought of another idea to bring him back into the world. She persuaded his father to buy him a bed with wheels, and for weeks after that youngsters from the nearby village pushed him around the country lanes, taking it in turns to jump on the mattress with him and Mr Binks.

Slowly, Jeremy began to regain his strength, but he didn't feel as powerful as before. He had been kept under sedation for eight weeks and been bedridden for eight months, during which time he had grown four inches.

One morning Bunny opened the front door and ushered him on to the steps leading down to the drive. He stood for a moment in the open doorway, his thin wrists protruding from the sleeves of a red silk dressing gown, his green eyes blinking owlishly in the waning light. As always the sight of his sometimes volatile father pacing across the shingle as if on a military mission acted on him like a spray of itching powder.

'Where's your mother?' his father barked.

Jeremy turned to Bunny, but she wasn't there. From that moment on he realised that she had a habit of just disappearing whenever she and his father fell out.

His father stepped inside, putting his hand on his son's shoulder as he passed. It was a fleeting touch, but enough for Jeremy to know that his father, who never really showed his feelings, loved him underneath.

His illness and weeks at death's door had made him feel grateful to be alive, and appreciative of people's kindness. Everything seemed wonderful. He wanted to know where he was, who he was and why he was there. There had to be a reason. Was he chosen? That feeling was to grow within him and flower in middle age. Facing death had changed his priorities and given him a deep regard for philosophy. Somehow God had given him a greater insight into the meaning of life than his friends possessed, as they still seemed to be preoccupied with football and girls. He felt he had been given a head start . . . and yet the truth was that the rheumatic fever he suffered following his murky dive into the Thames was to prove to be a time bomb ticking away.

The morbidity of his mind now was astonishing. Death and its accoutrements appeared to be his constant companions. He was obsessed by bodies and coffins and would talk about ghosts and spiritualism all the time. He began to believe that there was a fragile veil between life and 'the other side' and he felt blessed with an inner vision. He told everyone that he had touched 'the petticoats of comprehension'. It was his way of explaining that he had been on the very edge of understanding life itself . . . and yet the final secret was still hidden from him. With all the passion he was by now so well known for, Jeremy threw himself into a study of the star system. Astrology fascinated him and he began to believe that his own destiny was written in the heavens. His birthsign, he discovered, was Scorpio, with Leo in the ascendancy – which meant that he was passionate, emotionally unstable, suspicious and distrustful but loyal with tenacity and devotion once the suspicions were lulled. It was this experience and understanding which, in his own words, opened the door to an 'azure blue' world he was to live in for the rest of his life.

In one way, the rheumatic fever that nearly killed him was a stroke of destiny for the stage-struck teenager. For it ruled out the career his distinguished and proud army father wanted him to follow – that of a professional soldier. Dismayed, but trying to do his family duty, he went for an army medical but failed. Even the recruiting officers agreed that charging around a battlefield at the head of the infantry wasn't for this young man.

Most boys who left Eton went to university or military college; the proportion of those who went straight into business was fairly low. Jeremy's brothers went to either Oxford or Cambridge. Two were later to become painters and the third an architect. As the armed forces were obviously ruled out, his father changed tack, insisting instead that his youngest son should join his company, Tube Investments Ltd.

Jeremy felt rather sorry for his father, who had lost most of his close friends in World War II and found it hard to be a soldier in peacetime. His mother was always out of the house visiting someone or doing good works, and the colonel seemed to grow more isolated and lonely. He dozed off more than he used to. Jeremy was determined not to go into an office job just to please him. But when he told his father about his grease-paint ambitions the older man was furious. For the whole of the winter they were locked in a battle of wills.

The colonel could not believe that a respectable middle-class boy should want to do something so reckless. To him the world of show business was about drinking champagne out of slippers and it was full of those awful luvvies. With Jeremy's speech impediment and dyslexia, what chance did the poor boy have?

'I'll tell you what chance – no chance!' he told Bunny.

Bill was adamant that the whole exercise would end in failure and it was his duty to steer his son on another course. By this time Bill and Bunny weren't getting on at all, their rows growing ever more ferocious. Even in periods of truce they bickered and snapped at each other. Bunny became quiet and withdrawn and was taking medication for depression. Bill meanwhile sometimes stayed away from the house. Deep down the brothers knew that they loved each other but had become too familiar, much like brother and sister.

True to her Quaker nature, Bunny still understood Jeremy's passions. He was still her little boy. She would do anything for him. How could she ever forget his visits from Eton? He would always arrive on the doorstep with some early daffodils or sprays of mauve chrysanthemums. Jeremy believed that everyone in the world loved flowers. Once he bought her a huge wicker basket full of freesias and as she took it he presented her with a dozen red roses hidden behind his back. She just wanted him to do whatever made him happy, and she chipped away at her husband about an acting career for her son until he could stand it no more.

Finally one evening Bill stormed out of the house insisting that Jeremy changed his name from Huggins if he persisted with his intention to go on the stage. And persist he did. Instead of going to Cambridge as his father had planned, Jeremy enrolled at the Central School of Speech and Drama in London. But first he followed his father's wishes and changed his name. Wondering what to call himself, he rummaged in the pockets of his green tweed jacket for a pen and paper to make a list and found the answer there before him. The label of his first hand-tailored suit bore the name Brett. Jeremy was to wear the jacket until it was threadbare, a trait that was to stay with him all his life.

2 Strange Partners

When he was asked 'What is a friend?' he said 'One soul inhabiting two bodies'

Aristotle

JEREMY WINCED AS THE DOCTOR pricked his tongue with the needle. His mouth froze. It was as if he were in a dentist's chair – but it was worth it. Something was being done about his speech impediment at last. In two snips the doctor cut some flesh away under his petrified patient's tongue.

One of his tutors at the Central School of Speech and Drama had suggested the name of this GP who had been helping other students with their speech problems. His mouth was sore for weeks but gradually he began to sound his words better. With practice and tuition he began to pronounce his Rs and Ss, but the speech impediment had taken a hold on his mind and for the rest of his life he would subconsciously slip back into the old sounds. He would forever force himself to speak properly on stage and stretch his tongue in front of the mirror every morning.

It was during this period at drama school that Jeremy began to suffer the mood swings that were later to become so much a part of his character. Fellow students often found him on a high, full of energy, enthusiastic about the smallest thing, the minutest detail of a play. He was in love with being an actor and he acted on the set and off it. But one minute he would be the life and soul of the party and the next, in the middle of a drinking binge or birthday celebration, he would simply disappear and no one would know where he was.

Once again men showed their interest in him and he instantly responded, often falling deeply in love while still struggling with the guilt about what he felt to be unnatural sex. He so desperately needed to make love to a woman – and he knew they found him attractive. But he just didn't know how to approach them, how to get that close. He had begun to realise that the boys and now the men he had been with never really knew him – the real him. They didn't even want to know. It was never really love, and he was building up a feeling of resentment and anger towards his own sex.

Jeremy was also still heartbroken that his family looked on him as a mere strolling player, especially his father. He knew they were wrong; he had a feeling of destiny.

When he first arrived at the London drama school he stayed in Maida Vale with friends of Bunny but later moved on, living in a different area of the city every term. Once he lived in a mews just off Kensington High Street which cost him £2 10s a week, including breakfast. The morning after he left to go on holiday to Scotland the roof fell in, landing on his bed. Jeremy didn't care; he had a rendezvous with Mary Ure, the vivacious drama student who studied with him at Central. He absolutely adored her and dreamed of having a passionate affair. But he could never bring himself to go that 'extra mile' and spend the night with her, even though it was obvious she found him sexually attractive. In due course she went on to marry playwright John Osborne and later Robert Shaw. But Jeremy was to carry a torch for her all his life.

It was in London that Jeremy developed his love of buses, and throughout his life he would travel on one whenever he could, even when he became a household name as the TV Sherlock Holmes. It gave him pleasure, travelling with real people and not just Etonesque actors like himself. He was always aware that many of the boys he had grown up with at public school rather felt that they were above everyday people in the street; they believed somehow that public schoolboys were better and quite special. But Jeremy believed they were just privileged, tipped gently into life off the edge of a silver spoon. That's why he talked to people all the time – waitresses, bus conductors, people in the queue at the bus stop. Jeremy disliked snobs but understood that the 'old school tie' would never die in Britain. In the end his own aristocratic demeanour was to be a meal ticket when he was cast in so many upper-class roles.

During those first few months in the city Jeremy felt like a country mouse, and would daydream of returning to Warwickshire. In his mind's eye he would recall his brothers riding their horses across the fields, valleys of lush vegetation, sinister and brooding woodlands and haunted forests. He would enthral his friends with tales of holidays with his mother in Cornwall, driving to the tea shop and giving the waitress pennies for pasties fresh from the oven. As if in a play he would mime tasting scones, licking his lips and wiping off the jam and thick cream that spilled down his shirt. He would recall the drive across Dartmoor . . . the haunted wilderness of Conan Doyle's *Hound of the Baskervilles*. It was a long way from the throbbing, vibrant beat of his new world.

But Jeremy felt a buzz about the city and admitted to his pals that if he went back to Warwickshire he would slide into a world of dogs and horses and he knew it wouldn't be long before he would turn into a cauliflower. This, however, was a new beginning, a new act with new scenery, and he felt the anticipation of the curtain rising.

One evening, over several bottles of wine, Jeremy told a story that he was to repeat to others in later years. He had been in London a week and had no friends. So on his first Saturday he decided to go to the West End to see some life.

The day was bleak. A thin, sleety drizzle had been falling all morning and showed no signs of letting up. Jeremy stood at the bus stop watching as a pigeon flew down and landed on the road in front of him. He was thinking of the similarities between them – he had just flown down to London from the Midlands, not knowing anyone or where he really was, a bit like the bird which had just fluttered down on to the road. Suddenly a bus came along and squashed it. He stood for a moment looking at the dead pigeon. Perhaps it wasn't the best of omens. He climbed the stairs of the bus and sat at the front, thinking of the bird. When the conductor came to take his fare, Jeremy was crying. He didn't bother to explain to the man, who must have thought he had suffered a bereavement. He couldn't have explained anyway, he was choking with tears. When he got off the bus at Westminster, the conductor patted him on the back as if he were his father.

For the rest of the day the thought of the crumpled body, surrounded by blood and feathers, played on Jeremy's mind. For months he wondered why he should have been so affected by the death of a pigeon.

At drama school and perhaps all his life, Jeremy, six feet one inch tall, felt like an outsider. But unlike most outsiders he was brimming with confidence. Shortly after enrolling at Central he won three of its principal awards, even though he was still mentally dogged by his vocal problem. It didn't stop him in his new mission.

'Quiet, everyone, quiet! Let's start again!'

The words of the director brought a hush to the set and the spotlights dimmed. The small cast disappeared off stage leaving the elegant woman sitting on the sofa. There was a knock on the door to the left of the stage and she rose to answer it.

But there was another sound too. The director swung round to see a young man slipping into the back of the auditorium at the Manchester Library Theatre.

'Who the hell are you?' he shouted at the mysterious figure quickly settling himself in the back row.

The young man stood up. 'I'm Jeremy Brett. I'm going to be your juvenile next season, sir!'

'Oh, are you! Who says so?'

'I do, sir!'

The director was quite taken with the young lad's arrogant and powerful voice. 'Right, wait until the lunch break and I'll give you an audition,' he replied.

Jeremy swallowed hard and sat back in the seat as quiet as a mouse.

At 2.30 p.m. that day he had the job and for two years he would earn just £7 a week.

It was 1954 when Jeremy Brett joined Manchester's Library Theatre, the year in which a 25-year-old medical student and athlete named Roger Bannister broke the four-minute mile in Oxford and Lester Piggott became Britain's youngest Derby winner at eighteen on the American-bred Never Say Die at Epsom. Housewives burned their ration books in Trafalgar

Square as the government announced the end of war cutbacks after fourteen years and evangelist Billy Graham thrilled Britain with his hot gospels, drawing thousands to stadiums.

Jeremy's first stage production in Manchester was as Gerald Arnwood in the play *Bird in Hand* that September. It ran for three weeks and he was particularly proud of the programme which announced: 'Mr Jeremy Brett comes straight from the London Central School of Drama where he won the William Ford Memorial Prize and others.'

It was during this time that Jeremy met a man who would be his lifelong friend, 23-year-old actor Robert Stephens, whose life in many ways would mirror his own. Robert was a character juvenile when Jeremy was also a juvenile. Jeremy loved the tall, robust youth from Bristol from the moment Robert first made him laugh. Robert had never met an Old Etonian before and Jeremy's charm swept him off his feet. His new friend always seemed to be on a high. He had apparently inexhaustible energy and could go for nights on end with no sleep. He also had a voracious appetite for the theatre, talking and general revelry. Jeremy, just 21, was a handsome and athletic young man. Robert, coming from the working classes, believed Jeremy was the first true English gentleman he had ever met. They both smoked untipped cigarettes and drank the night away on cheap booze.

Robust Robert wasn't in the least impressed with Jeremy's looks. He burrowed away, digging deep into his new friend's psyche until he found the reality. It wasn't easy because Jeremy was obviously mixed up. In the end, however, Robert got so close to him that he won his trust.

Their upbringings had been so different, Jeremy from a background of money, love and prospects, Robert from a background of no money, no love and no prospects. They needed each other. Robert had been abused physically as a boy and Jeremy had been abused sexually. As they got to know each other, they each revealed their histories and came to believe that they were inextricably linked in space and time.

Ladies' man Robert would enthral and upset his Old Etonian friend with tales of his beatings at the hands of his mother

Gladys, a box packer at the Fry's chocolate factory in Bristol. Once she hit him so hard with the hot wet stick she used to prod the sheets in the copper washing tub that his grandmother thought his back was broken. Robert didn't laugh then, but he laughed now, especially as he and his new friend shared a past of mothers up to their armpits in chocolate.

His labourer father, Reuben, a huge man with a big nose, was prone to fits of violence. He once punched Robert's mother so hard she went right over the sofa.

Together Jeremy and Robert would walk to Manchester's prestigious Midland Hotel and press their noses against the window, vowing that one day they would stay there . . . and wine and dine in that great dusty womb where so many wonderful names of stage, business and sport would meet, get drunk and discuss life.

Robert was encouraged to act by his father and was spotted by a drama coach, who managed to get him a place at the Bradford stage school, unlike Jeremy, whose father believed the stage was a ridiculous, uncertain life. But they were to have a great deal in common. Throughout their lives they were to experience in full measure both the pain and compensatory pleasures of the acting profession. Both sought escape in the theatre, both filled any room they entered with laughter and high spirits. Who would have guessed that one day Robert's bid for film stardom would falter in a Billy Wilder movie with his portrayal of Sherlock Holmes, while Jeremy would find international fame with the same part? And who would have guessed that they would die within months of each other?

Thirty years later Robert's looks would be ravaged by time and the bottle . . . but he would give a crowning performance as King Lear at Stratford. At the same time Jeremy, ravaged by the drugs he took to fight his depression, would be a household name as Sherlock Holmes. In their early days they both felt the call of destiny – and they were right.

When Robert met Jeremy he was already married to a girl he met at drama school in Bradford, Nora Ann Simmonds. But he had fallen madly in love with actress Tarn Bassett. Nora had returned to her Londonderry home with their son Michael

Christopher and Tarn was starring opposite Robert in the farce *Not a Clue*, a touring production destined for London which never made it. Robert, wearing black make-up and a turban, played the villain, an Arab named Ali Chumna. But the sight of Tarn innocently disrobing on stage during a game of strip poker was more than he could stand. He was instantly smitten.

From that day on he adored her sense of fun and spirit. Tarn was everything Robert wished for in a woman at that time . . . a young, dark-haired, sensual actress trained at the Old Vic Drama School, a middle-class girl who really didn't need to work.

To Robert, the poor boy from Bristol, Jeremy and Tarn were two very important people. Life was good in Manchester for all three of them. Jeremy and Robert had a month to rehearse a production which gave them time to enjoy themselves, although they were both broke. A hot curry at the local Indian restaurant every Friday night was their big treat.

They rented a flat together over the last A in the Astoria ballroom's neon sign. It was so cold and damp that they would stuff tea towels around the gaps in the window frames to stop the draughts. In the morning the towels would be frozen rigid. Sleep was almost impossible because of the noise from the ballroom and the fights in the street outside. But that didn't bother Jeremy too much; after all, he had never been much of a sleeper.

He soon became great friends with Tarn, who would visit Robert whenever she could. She always ended up washing their jeans for them or trying to get them to eat properly. She hated the pot of 'broth' they kept on the stove all week. They would throw all their leftovers in it and she swore that even their old socks and pants were at the bottom somewhere.

'There's more penicillin in that than at my doctor's surgery,' she would shout at them.

Jeremy and Tarn found that they had a lot in common. Her father too had a military background, having served with the British Army in India. In fact Tarn was born in Ootycamund, in the Lilgri Hills.

Strangely, Tarn had met Jeremy's mother years before, just by chance. Bunny was staying with friends in Winchester and one morning they announced: 'Let's go and see the Bassetts – the colonel keeps excellent sherry.'

When the party duly arrived on the doorstep of the colonel's home they were disappointed to learn that he was out. Teenager Tarn and her sister invited Bunny and her friends in and they joked about coming for a glass or two of sherry.

'Oh dear,' said Tarn's sister. 'I'm afraid Father locks it up – because the cook is rather partial to it! But we do have some cooking sherry.'

They all hurried off to the kitchen to track down the bottle and spent a wonderful afternoon drinking and talking and laughing. Bunny was in fine form from the start. But Tarn and Bunny did not see each other again until many years later . . .

It was 1954 and the Manchester Library Theatre was packed for the First Night of *Othello*. Jeremy was playing Cassio in his first play for the company and Robert was Iago.

Tarn sat down in the stalls next to a stunning-looking woman with thick black hair.

'Hello,' the woman said, 'did you come far?'

'Actually I'm Robert Stephens's girlfriend. I'm staying with him at the Astoria ballroom,' she replied.

'That's nice, dear. I've heard he is really good.'

'But I actually live in Chilcombe near Winchester.'

'That's a lovely part of the world. I have some friends in Winchester – and I do believe I know some lovely people in Chilcombe. I think they are called the Bissetts or Bassetts.'

Tarn looked at the handsome woman again. There was something familiar about her. But Bunny beat her to it.

'I know who you are – you're one of those wonderful two sisters who gave me the cooking sherry that got me tipsy!'

The curtain rose and the play started on what was to be a memorable night.

The actor playing Othello forgot his lines and the seconds of silence seemed like eternity. Then suddenly Cassio, alias Jeremy, brought the house down when he pulled out a packet of cigarettes and said to Robert, playing Iago: 'Have a cigarette.'

'Thank you, don't mind if I do,' Iago replied. The applause was hearty, sustained and welcoming.

The next morning the *Manchester Guardian* ran the review under the headline 'The Have-A-Cigarette Othello'.

Over the next eighteen months Jeremy's roles included Mark Antony in *Julius Caesar*, Gerald Arnwood in *Bird in Hand* and Bruno Hurst in *Marching Song*. Next came Gerard in *Puss in Boots*, Brother Martin Ladvenu and Gilles de Rais in *St Joan*, the Duke of Aumerle in *Richard II* and Dick Tassell in *The Happiest Days of Your Life*. Jeremy was poor but happy, for the roles he was getting were good grounding for the English stage.

But he was still struggling with the guilt of his sexual feelings. The one secret he was keeping from Robert was that he was still a virgin as far as women were concerned. He had tried several times to lose his virginity. Once in Manchester he spent the night with a pretty actress he nicknamed his 'little princess'. They didn't sleep a wink – but he just could not make love to her.

Then he and Robert went on a weekend trip to see Tarn. Jeremy telephoned a girl he knew from drama school and fixed a date for the Saturday night. Before they boarded the train at Manchester station for the trip south, Jeremy bought some peanuts, because he had read in a magazine that they were a good aphrodisiac. When the train stopped at Crewe he jumped off and bought lots more. By the time he met his date he was practically poisoned by peanuts. Later that night, after going to the pictures, they went back to the hotel room. Jeremy was beside himself with anxiety. She gave him a little sticky circular paper thing as he went to the loo. He hadn't a clue what to do with the condom. He stuck it everywhere until eventually it lost its elasticity. He was totally perplexed. The night was an unmitigated disaster.

By now Jeremy hadn't seen his father for four years, so he wrote to him asking if he could borrow his army boots for the part of a foreign soldier he would be playing. When the curtain went up on the first night his father was sitting with his mother in the fourth row. After the performance they went to Jeremy's dressing room.

'If you're going to play a soldier can you at least play an

English one,' said his father. Jeremy was sure that he hadn't come to see him – he'd just come to see his boots. From then on he began to turn up sporadically at the theatre to see his son. But it was obvious he was never really interested in the stage – mostly because he just did not understand it. After the long drive to Manchester he would fall asleep in the stalls and Jeremy would catch sight of him in the front with his mother, dead to the world. He would be woken up by the applause, go round to the dressing room and announce to Jeremy: 'A triumph, old boy, an absolute triumph! Bloody awful play!'

In 1955 a photograph of Jeremy in *Spotlight* caught the eye of Hollywood film director King Vidor, who thought he had a face like Audrey Hepburn. Almost before he knew it he was invited to play Nicholas Rostov in the $6 million movie *War and Peace* with Audrey Hepburn and Henry Fonda. Jeremy couldn't believe his good fortune. It was the break every young actor dreamed of. He and Robert got so drunk that they fell asleep on a park bench.

The movie was being shot in Rome and when Jeremy arrived he felt lost. It reminded him of the first time he had left Warwickshire for the hard, unbending, bustling life of London.

He was chauffeur-driven to a beautiful house outside the city where Audrey was staying. The black Mercedes swept into the drive and stopped outside the huge whitewood door, surrounded by bougainvillaea and ivy. The door opened and there stood Audrey's husband, handsome Mel Ferrer, in a bright pink shirt and white slacks, with his hands on his hips. Suddenly a little girl put her head under his arm.

'You're Jeremy,' she said and, without giving him a chance to say hello, she blurted out: 'Goodness, you are Nicholas!'

Audrey, without make-up, looked as if she was about sixteen. Jeremy was smitten. All afternoon he swam in the pool with her and, as he bid her goodbye later that evening, he said: 'Audrey, I loved swimming with you – but I nearly drowned in your beauty.'

On the set he marvelled at her. She was the epitome of wholesome young love under benevolent aristocratic rearing.

Henry Fonda was starring as Pierre, the confused young liberal who aped the French as so many Russians did until Napoleon forced the Czar's armies to resort to a scorched-earth campaign.

Alone in his hotel bedroom Jeremy attempted to sleep, but sleep was a fugitive to him again that night. He lay in the darkness for ages, his thoughts moving away from the excitement of filming the next day. Instead he thought about Robert. How he missed him – and Tarn.

At 5 o'clock the next morning he was on the telephone to Robert: 'Darling, you must come to Rome. All you need is the air fare.'

Jeremy had already promised them that if they could pay for the tickets he would cover all their expenses. They didn't need another reminder and were soon on their way, spending three weeks in the Italian city with Jeremy paying for everything. They stayed in a flat with poet Robert Graves's daughter Diana, and Jeremy gave them pocket money from his salary. Then he went one better.

He persistently took Vidor aside and tried to persuade him to give Robert a part in the film. Finally the Hungarian-born director relented.

'I find it extraordinary that you English actors always stick together,' he laughed. 'That doesn't seem to happen in America!'

And so Robert got his first big screen part – a walk-on.

During the next three weeks he rehearsed the earth-shattering line that was to be spoken in the heat of the battle: 'Have you no room for these poor fellows in your cart?'

For that memorable moment he was paid a lot of money, but his dream of a movie debut turned to ashes because it ended up on the cutting-room floor.

But the three musketeers didn't care. They marvelled at the Sistine Chapel, walking in absolute silence around the fifteenth-century building and breathing in its beauty. They gazed in awe at Michelangelo's ceiling and the other wall frescoes of Botticelli, Pinturicchio, Ghirlandaio and Signorelli. In their hearts they hoped they would one day play the parts of these great men on stage.

Drunkenly walking back to Jeremy's hotel at night, two flamboyant and indiscreet young thespians abroad, they would quote Shakespeare aloud.

> Where both deliberate, the love is slight;
> Who ever loved that loved not at first sight.

When Robert flew home three weeks later Jeremy was no longer alone. He had become a firm favourite among the actors and production crew of the movie. He missed his friend Robert greatly but he had a sell-out audience . . . anyone who would smile along with him in the 5,000 bars of this wonderful, cultural city of wild flowers, fashion and history. His face was becoming well known too after he and Audrey appeared on the front cover of *Life* magazine and various Italian publications. But there was a secret desire burning deep within him and he could not put the flame of his desperately mixed-up feelings out. Coming from such a militaristic, responsible and loving family he felt the pain of guilt over his innermost desires. Then it happened. He met a wonderful woman he would remember with deep affection all his life. She was a voluptuous actress, quite a few years older than he was, and they spent the night together. Once again the feelings of guilt and anxiety swept over him and he was a disaster in bed.

'Don't worry, my husband failed at his first attempt,' she said, stroking his forehead. She was so sweet Jeremy felt perfectly at ease and fell blissfully asleep. In the morning he woke up – and it was happening. For the rest of the day he literally tingled with excitement. At last he was a man, a real man. He would swear his walk had even changed. From that wondrous moment on his life would never be the same again.

Sadly, Jeremy's hopes that *War and Peace* would be a massive hit were shattered. Vidor's three-and-a-half-hour epic showed little understanding of Tolstoy's power in depicting humanity on a massive scale through the observing eyes of individual characters. Only Hepburn's appealing Natasha saved the day. Fonda's portrayal of a civilian weaving in and out of the crude battery of bombardiers manning the buttress made the critics wonder if a little pruning would have been an advantage.

'Jeremy, I've got it!'

'Is that you, dear heart?'

'Of course it's bloody well me,' shouted Robert over the telephone. 'Did you hear what I said? I've damn well got it!'

'I never thought you wouldn't. The champagne is on you!'

All evening Jeremy had waited by the telephone to hear news of what had happened at their beloved Midland Hotel. Now Robert's dream had come true. He had signed for the London stage. The basher from Bristol was on his way to the Royal Court Theatre where he was soon to become a notable young actor in a company of rising stars, among them Alan Bates, Kenneth Haigh, Joan Plowright, Keith Michell, Tony Richardson and Nigel Davenport. They were to be the foundation stones of the English Stage Company who were to light up the moribund West End.

Months later Jeremy was on his way to the capital as well – to make his first London appearance as Patroclus, played as a notably seductive youth, in Tyrone Guthrie's Edwardian-dress production of Shakespeare's rarely performed *Troilus and Cressida* at the Old Vic. It was a small part in a production set just before World War I and the sixth play to be presented in the season, starring John Neville as Troilus and Rosemary Harris as Cressida. It aroused considerable interest in the national press but the reviews seemed to go over Jeremy's head. He never really read them. He seemed only to be interested in the *Manchester Evening News* and *Manchester Guardian* because his mother and father always read them. To him, they were the big newspapers and what they said counted.

Meanwhile, back in Manchester Jeremy had left behind a man who would one day, 30 years later, have a huge impact on his career and a huge impact on the world of television soaps.

Young Michael Cox had just joined the Manchester Library Theatre as an assistant stage manager, a role described unkindly by some as the lowest form of theatrical life. It was to be his vision of a truly authentic TV series featuring Sir Arthur Conan Doyle's creation Sherlock Holmes which was to make Jeremy a household name. But before that vision came true, Michael was to create a fictional TV community that would be remembered forever throughout the world. He was to produce *Coronation Street.*

A new phase was now opening up in Jeremy and Robert's lives and really it was all thanks to Tarn. In London, the English Stage Company was fronted by George Devine and Tony Richardson, who had at last managed to find a theatre in which to launch their plans. Tarn had recommended both Robert and Jeremy to Devine, a close friend of hers from her days at the Old Vic School. Devine never could resist her leggy charms and responded by opening the doors of the London stage to the two young thespians-about-town.

Jeremy's next roles at the Old Vic were as Malcolm in *Macbeth*, Paris in *Romeo and Juliet* and the Duke of Aumerle in *Richard II*, a part he had played with aplomb in Manchester.

In fact 1956 was a year the three of them would never forget. Jeremy was making plans to fly to New York where he would play Malcolm in *Macbeth* at the Winter Gardens. From there he would tour America and Canada with the Old Vic. But before he left he had his most important curtain call of all – as best man at Tarn and Robert's wedding in Chelsea. After the top-hat-and-tails nuptials he saw them happily ensconsed in a small town house owned by Tarn's parents just off London's King's Road, ten minutes walk from the Royal Court Theatre, which that same year gave birth to the play that would alter the course of stage history – John Osborne's *Look Back in Anger*, featuring Jeremy's teenage love Mary Ure, who would become the dramatist's second wife. The English theatre was changing – the council house and kitchen sink boys from London, Manchester and Liverpool were taking over. Authentic drama of the day was in vogue . . . and Jeremy was firmly lodged in the past.

Back at the Winter Gardens in New York, actor John Neville hadn't been very successful as the lead in *Troilus and Cressida* and didn't want to play the part any more. Jeremy jumped at the chance when he was offered it. The production was an outstanding success but Jeremy was to remember it more for the way it opened his eyes to the glitzy lifestyle of America than for its content. During the season he was invited to one Manhattan party after another. One evening, with his co-star Rosemary Harris on his arm, he swept into a hotel suite to see Stanley Holloway sitting at a piano tinkling the keys with Judy Garland singing along. He had hardly got his breath back when he saw Charles Laughton chatting to Edward G. Robinson in the corner. He was spellbound. But when he noticed Lauren Bacall and Humphrey Bogart having a drink together at the bar, he turned to Rosemary and said: 'I'm going to have to lock myself in the kitchen for a while – otherwise I will faint.'

These were heady times. Jeremy was only in his early twenties and he was walking out of the theatre on Broadway to see his name emblazoned on a cinema across the road where *War and Peace* had opened. His future as an actor could no longer be in doubt.

One evening, in his dressing room, one of the cast told Jeremy that a little girl was desperate to meet him. She had been a huge fan for some time and had seen him in his new film and on stage as Troilus. Jeremy agreed to see her and the next morning arrived in the coffee shop of his hotel to find a beautiful wide-eyed, red-haired Bambi-like creature waiting for him. It was Anna Massey. As they stepped out into the street for lunch, Jeremy took hold of her arm and suddenly said: 'Where are you?' It was as if his hand had gone straight through her coat to touch her bone. Anna was pretty but skeletal. Jeremy wondered if she were anorexic. She was dangerously, devastatingly thin and he felt instantly protective towards her. Anna was starring in *The Reluctant Debutante* on Broadway, a part for which she had received sparkling reviews in London. But this time her mother on stage was being played by her own mother, legendary actress Adrianne Allen, and it didn't seem to be helping her at all. Adrianne was dominant and outgoing and in Jeremy's mind Anna was living in her shadow. To him she seemed so frail and vulnerable.

A few months later Jeremy went on tour in America with the Old Vic and had an intense affair with a leading woman in the company. He was swept off his feet, obsessed with her, and they would spend almost every night together. But the woman was married and the affair ended like a Shakespearian tragedy at the end of the tour. She went off with her husband and he returned to England absolutely devastated. He had never experienced such a feeling of emptiness before. 'It is as if my insides have been taken out,' he confessed to Robert. 'It is agony for us both. We knew it had to end but that didn't really prepare us for this.'

On Jeremy's return to London in 1957, Laurence Olivier's outstanding performance as Archie Rice in the new Osborne play *The Entertainer* at the Royal Court was receiving ecstatic reviews. Jeremy, still locked in the past, was signed up to play Roderick in the musical *Meet Me by Moonlight* at the Aldwych. He enjoyed the part enormously. The comedy, set in an English provincial town in 1884, was about a pompous Victorian papa, his three daughters and his match-making sister, along with a number of gentlemen who sought the hand of his eldest child, Mary Ellen. She refused all her official suitors because of her clandestine romance with the handsome Roderick. Jeremy got good reviews but they weren't making headlines. It slowly began to dawn on him that he was already becoming typecast. Aristocratic leading men were passé. Scouse and cockney abrasiveness was still very much in style. Osborne's *Look Back in Anger* wasn't a one-off, it was a trend. As a distinguished-looking, archetypal aristo Jeremy found himself out of step. 'I am afraid I am as English as an oak tree,' he told Bunny.

Jeremy's face was now becoming both his fortune and his misfortune. Traditional, tall, dark and handsome with finely chiselled features, he had to deal with the whispers of the theatre set who would joke that as he had so much going for him in looks it was hardly likely that he could act too.

He despaired that his handsomeness was working against him, and fellow actors and stage hands would often find themselves sitting with him in his dressing room, listening to his sad story over a bottle of champagne and a packet of cigarettes.

'They all believe that pretty boys can't act,' he would grumble, staring into another empty glass, 'or so conventional wisdom, sometimes known as prejudice, insists.'

He was bored with playing handsome and he almost begged his agent to find him character roles. But they just didn't come.

Osborne's *Look Back in Anger* had been the English Stage Company's first outstanding success and its first night, back in May 1956, was already being considered a landmark of the modern stage. It had taken New York by storm with its angry-young-man hero . . . rude, eloquent and working-class. It marked a radical departure from Britain's traditional West End plays – and Britain's traditional West End actors, like Jeremy. At this time he was playing Sebastian, the 12th Duke of Chevron, in *The Edwardians* at the Saville Theatre. This was the moment when he finally realised that he was 'upstairs – and out'. In his heart he knew he was unlikely to be cast in working-class plays, as a working-class angry, even though he had started life with a Birmingham accent, picked up from the stream of city evacuees his mother had housed in the stables at the Grange. He was distraught. Not even Robert could console him.

'Dear boy, someone has to play royalty,' he would say kindly.

'That's very kind, but I feel my career is fading.'

'Jeremy, just remember that Albert Finney couldn't play a duke like you . . . his accent would give him away.'

Even the theme of his play *The Edwardians* seemed so out of touch. While Finney and his ilk were mirroring everyday life in Britain, he was a young duke in revolt against the strictures of his class in Edwardian England. Although the duke had socialist leanings and had further complicated his life by falling in love with the wife of a bridge-playing peer, the tradition of the ruling classes proved too strong for him and he finally accepted the heavy duty laid upon him and agreed to marry a young girl of good breeding specially picked for him. All of which was a far cry from the kitchen sink dramas so in vogue.

The play received a mixed reception from the critics. One said: 'In adapting Sackville-West's novel for the stage, playwright Ronald Gow set himself quite a task and appears to have been unable to make up his mind whether he is telling the story of the end of an epoch or of a love affair between a young duke and a married woman. Having failed to make this choice the resulting play rather falls between two themes and, lacking continuity, tends to be episodic.'

Jeremy sat alone in his dressing room reading the first-edition newspaper critiques. In one, most of the actors and actresses had been praised.

'This is the kind of play English actors do superbly well, especially the older generation,' he read. 'Ernest Thesiger's butler Vigeon rules below stairs more despotically and royally than any duke and he has achieved a marvellously intimidating portrayal. Ambrosine Phillpotts as the Duke's widowed mother Lucy is a regal matriarch; Athene Seyler's Dowager speaks her mind and meddles in the affairs of others as only duchesses in plays of this kind can, and Nicholas Hannen is a turf-loving Duke to the life. Helen Cherry is very decorative as the infatuated Lady Roehampton and one shudders at the poor woman's ultimate fate. As the young girl chosen to be the Duke's future wife, Patricia Rogers is charming and, of the younger players, catches most surely the mood and style of the period.'

Jeremy was deeply hurt by the reference to himself . . .

'Jeremy Brett on the other hand is too modern in manner as the rebellious and love-torn Duke, who is finally trapped by tradition and habit, and there is something oddly inexpressive about his handsomely moody face.'

He looked up at himself in the mirror. At that moment he doubted completely his ability to do anything well, traditional or modern. A dreary litany of his inadequacies and shortcomings raced through his mind, taunting him. What was the point of going on? He forced himself to read the last sentence of the review.

'His Duke becomes rather a bore and a prig – but perhaps this is not entirely his fault.'

That night Jeremy booked into a hotel just off Piccadilly Circus. He didn't want to talk to anyone; he just shut the door on the world.

He lay quietly in the dark staring at the ceiling, with a bottle of Krug champagne by the bed. Not an eyelash flickered, and if anyone had entered the room they would have rushed to his side because he hardly seemed to breathe. But he wasn't dying, he was wondering what he should do.

Later that week he returned to Warwickshire and confided to his mother: 'I suppose you shouldn't have let me go on the stage really, I'm too, too posh for it. Perhaps father was right after all. When Ernest Thesiger put the crown on my head in that play, I realised that I had taken on a far greater weight than just the coronet.'

But Jeremy pushed on the only way he knew how.

In 1958 he played Ron, the Birmingham-born ballet dancer to whom a consumptive society woman named Rose Fish, alias Margaret Leighton, took an adulterous fancy in Terence Rattigan's *Variations on a Theme* at the Globe Theatre.

'Young Jeremy Brett was excellent,' Noël Coward noted in his diary.

'Jeremy, you've won the acclaim of the master,' said Robert down the telephone.

But the new play, set in a crumbling château in Cannes, came in for a lot of criticism. Most newspaper critics felt it fell short of the author's accustomed skill and sense of theatre. Only the acting by Margaret Leighton as the desperate Rose, who had acquired the château through four husbands and was planning to marry a fifth, George Pravda, Michael Goodlife and Jeremy saved it. The play was produced by John Gielgud, who came in for some fierce criticism, and Norman Hartnell's strikingly up-to-date fashions were panned as a diversion rather than an asset.

By now Jeremy was dating elfin actress Anna Massey, who had returned to London. Time had partly healed the deep sadness he felt over his split with his lover after the Old Vic tour in America and he was living life to the full again. He and Anna were like little children. 'We are full of bubbles and mirth and youth,' he told Robert. But their relationship was strictly platonic.

Jeremy was torn at this time because his lifetime love Mary

Ure was back on the scene. They began to have a secret affair. Now that he had lost his sexual inhibitions their relationship was passionate and exciting.

One cold February morning, however, Jeremy realised that he had not sent Anna a Valentine's Day card, so he rang her. He had found an old card sent to him the year before by a young lady admirer at the Old Vic. Adopting his best French accent, he read the words over the telephone, ad-libbing his own thoughts: 'My darling, you are my pretty Valentine, my little bunny, the essence of the daffodil in spring and the fragrance of the rose in summer . . .' Then he suddenly put down the receiver.

He didn't know it then but it sent Anna into a frenzy, and she spent the entire day ringing everyone she knew, trying to find out the name of her mysterious romantic caller. Jeremy kept the game going for a month before he confessed to her. Then she cried with happiness.

'Oh, Jeremy, and I thought you had forgotten about me,' she said.

Jeremy realised then that he was deeply in love with the pretty, fragile young thing. And he knew that she loved him too. She even threatened to rent a room across the street from his house so that she could get closer to him. Every time she touched him he thought his heart would explode. But even though he was desperate to make love to her she remained a virgin.

Jeremy and Anna had totally different upbringings. Anna's childhood, though affluent, was a lonely one. Her parents separated when she was one and her father, actor Raymond Massey, departed for Hollywood. She did not get to know him until much later. But even then she was to meet him only ten times in her life. Her mother, actress Adrianne Allen, married her former husband's new wife's lover, as complicated an arrangement as could be imagined.

His name was Bill Whitney, and she first went to see him to start divorce proceedings against Raymond. He quietly told her: 'I'm sorry, I'm afraid I cannot represent you. Unfortunately, you see, you will be suing my wife!'

Anna's mother had always used her charm and energy professionally and ambitiously. With her exceptional organising abilities she soon became a busy London hostess as well as an accomplished leading actress. Noël Coward, who was the godfather of Anna's brother Daniel, gave her the affectionate nickname Planny Annie, forever used by him until their last meeting during his final days in Jamaica.

The nanny who looked after Anna and Daniel seemed more like their mother. Nanny Gertie and Anna shared a bedroom until Anna was fifteen.

This was the backcloth to Anna's life – a gregarious mother who was a more-than-generous hostess. Emlyn Williams once said: 'She will kill us all with her kindness.' But such kindness did not extend to her family. Daniel was later to compare her with Moors murderess Myra Hindley.

Nevertheless, Adrianne was always known as a giver. People flocked to her table . . . Somerset Maugham, Ivor Novello, Edna Thurber, Oscar Hammerstein and her greatest friend, his wife Dorothy. There were others too, not so famous. But behind the scenes there was another story. Anna and Daniel, who was at Eton at the same time as Jeremy, were left in the shadows. Their mother was cold to them, unable to show love. And later they were to find it hard to show love too.

Adrianne's cruelty was in evidence even when she was a child. At one birthday party she made her little friends form a circle before standing at the centre, flicking at their ankles with a whip to make them stop and start. Her children believed she was concerned only with her own happiness and what would make life right for her. But her coldness was not always reserved for her family. When a close female friend died she showed no emotion. For ten years she had spent every summer with the woman and her husband at their villa in Portugal. She was flying to London from her home in Switzerland for a West End opening when the news of her friend's death came. She didn't even telephone the bereaved husband herself when she arrived but instructed Daniel to call and say she wouldn't be going to the funeral. She never rang her late friend's husband again.

Adrianne starred in many top productions of the pre- and postwar years – plays by Emlyn Williams, Terence Rattigan and Keith Winter. In 1934 she was unforgettably moving on both sides of the Atlantic in Winter's greatest success, *The Shining Hour*, which starred Gladys Cooper and Raymond Massey as desperate adulterous lovers.

In her late teens, Anna had lived like a princess on a high hill in The Grove, Highgate, North London, a house her mother later sold to Yehudi Menuhin and which he in turn sold to rock star Sting. It was a beautiful house but remote. She used to complain that nobody would ever take her home – because it was 'six quid for a taxi!'

Anna was one of the last debutantes to be presented at court in 1955. Her 'coming out' party was a wondrous affair with elaborate decorations by Oliver Messel in the vast garden of the family's home.

Quiet, slim, virginal Anna was the Reluctant Debutante in more ways than one.

Jeremy put down the telephone, tears streaming from his eyes. His beloved Bunny was dead. Her car had spun off a road halfway up a Welsh mountain and she had been killed instantly. It was the first time that someone close to him had died and he was inconsolable. Death and Jeremy would become strange partners from that moment on.

3 Four Ladies

Do think, do perceive, do listen

Laurence Olivier to Jeremy Brett

'JEREMY, you can't go to your wedding dressed like that!' said Tarn.

'Darling, don't fuss.'

Tarn was adamant and even Robert agreed.

'I must say your trousers do look a little, well, odd. Of course, we would take no notice, but the Masseys, well, they have certain standards,' he said with a thespian wave of his hand.

He and Tarn looked again at Jeremy's trousers. He had tied ribbon around them to keep them up because he didn't have any braces.

'For God's sake, we'll have to leave now, and buy you some bloody braces!' exclaimed Tarn. 'Bob, get him in the car.'

They sped into the King's Road and stopped outside a tailor's shop. 'Honestly, Jeremy, do you really think you should go through with this marriage?' Tarn asked as they rushed in.

'Of course. Why?'

'Because you don't even seem to care if your trousers are falling down at such an important moment!'

The 1958 wedding was an elaborate affair with pictures by Lord Snowdon. Jeremy's best man was Robert, even though he and Anna were not the closest of friends. He felt she wasn't right for Jeremy – and his fears proved to be well founded. Anna wasn't Robert's cup of tea. He found her too reserved, a bit too moody for his tastes. Jeremy couldn't see it. Tarn meanwhile was matron of honour and the happy couple moved into a little house in Red Anchor Close, Chelsea.

Adrianne had decorated their bedroom as a gift and Jeremy, who still hadn't made love to Anna, had gone to considerable trouble to make the scene perfect for their wedding night. He put his little gramophone and a pile of romantic records beside the bed, champagne nestled in an ice bucket, and caviar was within reach. The crowning glory was a huge bouquet of flowers in the shape of a heart – placed carefully across the pillows. That afternoon, Jeremy was appearing as Ron in two performances of *Variations on a Theme* at the Globe Theatre and wouldn't be home until at least eleven o'clock. Anna went off to see Julie Andrews on stage in *My Fair Lady* with her voice coach and some other friends. When Jeremy arrived back at the house she was there in the bedroom waiting for him.

They had the most wonderful, passionate night, and Jeremy would remember it for the rest of his life. He never forgot the look on her face the next morning. 'When Anna is happy,' he told Robert, 'the sun shines.'

Jeremy knew that when Anna was on form she could walk into a room and turn every head. But there was another side to his beautiful wife and their happiness was threatened as the months went by and the rows began.

'There is a rage in her, Robert,' Jeremy told his friend, 'an anger that blazes and cannot be put out.' After each row they would make up and Jeremy would find the child in her again. She would settle down and go to sleep, putting little plugs into her ears so that she could not hear anything. As she slept Jeremy would lie awake all night staring at the ceiling, wondering if he could go on. But he was hopelessly in love and go on they did. For a while they found an unsettled happiness. Jeremy tried to understand Anna. He believed that she was suffering from rejection because her father had run off when she was young. And Anna tried to understand Jeremy, his non-stop energy, his constant need to party. They were two completely different people. Anna was private, quiet, reserved, Jeremy outgoing, generous and loud. Anna later admitted that she found married life a strain and underwent counselling.

At this time Anna's mother Adrianne was starring in Peter Shaffer's long-running first play *Five Finger Exercise* at the Comedy Theatre. The John Gielgud production was a huge success and introduced Juliet Mills, Brian Bedford and Michael Bryant to theatre acclaim. But Adrianne, playing the mother on stage, became wretchedly unhappy when she was not cast to play the part in New York, and she never acted again. In a fit of pique she had her name removed from *Who's Who in the Theatre.*

When Anna became pregnant she and Jeremy moved into a bigger house in Astell Street, Chelsea. But after their son David was born it was obvious to everyone who knew them that they were drifting apart. Jeremy adored his son and tried never to miss his bedtime. No matter what play he was doing, there was always time for a song by his cradle. Anna though was not the most maternal of women and admitted herself that she was not as good a mother as she should have been.

Gertie had always promised Anna that she would be nanny to her baby and she kept her word, moving into the couple's new home. Gertie was thrifty and took charge of little David immediately for the princely sum of £5 a week.

'Nanny,' Anna said a few months later, 'we must put up your wages.'

'But, Anna, whatever will I spend it on?' Gertie replied.

Anna went back on the stage to help out, as finances were tight for the young couple. She was secretly pleased. She had been desperate to get back to her career because she hated being at home, and had spent weeks losing weight and measuring her waist with a belt marked in inches, trying to get it down to her pre-pregnancy measurements. Jeremy was worried that she was becoming dangerously thin again. He was earning only £30 a week and they were struggling to keep up with their Chelsea-set lifestyle. They even had a cook because Anna wouldn't work in the kitchen. Now that they didn't see much of each other they drifted further apart. When they were home together the rows grew louder. Anna, it appeared, had secretly felt that the marriage was doomed from the start.

From the moment Gertie arrived, Jeremy felt that his wife had become a little girl again. She even dressed younger. To him, it was almost as if she were vying with David for Nanny's attention.

Gertie was totally in charge. One evening she marched into the master bedroom and told Jeremy and Anna to be quiet because they would wake the baby. She didn't even knock.

This, then, was a delicate time in their lives.

In April 1959, Jeremy played William MacFly opposite Paul Rogers as Cecil Fox in Frederick Knott's *Mr Fox of Venice* at the Piccadilly Theatre. He was pleased to land another role in London as he still wanted to be near David, although he and Anna had grown even more cold towards each other. He would dash in after matinée, see David, then dash out again.

Once again Jeremy's acting survived his latest play's panning by the critics. One wrote: 'How disappointing! A first rate cast, a luxurious set, a gay drop curtain, an intriguing opening full of pertinent references to Jonson's *Volpone* – and then a sudden descent to confusing and not very exciting thrillerdom. Paul Rogers, straining every nerve to avoid the pitfalls of a third rate farce and fifth rate murder mystery, turns in a remarkably lively performance as the latter-day Volpone of the title – an American millionaire living fabulously in Venice and scheming with the aid of his newly appointed secretary to hoodwink two old friends greedy for his fortune and his ex-wife in similar pursuit. Jeremy Brett as MacFly, along with the rest of the cast, brings distinction to his part.'

The following month, typecast again, he appeared as Archie Forsyth in Alan Melville's romantic musical *Marigold* at the Savoy. It was at this time that he turned to meditation to help him through his dyslexia, mild depression and periodic debilitated state. At first he would meditate once a week, then twice, but when he felt really troubled he would do it every day, squatting in the corner of the bedroom like a Buddhist monk and concentrating on the flame of a candle or a vase. He told friends he found the practice helpful and comforting.

Early in 1960 Jeremy was strolling down London's Strand one bright summer's morning, wondering what part he would be offered next. He had just finished playing the title role in *Johnny the Priest* and he didn't know whether to stay in Britain or try his luck in America. As he walked past the Savoy Hotel he heard a voice shouting to him. Frank Hauser was standing on the opposite side of the road, waving furiously.

'How are you, Jeremy?' he shouted.

'All right, but always looking for work,' Jeremy yelled back as the taxis and buses crawled by nose to tail.

'How would you like to play Hamlet, dear boy?'

'I'd like to play Hamlet very much.'

'I'll ring, then.'

With that, Hauser disappeared into the crowd.

Hauser had been impressed by Jeremy playing Marchbanks in *Candida* and believed the 25-year-old actor would make a marvellous Hamlet. So Jeremy joined the Oxford Playhouse Company as the prince, directed by Hauser on an almost bare stage.

On the first night, Jeremy stood in the wings, itching to go on. This would be the night on which Hauser would obtain from his lead the triumphant performance that he had failed to get from Alec Guinness in the same play a decade earlier. Jeremy was sure of it. Seconds later the slim, pale-faced, handsome actor with a Byronic air of melancholy was on stage.

By the time the curtain came down on the second act, with Jeremy standing alone on stage, his arms folded, gazing contemplatively into the wings, in an attitude that powerfully recalled the mountains looking on Marathon and Marathon looking on the sea, he had the audience in the palm of his hand.

After the performance Jeremy's father appeared at the dressing-room door. He cleared his throat and smiled. 'What a rotten part, Jeremy. Couldn't you have played the ghost – at least he's a soldier!'

None the less, his father was so impressed by his performance that he finally told Jeremy he could change his name back to Huggins. Jeremy was moved. 'But, Dad, it's too late, I have already established the name Brett,' he said. His father was crestfallen.

Described as pleasant and correct, Jeremy's Hamlet won praise for making the character's suffering understandable. But some critics found that the quiver of excitement was missing.

Overall his performance received such favourable notices, however, including a resounding endorsement from George Rylands, that in 1961 it transferred appropriately to the Strand Theatre for a successful four-week season.

One critic wrote: 'Brett was manifestly a prince among players. His voice was pleasant and pliable, and he never tired on stage right up to the dramatic moment when news arrived of Laertes' treachery. Somewhat taller than most, Brett was princely in looks, manner, speech and authority and had an easy transition of mood. His turns of humour were perhaps too light. He did not appear to suffer in spirit severely. He was not obviously lonely and tortured but rather at ease, master of himself and his surroundings. He portrayed Hamlet's youth, but Hamlet's psychological progress had made him old beyond his years.'

This should have been the making of Jeremy as a star but somehow the transformation never quite took place again. He still looked and sounded like a handsome Bertie Wooster.

Such typecasting was unfair to the zestful Jeremy, but after two years at the Old Vic he was finally rescued from well-bred obsolescence by Robert, who persuaded the Royal Court Theatre that his friend was the best man to replace him as Peter, the German fish cook who goes berserk in Arnold Wesker's *The Kitchen*. He was off to find film stardom in *A Taste of Honey* with Rita Tushingham, for which he was paid £500 a week.

Director John Dexter wasn't convinced at first but Robert and Tarn, who knew Dexter well, were persistent. In the end he told Jeremy: 'I think you can do it, but you must put on two stone and have all your hair cut off.'

Jeremy was beside himself with joy. At last he could shake off his pretty-boy looks. From that moment on he ate and drank everything in sight.

'Soon even I won't recognise you,' said Robert, prodding Jeremy's beer gut after a large supper one evening.

But sadly the play, set in the kitchen of a big London restaurant called the Tivoli and very much an ensemble piece, was not enough of an actor's vehicle for Jeremy. He was soon back with the classics.

But yet another door opened . . . his television career was taking off again with a stream of appearances for both the BBC and ITV. For the BBC Jeremy played Julian Bennett in *A Kind of Strength*, the student in *The Ghost Sonata* and Jacques in *Dinner with the Family*. For ITV he appeared as Pascal in *The*

Typewriter and was voted Tomorrow's Star Actor in *The Award Show* presented by Bruce Forsyth.

Then, at last, came Jeremy's chance to appear in a film in the down-to-earth Finney mould – *The Wild and the Willing*, a movie directed by Ralph Thomas, taken from a play by writers Laurence Dozie and Robert Sloman, about youth trying to find its place in society. Spiced as it was with humour and sex, Jeremy believed it would be a box-office hit, even though Robert had said it was a little late in the Angry Young Man series. Nevertheless Robert was thrilled for him.

It was a well made and exciting picture produced by Betty E. Box, who claimed she was unleashing half a dozen potential new stars. There wasn't much new for it to say on its chosen theme but the screenplay was lucid and the university background authentic. Jeremy believed that the storyline would finally catapult him into the modern world. It concerned a brilliant young student from a poor working-class family, played by newcomer Ian McShane, who was acutely class-conscious and rebelled against the university, its professors and the opportunities they offered. He did not know where he was going and was arrogantly content to drift along, creating commotion, drinking beer, playing football and fondling his student girlfriend. He was a leading light on the campus with a particular influence on his roommate, a shyer, more introspective young man, played by newcomer John Hurt. They were surrounded by the 'in crowd' – that little group of students that seemed to run every university at the time. Jeremy, in the role of upper-crust Gilbey, was utterly convincing as the youth who was desperate to have fun. Rebel McShane's professor, alias Shakespearian actor Paul Rogers, recognised the boy's ability but disliked him for his brashness. Things came to a head at a cocktail party thrown by the humourless and rather cold don, at which they openly insulted each other. The professor's young, unhappy wife, played by Virginia Maskell, found the boy's youth and wildness attractive. Her marriage was virtually on the rocks and she spent her time drinking and dallying with selected students. Her husband knew about her indiscretions but chose, contemptuously, to ignore them. The wife and the student went on to have a brief affair, but when she rejected his pleas to run off with him he was stung into engaging in a reckless, rag-week stunt. He and his roommate climbed the school's tower with the result that his shy friend fell to his death. The film ended with McShane being sent down in disgrace, although the audience was left with the impression that he might be on the threshold of a more useful and understanding life. Norrie Paramour provided a lively score with a closing calypso that seemed to sum up the whole film in a touching finale.

At the end of shooting Jeremy was concerned that some of the opening student scenes were rather too hearty, but gradually the film seemed to settle down into a thoughtful pace, accelerating to the climax of the tower climb.

He and Robert watched the movie together when it opened in London and agreed that there was a complete air of realism throughout. The students, the professors and the townsfolk were real people about whose problems audiences must surely care. Robert was particularly impressed by the performances of the little-known cast, especially McShane, who 30 years later would be known to millions of TV viewers as Lovejoy, the impertinent roving antique dealer.

McShane, with his broad Manchester accent, had come straight from drama school to play the lead. He was a virile, good-looking young man with an air of authority, and was already being hailed by the production crew as a real discovery, along with the slim and wiry John Hurt.

Johnny Briggs, John Standing, Johnny Sekka, John Sumner and Jeremy all clicked as the other students, and other newcomers included Samantha Eggar and Catherine Woodville.

Sadly, at the end of the day, this down-to-earth, well-presented British movie, with its perceptive take on the Angry Young Man theme, did nothing to further Jeremy's career. Robert had been right all along. It was too late in the series to make an impact. The public had seen it all before, although it was a well-acted film with an intriguing storyline. Jeremy soon found himself back in breeches and ruffs.

In 1963 he went to Chichester where Sir Laurence Olivier

was preparing the National Theatre Company's repertoire for its opening season as the Old Vic. Olivier had now married Joan Plowright following his divorce from Vivien Leigh.

'I expect every young actor who works with me to have the body of a god and the vocal range of a full orchestra!' Olivier boomed at Jeremy, who didn't disappoint his movie hero. But for those actors who did not measure up, Olivier had his own special recipe – full-time access to a gymnasium and a voice coach. Jeremy soon came to learn the hard way about Olivier's mood swings. The Heathcliff and Henry V of his boyhood could be as gentle as a kitten one minute and roar like a lion the next, splitting the air with a seemingly endless torrent of swear words. But his professionalism could not be doubted. Jeremy, who originally adored him, now came to admire him. Olivier would rehearse with the actors and eat with them in the staff canteen. He would nurture them, talk them through any crisis of confidence, send them bouquets . . . or verbal strands of barbed wire.

Olivier stretched Jeremy's abilities to the limit. When he forgot to trill his Rs, Olivier would snap at him.

'Come on, boy, that's enough of that. Move your tongue, move it, sound it!' he would bark. It was like a military command and Jeremy would obey it, to the extent of stretching his tongue in the morning for half an hour before arriving at the theatre. Then he would be barked at for something else . . . how he held his arms, the way he walked to the front of the stage, the look on his face.

'No! I want more, more than that, give me more!' Olivier would shout. Jeremy found him an intuitive leader with an almost animal-like quality.

He and Robert believed he was a powerhouse who could terrify an actor or break his heart.

At the time nobody was more closely connected to the National at its Olivier best than Robert. He had joined the company to play Horatio to Peter O'Toole's Hamlet in the opening production . . . and Olivier both adored and admired him. It was a marvellous link for Jeremy.

Jeremy's first role was Dunois in Shaw's *Saint Joan* opposite Robert as the Dauphin (later Charles VII), at the Chichester

Festival. It was a star-studded cast: Joan Plowright as Joan, Frank Finlay as Chaplain de Stogumber and Derek Jacobi as Brother Martin Ladvenu.

Jeremy and Robert had just returned from a holiday in Ibiza, very fashionable then, where they had found a cheap tailor who had fitted them both out with white trousers, matching white jacket and white shirt. They were so delighted that they bought three suits each. They weren't good enough to wear on big occasions, but Chichester was their big chance and they decided to use them as rehearsal suits.

Jeremy moved in with Robert and Tarn for the festival. Each morning he and Robert would trot off to the theatre for rehearsals looking like chefs. But it must have been one of the worst plays in the English theatre to act out in pure white.

There were scenes at the trial of Joan at the castle at Rouen in May 1431, with people kneeling on dirty, painted steps. Jeremy and Robert would return home looking as if Joan had put a curse on them, their white outfits grubby and grey.

'All I bloody well do is wash your clothes,' shouted Tarn up the stairs to them before throwing their trousers and shirts into her tiny little washing machine. Minutes later Jeremy and Robert would rush down the stairs in their spare clean white clothes, give her a hug and a kiss and go out on to the lawn to rehearse over a bottle of champagne. They were as irresistible as ever.

No one was really impressed with Jeremy as Dunois. One critic said that all his roles seemed to be thankless ones. And yet he had thrown himself into the part as he always did. The fact that proper acclaim still wasn't coming his way hurt him tremendously. One night, back in London, tired and wanting to be alone, he left his friends in a restaurant in the middle of the main course and walked home through the rain. He felt a sense of both destiny and loneliness. What would he do now?

He picked up the bottle of shampoo and started to read the label.

'Does this work, Larry?'

Laurence Olivier turned away from the mirror in his dressing room, still scraping off his make-up. 'Yes, dear boy, it's the best.'

'Philip Kingsley shampoo. Never heard of him,' said Jeremy.

'He's the best trichologist in London. Has a salon in Mayfair where I go.'

'Is he good?'

'Been going for years – his scalp massages are wonderful.'

'Then I'll go too.'

'But you already have a fine head of hair, dear boy.' And he had. Jeremy's thick, brown mop was the envy of many an actor.

'But I want a massage.'

A few days later he arrived for an appointment. Within an hour he had the staff at his feet. From that day on he became a regular customer and the Kingsley girls would squabble over who was to massage his heavy locks. Jeremy found the treatment so relaxing that he would fall asleep as they worked on his scalp.

'My angels, you must come and see my play,' he would say afterwards, leaving tickets for them at the box office of whichever theatre he was appearing at, with backstage passes thrown in. Then there would be dinner for them all later somewhere in Soho. But often, without rhyme or reason, he would suddenly disappear in the middle of the proceedings without finishing his meal, blowing kisses to them on the way out.

Jeremy became Philip Kingsley's super-salesman, telling everyone to book an appointment. Soon an array of stars was turning up for treatment, including Robert, John Stride, Derek Jacobi and Penelope Keith.

It was the start of a lifelong friendship between him and Philip. At weekends they would visit each other for bridge evenings. Penelope Keith and actors Charlie Kay and John Saunders would join them. Jeremy was a wonderful but erratic bridge player, totally unpredictable, at times even manic in his quest to win.

The first time Jeremy ever played Philip he called seven spades as his bid. It was almost unheard of. Everyone was shocked at the table at his house in London's Campden Hill. They couldn't tell whether he had the cards or was being typically Jeremy and just having fun. But in the end he made all the tricks. Philip and Penelope were quite rattled.

In 1963 Jeremy was given the role of Maurice Sweetman in John Arden's *The Workhouse Donkey*. Now the critics were impressed; it was one of his finest performances and it prompted Olivier to ask him to become the National Theatre's juvenile lead.

But after playing Hamlet in the West End to rave reviews, Jeremy, now 30, was unwilling to accept the role of Laertes when offered it, especially when it was not yet certain who would be Hamlet in the opening production. Why, why, why hadn't Olivier offered him the lead role? Jeremy was crestfallen yet again. But he believed in himself and turned the great man down. Days later he was having second thoughts – what if the master never employed him again?

The following month things looked up. Jeremy was being seen on British TV in Cocteau's play *The Typewriter*. It was one of the most testing parts – or rather two of the most testing parts – of his career so far. He was appearing in the dual role of two brothers, Pascal and Maxime.

He had adored the script and pace of the play, which had been specially translated and adapted for Independent Television by Giles Cooper. Jeremy thought that Cooper had managed to bring out all the drama and tragedy that followed an anonymous letter circulating in a small French town. The poison-pen note had resulted in many suicides, and when a detective friend of one of the town's families arrived to investigate, events moved swiftly to an unexpected climax.

Jeremy did not leave his part behind in the rehearsal room. He stayed up night after night, standing in front of his tall mirror, first as the delicate, self-centred Pascal, and next as the ill-balanced, ex-convict Maxime, jailed for mutiny and nursing a grudge because he had been cast out by his family.

Patrick Wymark was the detective, human and understanding, ahead of his time in the world of TV crime-fighters.

The ending of the play, exposing a rich, nubile widow in a château as The Typewriter – the poison pen – was not as important as the implicit moral, which was that all of us are responsible for the atmosphere in which poison can circulate.

Jeremy found the role exhausting, but prayed it was worthwhile.

He was half right.

The day after it was screened the critics were kind.

'Jeremy Brett portrayed both parts with singular ambidexterity. The greatest triumph was his,' said one. And another: 'This play was notable for the fine performance of Jeremy Brett, a young actor who has already appeared in a number of television dramas.'

Sadly, that seemed to be the end of it. Jeremy's TV career did not immediately take off as he had hoped and soon he was to find himself back on the stage.

The following year his drifting marriage finally broke up when Anna discovered that he had been having affairs. Jeremy had been kind and considerate but perhaps the relationship between himself and Anna was doomed from the start, as she had once said. Anna felt that she was not a good enough mother to their son David, or a good enough wife. Jeremy's mood swings and unpredictability must also have complicated their relationship.

One evening they had been for a meal and as they were leaving the restaurant a couple smiled at them from another table.

'It's so nice to see you two together, enjoying yourselves,' said the man. 'We used to lie in bed at night listening to you both going at it hammer and tongs. We could almost tell the time by your rows. But we all grow out of those in the end, don't we?'

Jeremy was dumbstruck. He and Anna lived at number 21 Astell Street – the couple lived at number 1. The whole neighbourhood must have been listening to them.

One morning a few days later Jeremy lay staring at the sun streaming through the bedroom window, waiting for Anna to wake up. As she took out her earplugs he announced: 'I'm sorry, Anna, I am no longer involved. Our marriage is over.'

Jeremy moved out that day and went to stay with Robert and

Tarn where, unusually for him, he slept solidly for 48 hours. Anna was devastated, ringing her friends and blaming herself. She refused to let anyone touch anything of Jeremy's, even the ash in the ashtray. She herself admitted that she was always 'too obsessed, too pained from her past'. She would even feel guilty recalling how cold her own mother had been to her and Daniel when they were children, although she had tried to get closer to her before her death. In the end, however, both she and Jeremy believed it was better for David's sake that they should part.

Anna went on to bring him up on her own. She was fiercely independent and proud and refused to take any money for herself from her actor husband after the split – only enough for her son. Anna was to spend the next 27 years alone and for twelve years, three times a week, she was in analysis. She became cocooned in her own loneliness, feeling guilt, especially over the irregular hours she worked as an actress, which meant that she wasn't near her son.

Anna became even more isolated when her brother Daniel stopped speaking to her for no apparent reason. He would go on to develop Hodgkin's disease and spend years in psychotherapy himself. But Jeremy always told everyone, 'If any of the Masseys need my help they only have to ring.' He was always haunted by the thought that his relationship with Anna might have worked – if only they had become friends. He hated hearing rumours around the acting world about her being romantically linked to someone else. Finally Anna sued for divorce on the grounds of Jeremy's desertion and adultery.

Jeremy threw himself into his career again going before the cameras to play a sex maniac in a British film called *The Very Edge* – yet another big chance for him to break into the movie world he longed for. This time, however, he was playing one of the leading roles. Surely he was on the edge of superstardom now. But for some reason he could never work out himself he did not feel comfortable with the part, and he flopped along with the film, even though there were some nail-biting moments for audiences.

The Very Edge starred Anne Heywood as an ex-model and

happily married young wife of architect Richard Todd, pleasurably awaiting her first child. One day, in Todd's absence, a young sex maniac, played by Jeremy, broke into her house and assaulted her. On the verge of a nervous breakdown she lost her child and bitterly turned against men, even rejecting her husband. Perhaps understandably, though somewhat hurriedly, he turned to the warmth and understanding of his secretary, Nicole Maurey. But behind the scenes the problem was: 'Will the maniac strike again?' Life for the wife became a wretched affair. The attacker was caught but escaped and the terror began again. The climax was a rather corny but tense cliff-hanger that finally brought the wife and husband back together.

The acting was sound, with Anne Heywood running a gauntlet of emotions and Richard Todd playing his fairly colourless part adequately. Jack Hedley meanwhile almost stole the movie as a believable Scotland Yard man. But Jeremy never fully captured the menace of his part and he was panned by the critics.

On screen it looked as if he had yellow eyes and a green skin. His appearance shocked his father so much that he told him: 'Son, if you're going to do such terrible films, please make sure they don't come to our village!'

Jeremy wondered if he would ever make a movie again.

Then Sean Connery announced that he was giving up the role of James Bond. Debonair Jeremy was tested for the part – but was turned down. 'If I had been chosen as Bond it would have spoiled my life,' he stated afterwards. Privately, however, he admitted it would have changed his life for the better. In his mind he would have been a star his son could have been proud of.

But that year he was voted the *Daily Mirror*'s Most Promising Actor on TV for his BBC performance in *The Picture of Dorian Gray*. It was the first of two dark Victorian stories that led him to Sherlock Holmes.

Then Jeremy packed his bags for Hollywood to play an admirably ardent Freddie Eynsford-Hill in George Cukor's film *My Fair Lady*, starring Audrey Hepburn and Rex Harrison.

Laurence Olivier tried to dissuade him from going but his arguments were singularly unconvincing. Jeremy was still hurt that he had not been asked to play Hamlet at the National.

'Darling, if I can't play Hamlet then I will play Freddie, even if he is a bit of a chinless wonder. Perhaps I can bring some sensitivity to the part,' Jeremy told Olivier's wife, actress Joan Plowright. Joan was also unmoved by her husband's feeble pleas to make Jeremy see sense and stay in London.

'Larry, you've sold this so badly to Jeremy that if Eliza Doolittle had a sister, I would go with him,' she said.

Olivier, however, didn't fret for too long. The studio agreed to pay the National £10,000 compensation for Jeremy to break his contract, which settled the debt from two plays that had failed the year before.

Jeremy booked his flight to America with nagging doubts. The National, under Olivier, was at its absolute height and the great man could do no wrong. But privately Olivier was worried and Jeremy knew it. Robert had told him of a private conversation he had had with 'the Bard of the South Bank'. Olivier was in one of his low moods and admitted to Robert: 'This won't last, you know, no company survives more than about seven years in Britain without falling apart.'

One of the problems was that the National was creating stars who then, understandably, wanted to go off and work elsewhere to achieve fame and fortune. People like Michael York and Tony Hopkins went off to seek their fortunes on the big screen and somehow the fireworks began to fade, especially when some of the top directors, like John Dexter, left too.

Meanwhile, Jack L. Warner had forked out $6 million for the rights to *My Fair Lady*, the stage musical derived from Bernard Shaw's original play *Pygmalion*. It promised to be stunningly creative cinema entertainment, in Technicolor and Super Panavision 70, a Hollywood wide-screen breakthrough at the time.

Jeremy at once felt at home with the colourful Edwardian costumes and scenery created by Cecil Beaton for the expensive set. Beaton had designed the backdrops for the original stage play starring Julie Andrews as Eliza Doolittle, the cockney flower girl plucked from obscurity into high society for a bet. Both Jeremy and Robert had sat spellbound before her performance in London.

The only difference now was that everything was expanded, Americanised. The small Covent Garden set Jeremy had seen on stage became a stunningly populated market, full of characters and movement. The embassy ball, to which Eliza was whisked in Cinderella style, became a dazzling array of regal splendour. This was Jeremy's world, a slice of romance from a bygone age. He felt comfortable in this period just before World War I and loved the glamour, the women's gowns, the comfort and service of upper-class pre-war England.

He watched the shooting with Rex Harrison as the distinguished Professor Higgins turning a guttersnipe of a girl into a lady by teaching her manners and how to speak, in league with his urbane associate Colonel Pickering, alias Wilfrid Hyde-White. Harrison brilliantly captured the egotism and ferocity of his character, just as he had on the stage, and Stanley Holloway rolled through his scenes like thunder as Eliza's antisocial dustman dad. Jeremy nicknamed him The Titanic because he appeared larger than life and seemed to take over the set as soon as he walked on it. He wished he could have joined in with the bevy of boozers as the film reached a high point with the immortal song and dance routine 'Get Me To The Church On Time'.

Audrey, meanwhile, simply became Eliza, struggling to come to terms with the pomp and grace of this confusing but wonderful time. Jeremy watched her with total admiration. When they tried to plunge her into a bathtub she fought with the fury of a tigress and he thought someone would get hurt. She was utterly convincing as the girl who would not submit to the obscure customs and refinements of a society that was alien to her. In another scene, when Eliza reached the point where she could parrot the correct words to describe the rain in Spain, she acknowledged the thrill of her achievement with a wonderful electric gleam in her eyes and Jeremy wanted to cheer and clap for her.

Jeremy was always to be remembered in this award-winning,

unorthodox movie for his rendering of the song 'Street Where You Live'. The only reason it was in *My Fair Lady* was that in the original stage play time was needed for a set change, and so Freddie sang it with a frontcloth. Behind it, everyone was dashing around taking out the scenery for Covent Garden and replacing it with Ascot. Many people who saw the musical play, especially in Manchester where over 200 performances were staged, thought Freddie's rendering stuck out like the proverbial sore thumb. They were confused. They hadn't even figured out who Freddie was by the time the song was featured. But it stayed in the movie, and worked. Jeremy was lucky by default.

The one thing that always irritated him, however, was that he did not sing the song on screen. When he arrived on the set he discovered to his horror that a man named Bill Shirley had already recorded the number. Jeremy was placated only by the thought that Audrey did not sing a single note in the whole movie. The wonderful songs that flowed from her lips were dubbed by singer Marni Nixon. She too was furious. Jeremy kept his dubbed song a secret for nearly 30 years.

During his spell in Hollywood Jeremy had hoped to meet a lot of film directors but he was amazed to discover that most of those that would be interested in his very English talents lived in the Cotswolds or Berkshire. It should have been the highlight of his career – a Hollywood movie opposite two of the world's biggest stars. Instead all he did was sit around, waiting to play his part, and his agents subsequently turned away other offers that could have led to something bigger. No matter what they said, Jeremy was convinced he would be the star of Tinsel Town. He felt the call of destiny. New roles back in England were not the way forward. He would show them all. But while Jeremy was smitten by the talented Audrey, his stay in Hollywood proved to be the most miserable six months of his life. At one point he fell out with Rex, who wanted to cut Jeremy's scenes even more. Jeremy believed he saw them as a threat and didn't want them to outshine his. But even though he was bored by Tinsel Town, Jeremy was very aware that he was there at the same time as the last of the greats, people like

Cole Porter and Mary Pickford. One morning he looked up from idly reading a newspaper on the set to see a man in a straw hat talking to Cukor by a camera. The man then lit up his pipe, bid Cukor farewell and walked past Jeremy, nodding to him. It was Bing Crosby, and it made Jeremy's day.

Once the afternoon shooting was finished, however, Jeremy couldn't wait to get on a plane to New York and Broadway. He arrived there to play Father Riccardo Fontana in German author Rolf Hochhuth's provocative and powerful play *The Deputy* at the Brooks Atkinson. It was a visit he was never to forget. The play was about Pope Pius XII and the Jews trapped in Nazi Germany. It had been shrunk drastically from its original five-act length, which would have taken around eight hours to perform, and it wasn't long before Jeremy began to wonder if he had made a huge mistake. The play suggested that the Pope was wanting as God's vicar on earth when he failed to denounce the Nazi extermination of the Jews in the death camps. Jeremy believed it was too soon for such a production to be staged in the United States, although he subscribed to the view that the theatre should be a platform for charges and pronouncements of this kind. And he enjoyed the fact that the play was controversial; that would at least get him noticed. He was noticed, but for the wrong reasons, and he ended up having a terrible time. For a start the production had difficulty securing a theatre. Refusals were generally accompanied by excuses, some of them credible, but in the end it was all down to nervousness and fear on the part of the theatre owners. No play in modern history had ever blown up such a storm. When the Brooks Atkinson agreed to stage it, thousands of letters and telephone calls bombarded the theatre office. Newspapers and magazines ran editorials on the rights and wrongs of the production.

On the first night some Germans demonstrated and threw bottles outside the theatre. The next day Jews demonstrated and then came the Catholics. All the cast had police protection, and one night Jeremy was nearly pushed under a car opposite the Broadway cinema where his name was emblazoned on the credits for *My Fair Lady*.

The protesters saw him very much at the centre of things as he was playing a young Jesuit priest who believed himself to be God's deputy, expressing the harrowed conscience of those in the faith who wanted openly to protest about the death camps.

The edited version of the play had lost many of its original complex strands and got straight to the point. It introduced the young priest as he reported for duty to the papal nuncio in Berlin in December 1942. There he met an intense, distraught SS lieutenant, Kurt Gerstein, who had virtually forced his way into the papal legation. The author based Gerstein on a real-life figure who had infiltrated the SS to fight Hitlerism. He had just arrived from Poland where he had obtained proof of the mass murders being committed at Treblinka and Belzec, and he pleaded with the papal nuncio for a protest from the Holy See. It was here that Father Fontana learned for the first time of the monstrous crimes the Nazis were committing. Thereafter the play followed the priest as he discovered more about the Nazi evil and sought to persuade others of the urgency of the situation.

As the Nazis began to round up Jews for deportation, following the overthrow of the Mussolini Government in 1943, gathering them virtually under the shadow of St Peter's, Father Fontana got his chance to put his case directly to the Pope. But when Pius refused to alter his policy of silence, the young priest pinned a yellow star on his soutane and joined the miserable passengers to Auschwitz. The play left no room for doubt about the author's contempt for the Pope, and it was this which led to the Broadway riots. People just did not believe that the Pope was as cold, sanctimonious and insipid a creature as he was made out to be in the production. He was presented by the author as a ditherer and Jeremy, as the young priest, had no trouble in making the head of the Church look bad. The author did not give Pius the chance to state his position with any sort of clarity or eloquence. In the end, however, Jeremy agreed with many critics that it was impossible to believe that the Pope, a man noted for his aristocratic, intellectual background, could not have argued his case with force, if not brilliance. Finally Jeremy had had enough and could not wait for the play to end.

A few months later he saw Robert again. On hearing that his old friend was starring as Atahualpa, King of the Incas, in the Chichester Festival production of *The Royal Hunt of the Sun*, he flew back to England and sneaked quietly into a front-row seat at the National Theatre. The play was about the conquest of the Incas by the Spaniards and their subsequent corruption of them. The last time he had seen Robert, the Bristol bruiser had been flat-footed with a huge pot belly. But it was obvious from this performance that he had been to the gym. Jeremy sat spellbound, watching the gleaming, shaved creature on stage speaking an extraordinary language of clicks which he had invented as the Inca tongue. Robert was unforgettable. It was a performance full of rage and fury. Jeremy was to describe the evening as 'seeing an incredibly brilliant orchid on the move'. The production, by Peter Shaffer, was to be one of director John Dexter's most brilliant *coups de théâtre*.

After the performance Jeremy and Robert embraced backstage and Robert seemed relieved to hear that his portrayal of Atahualpa had impressed the house. Jeremy learned that his friend had been training with heavy weights for ten weeks and that he had been worried about the part from the start.

'It could so easily have been stiff, silly Indian-chief stuff,' he said.

Instead Robert had emerged as a perfectly sculpted icon of burnished flesh, with a curious high-pitched, musical voice. Thirty years later his looks would be ravaged by the bottle and time, that deadly combination. He was to become a lovable rogue, a womaniser, an actor with a self-destructive streak, a fascinating, romantic ruin, none the less loved by his peers and royalty . . . an actor who would be knighted and achieve esteem. Jeremy would never achieve the public esteem of his friend. But there was no jealousy. Jeremy loved him deeply.

Visiting the theatre always excited Jeremy and by now he was going out a lot to watch other people. Sneaking in quietly was always to be one of his great joys, but as time went on it became difficult as practically everybody in the business knew him and would expect him to turn up backstage with a bottle of champagne.

Jeremy returned to England early in 1965 to appear at the Birmingham Repertory as Gilbert in *A Measure of Cruelty*. But his arrival back on the English stage was tinged with sadness.

He had bought himself out of *The Deputy* and signed up in Birmingham to be near his father, who was fighting a losing battle against heart trouble. Bill hated hospitals and Jeremy virtually had to drag him along for tests. Somehow the fight had gone out of the old man, who was still pining for his late wife.

'Life's not the same for me now that I have lost my sparring partner, Bunny,' he confessed to his son.

On 22 April he died. Jeremy and his brothers returned to their family home for the funeral service at Berkswell Church, and saw his ashes interred in the graveyard. A memorial plaque for their father and mother was later mounted on a screen in the Lady Chapel in the church and the lychgate in the graveyard dedicated to their memory by the Bishop of Coventry.

There was no need for Jeremy to be in Birmingham now. The wonderful old Grange, which held so many fond memories for him, was sold and he returned to London to play the young aristocrat Sir John Maltravers in the ITV production *The Lost Stradivarius*, part of the station's 'Mystery and Imagination' series. Next he took the West End by storm playing Beliaev in *A Month in the Country* at the Cambridge Theatre. It was produced by Michael Redgrave and starred Ingrid Bergman.

Outside the theatre, the bustling capital was covered by one of those clear, light blue skies that September occasionally brings. Inside, Jeremy sat in his dressing room staring at himself in the mirror, as he had done so often before, becoming the part, becoming Beliaev. He imagined himself oppressed by the heat of the Russian plains. The plot was typical Chekhov, stories within stories.

Rakitin, the servant, played by Michael Redgrave, was departing after four years of platonic friendship with Natalia Petrovna, with nothing achieved and no wisdom gained. Vera was marrying Bolshintsov, 30 years older than she was and left on the shelf for the same period of time for reasons only too obvious. Shpichelsky, the incompetent Machiavellian doctor, played by Emlyn Williams, would carry off Lizaveta to console him in his declining days. This devious manipulator, a man by his own admission 'not of a high degree', was the only one to derive any personal benefit from the emotional mess on the Yslaev estate. Meanwhile Beliaev, the young tutor, had returned to Moscow after his month in the country, a little wiser having unwittingly fired two hearts he never believed susceptible. Remaining on the estate were the Yslaevs themselves, picking up the pieces of a dull marriage.

During rehearsals Jeremy was mesmerised by Ingrid Bergman's Natalia. She had given a physically radiant performance of a woman in her thirties who had scarcely been touched emotionally until the 20-year-old Beliaev arrived. Up until then both her husband and Rakitin, her servant, had only the status of friends, not lovers.

Jeremy's admiration for Michael Redgrave also knew no bounds. It seemed to him that Michael gave a performance of tact and delicacy, revealing inch by inch the position of a man who was kept at rather more than arm's length from the woman he adored both by her coldness and by his ingrained reticence. By temperament he was the outsider who would always be accepted and liked rather than loved. Jeremy was struck by the importance of Michael's impulsive swallow when Natalia announced that she had been touched by Beliaev and then his quick return to composure. It was a masterpiece of acting. So too was the look on Ingrid's face the moment she succumbed to jealousy after realising that her young ward was her rival in love.

Jeremy battled hard to get his Russian pronunciation just right. He succeeded, giving a magnetic performance.

As the champagne flowed backstage, the cast read the reviews. One, in the *Financial Times*, was unforgettable.

It read: 'But perhaps most impressive of the newcomers is Jeremy Brett as Beliaev. In a production notable for the way in which each of the actors slides into his role like a hand slipping into a well-made glove, Mr Brett is still outstanding. His tutor is still basically a student, even a peasant, as the muzhik costume suggests. Yet he, like Vera, becomes aware of his sexuality for the first time, his power to move others when they want to stand still. Here is Beliaev, gauche and shy, yet with the quick smile of those who are charming by nature rather than by adoption, and here was the perfect leave-taking – sad, surprised, yet totally courteous.'

'Where's Jeremy?' asked Ingrid excitedly, after reading the review.

No one could find him. He had simply vanished into thin air, just as he always did.

By now Christmases weren't so manic for Jeremy. While his father was alive he would insist on driving up to Berkswell to see him first thing Christmas morning, then speed back to London for lunch with his young son David. In the evening he would rush off again, this time to Winchester for dinner with Tarn and Robert. By ten o'clock at night he was exhausted. Tarn believed it was the only time he ever slept.

Over the next few years, as Jeremy battled to establish himself on the stage in Britain, he felt at rather a loose end. His mother and father had died, the Grange had been sold, his marriage was just a fleeting memory. The only stability in his life were David, Tarn and Robert.

Early in 1967 he played Ronnie in *Any Just Cause* at East Grinstead, to no great acclaim. He was becoming depressed again, his up-and-down nature coming ever more to the fore. One day he would be on a high, ordering champagne for the cast and buying presents; the next he would shut himself away or simply disappear to be by himself. Then came a turning point.

A few weeks after *Any Just Cause* closed he was invited to the dress rehearsal of *Much Ado About Nothing*, where Joan Plowright was taking over from Maggie Smith. It was then he realised that there was only a certain amount of gamesmanship he could indulge in with Olivier. He had learned now to take the opportunities as they came. He knew that Orlando hadn't been cast in the all-male *As You Like It* and he adored the play. It was always popular on the stage with lively dialogue and contrasting parts. It had a pastoral charm all of its own.

While Olivier was watching Joan reading her lines on the stage, he sneaked away from the rehearsal and found an empty dressing room. Closing the door, he looked in the mirror, picked up a pair of scissors and cut a fringe in his hair.

'There, that's more like Orlando,' he said, standing back and admiring his new look.

He stared hard at his reflection, remembering the lines from *As You Like It* that seemed to sum his life up: 'What, wouldst thou have me go and beg my food, or with a base and boistrous sword enforce a thievish living on the common road? This I must do, or know not what to do.'

At the end of the rehearsal Jeremy walked into Joan's dressing room sporting his new fringe and shook Olivier's hand. Larry took one look at the new hairstyle and let out a throaty roar of approval.

'Dear boy, come with me, we must talk,' he said, slapping Jeremy on the back as if he were a long-lost brother.

He took him to his own dressing room, shut the door and asked: 'Will you play Orlando for me?' Jeremy could not contain his excitement. He leapt at Olivier and practically knocked him over before lifting him off the floor in a huge bear hug. And so began what he thought would be the happiest time of his career. His only sadness was that Tarn and Robert had split up over his friend's affair with actress Maggie Smith, who had fallen pregnant.

Jeremy felt secure after joining the National Theatre Company again and promised himself that there would be no more Hollywood Freddies for a while. This was the heyday of Laurence Olivier's rule. But it wasn't smooth sailing for those with the vision of a home for the great plays of theatre history on London's South Bank.

Rising costs had caused a drastic rethink of the National Theatre building scheme. Plans for an opera house to be included were abandoned because of a £250,000 overdraft on the project.

Meanwhile the Old Vic was still the company's temporary home and Olivier ran it with a rod of iron.

Jeremy quickly became embroiled in the politics of the day, arguing until the early hours with fellow actors and politicians over the importance of establishing a permanent base to represent the golden age of English drama . . . writers such as Shakespeare, Marlowe and Johnson.

He knew that the first plan for a British National Theatre had been put forward in 1848 by a bookseller named Effingham Wilson who wanted a house for Shakespeare to be owned by the public. And yet more than 100 years on they were still arguing.

Meanwhile Robert had been seconded to the planning committee for the new building, as a 'token actor'. The committee was bristling with radical ideas. It sent round questionnaires to all the casts at the Old Vic asking what shape of dressing room they found most useful and what sort of furnishings it should have. When someone suggested 'Marilyn Monroe' the idea was dropped.

When the curtain went up on Clifford Williams's provocative all-male version of *As You Like It* there were plenty of adoring female fans in the front row at the Old Vic who had come to see the tall, well-built, handsome Orlando who strutted around the stage half naked. But they were wasting their time. At that time Jeremy just wasn't interested in women. He was consumed by his role. Secretly he felt that he was too old for the part and found himself having to regard it as a 'character role' to make any sense of it.

The play was camp and very sixties ... a wintry, futurist dreamscape of glistening synthetic materials, populated by courtly astronauts in gleaming PVC, Lurex and snowy, nylon fun furs. The trees were thin transparent reeds, suspended from above the stage. Two movable, fungus-like canopies formed an ever-changing ceiling suggesting tree tops or the movement of clouds, and most of the set consisted of a steeply raked rostrum, highly polished with lights reflecting the mood of the scene. At one point the stage was bathed in a golden winter glow, at others in silver, red or, for the nuptial celebration in the last act, an almost psychedelic profusion of colour. Most of the furniture consisted of straight or jagged Perspex cubes.

The performance was also dotted with camp in-jokes. Adam was a silver-maned Dr Who and Frank Wylie's usurping Duke Frederick a platinum-wigged parody of Dirk Bogarde in *Modesty Blaise*.

Visually, the production, designed by Ralph Koltai, was one of the most beautiful Jeremy had ever worked on and certainly the most fun. The cast were a jolly bunch. Celia, played by Charlie Kay, looked disconcertingly like *Daily Mirror* columnist Marjorie Proops; plump Audrey, played by Anthony Hopkins, was taciturn but a devil when roused; and Richard Kay's Phoebe, a nightclubbish, lipsticked sexpot, had to overcome a schoolgirl crush. Touchstone, played by Derek Jacobi, had the sharpness of a cockney taxi driver and was genuinely funny on stage. But Robert Stephens's Jaques was one of his finest performances to date. He came across as a white-suited, fastidious, apparently sour old man, fundamentally lonely and kind, picking his way through the plastic wood with a civilised disdain. The play was so robust at times that Jeremy broke his nose in the on-stage wrestling match. Olivier was surprised to find that Orlando appeared to be thrilled by his misfortune.

'At least my new-shaped nose gives my face character at last,' he joked – and he meant it. Nevertheless Olivier paid to have it fixed.

Next at the Old Vic came *Much Ado About Nothing*, with Jeremy appearing as Claudio, followed by Valere in *Tartuffe*. That same year he had small parts on television – Tressilian in *Kenilworth* for the BBC and Gino in the ITV play *Quite an Ordinary Knife*, followed by The Bey in *The Champions* for the same channel.

Olivier, however, like Donald Wolfit, did not relish rivals near his throne. At this time he was Britain's most acclaimed actor. A ticket for his performance in *Othello* was described as 'the most difficult piece of paper to get hold of in Britain today'.

Consequently the roles Jeremy began to be given were sometimes thankless ones. Both Peter O'Toole and Jeremy noticed that no one played the parts that had made their mentor famous . . . Henry V or Richard III. Soon Jeremy's depression set in again.

When he played Kent, John Stride's small, weak brother in Brecht's *Edward II*, Olivier came to a rehearsal and told him: 'I've never known an actor who has claimed the limp, the stutter, the glasses and the sway so boldly because he isn't quite sure what part of the role to concentrate on. Don't you think you could concentrate on just two idiosyncrasies?'

Jeremy was crestfallen but knew that the master was right.

In 1968 came Berowne in *Love's Labours Lost*. It was one of Jeremy's all-time favourite roles. He had played it four times at drama school and was always excited by the thought that Shakespeare was a young man when he wrote the play and apparently unable to resist dazzling the intellectuals of his time.

Olivier's production was brilliantly rehearsed. He was like a conductor with a symphony, taking the cast minutely through the intricate word-play of the showy comedy, masterly mingling lightness, sorrow and conflict. Jeremy brought to the part of Berowne an almost mocking strength and the audience was won over by the depth of his love. Rosaline, played by Joan Plowright, was bustling and bubbling, and the two of them seemed made for each other.

After the opening night Laurence Olivier sent Jeremy an index card covered with performance notes. It read: 'Do Think, Do Perceive, Do Listen, Do Blaze, Don't Be Soft, Don't Be Polite, Don't Be Gobblesome'. It was signed: 'Love Wishes, Love Gratitude, Love Admiration – from Larry.' The instructions were clearly intended to encourage Jeremy's self-confidence and spontaneity, but also to encourage him to think and not rush his acting.

Jeremy was to keep that note all his life. His notes were one of the things he loved about Olivier. He would write them to anyone whenever he had something to say, even to someone who had just walked on stage to put on a pair of gloves.

But Jeremy wasn't getting love and admiration from the public. They seemed to be looking for something else in the play – a sort of hidden agenda. This was a new, exciting beginning for Britain, a time when everyone seemed to be equal. *Coronation Street* had already established itself as TV's most successful soap opera, bringing a new breed of kitchen-sink actors to the screen. The Beatles had captured the hearts of the young and youth was having its say.

John, Paul, George and Ringo had set up Apple Boutique, a psychedelic shop in London's West End which Jeremy couldn't resist the temptation to visit and rummage around in. He loved the expensive, exotic fabrics of the Dutch hippie designers

Simon and Marijke and would often walk out with a bright yellow shirt or silk kipper tie.

In a way the fantasy of the flower power sixties was very much Jeremy. Everything was being questioned, not just the theatre – peace, war, love, politics, sex, the office, suburbia . . . The Bomb. Off stage Jeremy was in his element in this new psychedelic world of brightly coloured clothes and spiritual love. He adored the paisley shirts of Carnaby Street, the black Cuban-heeled boots made to measure in Covent Garden, the swinging West End with its new discos – the Whisky A-Go-Go and Georgie Fame singing in the Flamingo.

But the boy from the Black Country was two people – the bright, fun-loving young man about town in garish clothes and the thespian trapped in the past. He sported breeches on stage and white hipster jeans on the street. He found it impossible to bring the two worlds together. The parts kept rolling in through his agents, as did the money – and he needed to earn a good living because of his gregarious and generous lifestyle. But he was still being sold as an aristocrat in a ruff, and Shakespeare was becoming old hat, except to academics.

Many of the new red-brick intelligentsia considered *Love's Labours Lost* to be an early document of student revolt, with Berowne leading a bearded sit-in for co-educational residences and Don Armado turned into a visiting professor from Havana, wreathed in cigar smoke, argumentative and quoting Che Guevara.

Olivier would have none of it, and the cast knew it in no uncertain terms. Jeremy was moved by his mentor's vision and stubborn refusal to bend the Bard's works.

Like Olivier, Jeremy too saw the play as a reflection of historic shadows drawn from the mind of Shakespeare . . . the forests of Tudor England, a wilderness of violent possibility where criminal and lover could escape beyond the law and be instructed in man's primitive resources, nature and morality. He adored the escapist world of forests and archery and wondered whether that was why he loved Shakespeare so much. The Bard offered him an escape route into a fantasy world.

* * *

The tears cascaded down Jeremy's face and he made no attempt to wipe his eyes. The emotion of the moment, as he sat at home in front of the TV screen, had rendered him completely powerless. Bobby Kennedy had been shot dead. He had cried when Martin Luther King was gunned down a few months earlier. Now this. What was happening to his beloved America?

A few months later Olivier was knighted and Jeremy was on a plane to New York.

4 New Beginnings

America is a country of young men

Emerson, 'Old Age'

JEREMY FOUND NEW YORK packed with humanity and he loved it. He was older and wiser now than in his days appearing in *Troilus and Cressida* at the Winter Garden and as Father Riccardo in *The Deputy* at the Brooks Atkinson. He wasn't quite so star-struck or big-headed. He quickly realised that if you were not gregarious, New York could be the loneliest city in the world. But he was as gregarious and as energetic as the natives were and, as he hardly slept, the city's lifestyle suited him. There was something going on 24 hours a day.

He adored Greenwich village with its bustling cafés and tiny restaurants, bounded to the east and west respectively by Broadway and the Hudson River. The illogical nest of streets west of Sixth Avenue made it an entirely appropriate setting for Bohemia, where people like Poe, Thomas, Dreiser, Melville and a host of others had lived, worked and played. And now Jeremy was working and playing there too.

He hated the subway, although the underground trains got him where he wanted to go quickly. But the system was to his mind unparalleled for grime, poor signs and crime, and anyway he was beginning to suffer from claustrophobia now. He didn't know why but he was experiencing anxiety states in confined places. Somehow he needed to see a doorway out, know that he could leave a place any second he chose. He hated to feel trapped. He preferred to take a Yellow Cab whenever he could, although the rudeness of some drivers made his English gentleman's conscience wince. Once, as he sped away from Kennedy Airport, the driver, with one hand on the wheel and the other across the back of the front passenger seat, said: 'You from

London, buddy?' At that moment a little old lady with two airport carrier bags stepped into the road.

'Watch out!' shouted Jeremy.

The driver, with one arm still over the seat, slammed on his brakes, managing to stop just a few feet from her. The old lady, rather shaken, stepped back on to the sidewalk and the driver pulled away.

'You know, buddy, if we hit one of them now we have to sign three forms!' he said.

Jeremy had fallen in love with Broadway from the moment he first set eyes on it. The longest street in the world ran the entire length of Manhattan and bustled with theatres, cinemas, night-spots and bars and something New York was never without – people. He mingled in the gay clubs and shopped in the best stores.

New Yorkers love a parade and so did he. They seemed to be the city's answer to the blues, and quickly became his. Every ethnic and national minority took its annual trip along Fifth Avenue and a host of political, social and religious events were celebrated with brass bands, drum majorettes, banners, clowns, exotic millinery, outrageous costumes and assorted monkeys. There was the St Patrick's Day Parade, the Easter Parade, Brooklyn Bridge Day and Martin Luther King Jr Memorial Day. What he liked about them best of all was the colours – the bright reds and greens, yellows and blues.

In the mornings Jeremy would stroll through Central Park. To his mind it shaped the city's spirit. It was the font of everything beautiful about New York, a sort of democratic free zone at its heart, explored and admired by all – a tranquil pond in the south-east corner, magical at dusk; the vast pastoral sheep meadow, without sheep; the maze of wooden paths through the Ramble; the washed-out brick and sandstone elegance of the Bethesda Fountain. Jeremy found a sort of comfort and spiritualism there, much as he was to many years later on London's Clapham Common.

It was 1970 and Jeremy was in New York to play Bassanio in *The Merchant of Venice* for CBS TV. Some American actors found his eccentric English character irritating. Others found him, and spoke of him as, a true professional. Earlier that year

Eton. Parents and pupils gather on 4 June 1933

The newly married, youthful couple. Jeremy Brett and Anna Massey on 24 May 1958

17 August 1959. Jeremy and Anna with baby David

Two years later the fashionable couple pose for the cameras in their Chelsea home

Anna Massey - the young, gamine actress

The first big break. Jeremy Brett in *War and Peace* with Audrey Hepburn, 1956

'He was princely in looks, manner, speech and authority.' Jeremy Brett in the Oxford Playhouse production of *Hamlet* at the Strand Theatre, 20 June 1961

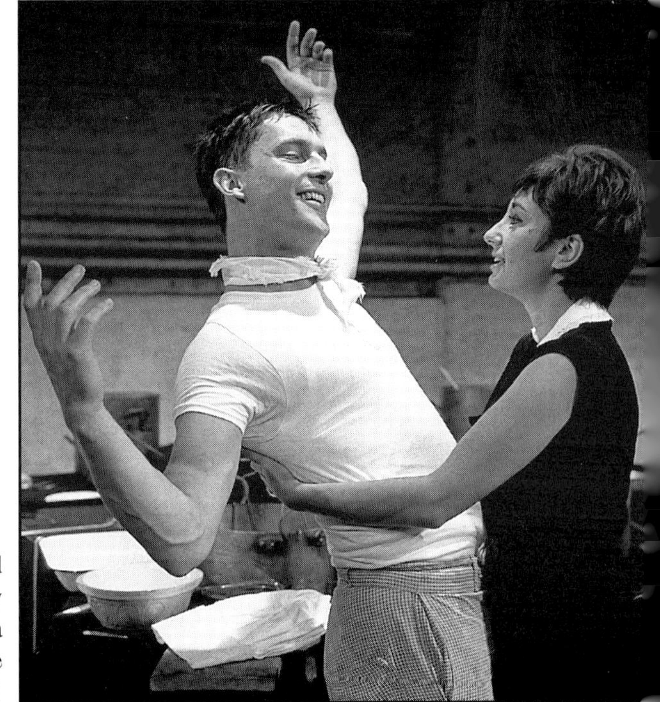

Having put on two stone and cut off his hair, Jeremy appeared alongside Sandra Caron in *The Kitchen* at the Royal Court Theatre, 1961

A very British young actor. Jeremy, with the world at his feet and his dog on his lap

Fast asleep with Mr Binks

Jeremy sorts through the fashionable and antique clutter of his west London top-floor flat in 1962

With Anne Heywood in *The Very Edge*. 'If you're going to do such terrible films then please make sure they don't come to our village,' said Jeremy's father

Once again on screen with Audrey Hepburn. Jeremy Brett as Freddie, at Ascot, in *My Fair Lady*, 1964

n conversation with *My Fair Lady*'s director George ukor, on Stage 7 in the Warner Bros Hollywood studios

'Hollywood has seldom looked lovelier' - *Variety*

Jeremy, dashing in seventies gear

he had played Bassanio in Jonathan Miller's Victorian production at the Old Vic for the National and received wide acclaim. Olivier sent him a note, written on the back of a programme, endorsing the critics' words.

By now Jeremy had experienced a stream of lovers, men and women. But he was never able to sustain a relationship. For some reason the sparkle seemed to fade and he would move on to pastures new. And yet he was looking for something more permanent – he didn't know what. He began to doubt himself, wondering why he couldn't get close to one person properly. He didn't feel comfortable having a relationship with a man, didn't like people knowing – it just wasn't socially acceptable.

Nursing these contradictory feelings, Jeremy returned to the UK to give one of his best performances – a masterly portrayal of feeble devotion as George Tesman to Maggie Smith's Hedda Gabler under Ingmar Bergman's direction. Maggie had now married Robert and they had a son, Christopher.

Jeremy created a wholly credible character, not the usual bungling fool but a very presentable, handsome young man who just happened to be too dull, too scholarly and too conventional for his wife.

'I feel I've woken up at last,' he told a theatre critic. 'I've never really given myself credit for being an actor until now. Suddenly, I've aged a bit, I believe that I'm not a pretender. I'm more determined, more experienced and I've learned to state what I mean and surmount all sorts of things with the use of positive thinking.'

It had taken him a long time to be happy with his role in life – that of actor. As Olivier had advised, he no longer needed to be 'polite' and justify himself or be 'gobblesome' because he was sure it wouldn't last.

The production was a brilliant conception. The scene, essential pieces of furniture only, was all blood red. A small movable screen indicated that the set represented two communicating rooms in Tesman's house. It enabled Bergman to show the characters who were not on stage, alone in the next room. The audience could see two sequences of events happening side by side. The play opened with the dialogue between Aunt Julia and the maid, happily gossiping about the returned honeymoon couple. As the audience listened to their sentimental chit-chat they watched Hedda standing, looking at herself in the mirror in despair, expressing her utter disgust at being pregnant.

Robert played Loevborg, a man of immense charm whose passionate nature had led him into brothels because women of intelligence and breeding were seemingly unattainable. It was a chance for the two old friends to be together again and swap stories. Jeremy was no longer just a Black Country boy who had come up to town.

'In the early days I tried too hard,' he admitted. 'I wasn't sure. I felt inadequate. I used to say to myself – I fooled them! But now I know I am on my way.'

And soon he was on his way to play the son of a blind barrister in John Mortimer's *A Voyage Round My Father* at the Haymarket, where he was a resounding success.

Robert meanwhile was appointed an associate director of the National Theatre and was considered to be Olivier's most trusted protégé. But his relationship with the guru of the English stage was under great strain, owing in some measure to Robert's own popularity with actors and audiences alike.

In 1973 Jeremy transferred to Greenwich where he starred opposite Joan Plowright in Ibsen's *Rosmersholm*. The story was set around the hypocritical John Rosmer, played by Jeremy, and Joan's domineering Rebecca West. True to his usual form, Ibsen had presented the distasteful and deranged pair as sympathetic, letting the audience see them as they saw themselves. Once again Jeremy had thrown himself into the role, reading his lines throughout the night, studying Ibsen, understanding him, digging deep into the character of Rosmer, even inventing a childhood for him. He wanted to become the part. What fascinated him in the early stages of the play was that the couple appeared intelligent, articulate, responsive to all that was new and humane and genuinely reforming in their society. But gradually they were revealed as self-indulgent, self-deceiving, morally evasive and literally murderous to anyone standing in their way.

It was a play built around a dazzling irony. Having destroyed a whole family to attain her ends and spur Rosmer into a life of public action, the Machiavellian Rebecca found that her own will was crippled by ennobling idealism. It was, as Freud said, a classic study of psychological failure at the moment of success, comparable to the crack-up of Lady Macbeth.

Jeremy found it a complex and difficult part to play, but he began to recognise bits of himself in the role. Rosmer was an ex-pastor, an intellectual sceptic and moral do-gooder whose crusade consisted of sitting for hours in his study reading uplifting books. He was a sexually inadequate husband and lover and a vacillating liberal who renounced his liberalism at the first sign of pressure from the opposition. Finally, almost in spite of himself, he was an ennobled individual accepting self-judgement and suicide. Into this part Jeremy was to bring the hand-wringing mannerisms he was later to use to convey the black thoughts of Sherlock Holmes. The play was a resounding success, even though some critics felt that Rosmer and Rebecca's agonising decision that they must both embrace their deaths did come a shade too easily. Others thought the open-plan set did not really embody the brooding presence of Rosmer's house, where his wife had died.

But Jeremy was thrilled to read in the *Guardian* the morning after the opening night: 'Robin Phillips's production is admirable. Rebecca herself is a vessel for implicit rather than explicit emotion; and Joan Plowright conveys this perfectly by starting outwardly serene; slowly cracking apart with the words coming in a throttled rush, the body losing all coordination; and then finally achieving fulfilment in death. And Jeremy Brett's Rosmer is a revelation; a bookish, private, ravaged individual with just enough latent sensuality to make you understand his magnetic attraction for Rebecca . . .'

Jeremy sat in the audience spellbound by the talent and sexual chemistry of the young man blessed with seemingly ageless good looks. Gary Bond reminded him of Michael York.

His performance as Joseph in the new Tim Rice and Andrew Lloyd Webber musical *Joseph and the Amazing Technicolor Dreamcoat* at the Albery Theatre was sensational. Gary, 32, made a convincing adolescent as the youth stranded by his brothers in Egypt. His ease, his intelligence in the role and his lightness of foot made him an instant hit with the audience. At the end of the show Jeremy stood and cheered with them as the cast took curtain call after curtain call. The show was to be such a success that it propelled Gary to a new level of public popularity. Princess Margaret saw the production five times and soon she and Gary became friends. What she didn't know then was that Jeremy and Gary had become lovers. They had hit it off immediately they met at a backstage party. Jeremy loved Gary's sense of fun and Gary adored Jeremy's infectious laughter. Slowly their relationship grew and they decided to live together. They had a lot in common.

Gary, born in Liss, Hampshire, and educated at Churcher's College in Petersfield, came from an army background, just like Jeremy. All his mother's brothers were in the service and his father was also a professional soldier, who wanted his son to pursue a steadier career than acting. But he died when Gary was just sixteen, leaving his son free to follow his own inclinations.

Gary also trained for the stage at the Central School of Speech and Drama, after winning a scholarship. Soon he was ploughing a steady if unspectacular course on the London stage in the late 1960s, mixing contemporary works with Shakespeare and Shaw. His first television role came in *War and Peace*, which was followed by his first film, *Zulu*. Other TV roles had included Pip in *Great Expectations* and Boswell in *Highland Jaunt*.

Joseph had originally been written as a 20-minute end-of-term school concert and premiered at the Edinburgh Festival in August 1972. It was the success of the festival and transferred first to the Round House on London's Haverstock Hill and then to the Albery the following year as a full-length production.

All Jeremy's close friends knew of their relationship and the two actors were frequent party guests, especially at the home of hairdresser Philip Kingsley. They were very close for five years. But Jeremy, approaching 40, still didn't like cohabiting with a man. He found it too complicated and always felt more comfortable and happier with a woman, both at home and in public. But he adored Gary and couldn't bear to be without him, until the moment the spark died. Jeremy's guilt had risen up inside him. And the truth was he no longer felt sexually attracted to the talented young actor. One night he engineered a row and walked out. But they were to remain friends for ever.

During this period Jeremy was the epitome of the seventies man. The vision of the typical Englishman to those who flew in from abroad was still a cross between Sherlock Holmes and a university don, wearing an old tweed jacket with a leather patch at the elbow, baggy trousers and maybe even mismatched socks. He would be a comfortable kind of man, a sort of lovable shaggy dog, perhaps a bit eccentric but someone you could depend on. He was personified at this time by people like actor Richard Briers, who would often be seen walking around London in a safari suit he had worn in a TV play. He liked it so much that he bought it.

But Britain had changed radically following the blaze of the sixties.

Jeremy was now talked about in the theatre world as the seventies thespian about town ... colourful shirts, cravats, flared trousers and battledress jackets. In fact he was such a fashionable, romantic figure in people's minds that mannequin-maker Adele Roostein, who had already made window dummies of Twiggy and Lady Jacqueline Rufus Isaacs, decided that he had the look of the moment and convinced him to model.

Soon there were life-size copies of him in shop windows all over the world, and he even represented modern man in the Bath Museum.

But the truth was that Jeremy never spent a lot of money on clothes. If he found something he liked he would flog it to death. Most of his cashmere sweaters had holes in them at the elbow and he still wore the suit he had taken his name from, which was given to him when he was seventeen.

He boasted to friends that he bought a couple of pairs of trousers, three pullovers and four shirts each year and that was all. 'If you have just a tiny bit of flair you don't really have to dress up,' he said.

The one fashion item that really did appeal to him was platform shoes. 'I fall about and hit my head on doors,' he said, 'but they're fun. Now I'm taller than all my three brothers.'

By this time Tarn was in Paris. She had married again, this time an American cancer specialist who worked in France. She had taken Robert's daughter Lucy with her and Jeremy visited them whenever he could. He adored her apartment with its high ceilings and antique furnishings. They would dine out at the best restaurants and true to style he would send bottles of champagne to other people's tables on a whim. Then he would spend ages asking the wine waiter how many children he had, or how his wife or mother was. Tarn would get irritated. Somehow it had seemed fun in the sixties. They were all young and carefree. Such behaviour was tolerated then but now it was embarrassing.

'Jeremy, do you have to do that?' she would ask after he had stood up at the restaurant table without warning and performed a song from *My Fair Lady*.

'Tarn, my dear, I didn't realise you had come to Paris to be a snob!' he would answer.

Sunday afternoons were not for the sleepy. Jeremy would arrive for lunch and insist that Tarn and her other guests spend the rest of the day engaged in a treasure hunt. He would rush around the apartment with safety pins, sticking them in unusual hiding places with the aid of Blu-tack – behind a mirror, under the seat of a chair, on the end of a curtain pole. The children would join in too.

It was around this time that Jeremy stood in for a short time for Alistair Cooke as presenter of *Masterpiece Theatre* for the Public Broadcasting Service of America. The American producer was Joan Wilson, known as Joan Sullivan, who was so overwhelmed by his handsomeness that she vowed to get to know him better. She had seen him on stage at the Phoenix Theatre in London, playing Otto in *Design for Living*.

But behind Jeremy's jokes and bonhomie at this time was sadness.

Robert was in despair. His portrayal of the title role in the Billy Wilder film *The Private Life of Sherlock Holmes* was a disastrous flop. He had believed it was going to be his greatest statement, like O'Toole's *Lawrence of Arabia* or Finney's *Tom Jones*. Wilder had told him it would make him a star. But it didn't. It took 29 weeks to film, seven years to write and had a budget of £5 million. It was cut from three hours to less than two, was a disastrous failure and made him ill.

Wilder had nursed the project with his scriptwriter, Izzy Diamond. Robert didn't need to audition because Wilder had seen his films. They met at London's Connaught Hotel and the deal was done over drinks. But Robert had to lose weight for the part and he went on a crash diet which sapped his strength. His only brief for the role was that Holmes was very tall, played the violin, was terrible with women, lived alone, took cocaine, described himself as a thinking machine and had a brother called Mycroft, who was much cleverer than he was and worked for the Foreign Office. With those facts in the back of his mind Robert suffered a crisis of confidence. He read everything he could on the great detective but the script presented a character totally different to Conan Doyle's. In the middle of shooting the film got on top of him. The demands Wilder made were too severe. The director himself wasn't sure how Holmes should be played. The movie was meant to be an affectionate, light look at the character, but Wilder had asked Robert not to try to be funny. Then he ordered the actor to slim down even more and try to look as thin as a pencil.

Robert was shooting for twelve hours a day at Pinewood Studios, going home to an empty house, getting his own food and then sitting up all night learning the complicated dialogue for the next day's work. And the lines had to be perfect, right down to the pauses for a comma, because at 6 o'clock the next morning Wilder would be on the set with Diamond behind him on every shot. As Robert did the scene Wilder would shout: 'Cut!' then turn to Diamond and say: 'Are all the words there, Izzy?' If they weren't, or the emphasis on a certain word wasn't right to his mind, then just one little scene would require 35 takes. Robert was exhausted both mentally and physically. His doctor gave him sleeping pills and he began to wash them down with alcohol. Then one evening he just drifted off in a haze in front of the television, waking up in hospital. Executives from the studio had broken in and found him slumped in the chair.

Things got worse. His relationship with Olivier had soured to such an extent that he resigned as associate director of the National Theatre. And if that wasn't enough, he and Maggie Smith appeared together in Noël Coward's *Private Lives*, the story of a couple whose marriage had failed. Unhappy together and unhappy apart, the play mirrored their own situation unbearably.

Everyone in the acting world felt that they had worked together too much and Robert had run out of cupboards in which to conceal his numerous sexual escapades. Off stage they had become like the characters in the Coward play . . . 'two violent acids bubbling about in a nasty little matrimonial bottle'. During the production they quarrelled bitterly. Maggie, in Robert's words, started 'messing about' on stage. He retaliated with a two-minute pause in the middle of a scene. When the curtain came down he claimed the pills she had been given made her work at double the pace of everyone else.

Jeremy supported his old friend, telephoning him almost every day, trying to wean him off the bottle. He would sit with him for hours, talking things over, chatting about the old days. Robert gradually came together a bit, but not much.

To see his old friend like that was breaking Jeremy up. Robert was a performer of pure instinct and self-assurance, hailed as a possible successor to Olivier, who had once described him as a natural heir. Now he was failing to live up to the accolade. But as always, he was failing in style.

The telephone rang and Jeremy picked it up.

'I've been to see him, old boy.'

'How is he?' Jeremy asked.

'His usual self, sometimes cutting, sometimes humorous. But I've got a surprise for him.'

For weeks Noël Coward had been ill in his suite in the Savoy. Everyone knew he was dying. Robert had visited him every day

– but in true Cowardesque style he was only allowed to see him if he brought up a present each time . . . flowers, chocolates, cologne.

'What's the surprise, then . . . two tickets to an opening night?'

'Twiggy,' said Robert with glee.

'What, he's going to sleep with Twiggy? I didn't think he liked women that way.'

The wafer-thin model was rehearsing for *The Boyfriend*, her first West End stage musical.

'No, no. I've just been to her twenty-first birthday party and I had the most wonderful idea. I told her that she was Noël's present for tomorrow. She's such a wonderful little thing . . . I think I'm in love with her, you know.'

Robert was as good as his word and he took Twiggy along the next day. Noël had the carpet rolled back in his suite and she tap-danced around his bed as he clapped with joy.

Noël died in 1973. It was yet another blow for Robert, who couldn't control his grief. He went to the Queen's Theatre where he and Maggie Smith were appearing in *Private Lives* and sat alone, weeping in the empty auditorium.

'How dare you die!' he suddenly screamed when it hit him that he would not be able to talk to his great friend ever again. Now, from being a gregarious, if over-indulgent, drinker, he began to take to the bottle more seriously – pints of beer topped up with double whiskies day and night. His looks changed dramatically and he began to develop a bulbous, bourbon nose.

He finally ended up in a London nursing home. Jeremy took him in but at first they wouldn't accept him because he was so drunk. He had been so desperate that he had found a bottle of vodka in Jeremy's flat and drunk most of it. Eventually he was hospitalised and given sedatives. Jeremy was mortified. He couldn't stand to watch people in pain, physically or mentally, and seeing his friend like that was more than he could take.

Two nights later Robert slipped out of care and turned up in his pyjamas at a theatre where Jeremy was appearing. He was in a terrible state and they both cried. Jeremy eventually persuaded him to return to the nursing home. Finally, after two months, he couldn't stand to see his friend there any more and took him home to look after him.

Over the next year or so there was no need for Jeremy to find work. Work always found him, but the roles, mostly for television, were never modern ones . . . Count Kinsky in *Jennie, Lady Randolph Churchill*, Father Daley in *The Prodigal Daughter*, Willie Edwardes in *Ten from the Twenties* and Captain Absolute in *The Rivals*.

It was a wonderfully warm June afternoon in Stratford, Ontario, that rather puritanical part of Canada. The sort of afternoon for barbecues and martinis on the patio.

The chattering ladies sitting at the bottom of the garden were passing around egg-and-cress sandwiches and stirring their bone-china teacups with clinking teaspoons. They were discussing the price of summer frocks and winter boots when the hostess of the afternoon, Yvonne Masters, suddenly dropped her plate. Her friends followed her gaze . . .

Wandering around the garden next door was a man smoking a cigarette, sipping a glass of champagne and wearing a smile – and that was all. 'Good afternoon, ladies,' said a naked Jeremy, waving to them in his grand, dramatic way. Suddenly the garden party was over.

The next day Jeremy made amends for his outrageous appearance in the rose bed and invited all the ladies round to tea, where he appeared fully clothed and was his normal gregarious self. They adored him.

It was 1976 and Jeremy, now 41, had rented a house in bustling Perth County. He had left England and moved to North America to become 'a movie star'. He had finally decided to uproot himself because he believed that he had become a sort of 'semi-establishment' figure. He had a big house in Campden Hill Square, Kensington, a nice racy car, a growing tummy and by now more than enough money. But he had come to realise that he was actually full of 'bluff, plonk and Polyfilla'. The moment of acute realisation came when his son David drew a caricature of him which dwelt on all his worst points – including his newly acquired earring!

Jeremy was playing Mirabell in *The Way of the World* and Oberon in *A Midsummer Night's Dream* and at the same time trying to settle into the way of life of this south-eastern Ontario city, named after Shakespeare's birthplace, nestling on the banks of the Avon River. The hotchpotch of factories producing car parts, furniture, clothing and metal and plastic goods was the backcloth to an art-loving society. The Stratford Festival, an annual event since 1953, was a world-famous drama extravaganza that lasted more than six months, featuring plays from the Bard and other English writers. Jeremy was glad that he had made the break from England. The previous year had not been a good one, culminating as it did in the death of his childhood sweetheart Mary Ure at the young age of 42, which left him heartbroken.

He was by now becoming well known to American and Canadian TV viewers because he introduced a popular programme called *Piccadilly Circus* produced by Joan Sullivan, on the Public Broadcasting network. It featured some of the best of British TV shows, among them *The Goodies* and *The Stanley Baxter Show*. He was, he believed, a sort of 'poor man's Alistair Cooke', and he felt that Joan had rather stuck her neck out to get him the job. She had argued to her bosses that his performance in a Sheridan play shown on *Classic Theatre* was outstanding, and during her interview with him he had proved that he had what it took to be a presenter.

Joan, originally a milkmaid from Wisconsin and one-quarter Cherokee, was very taken with the handsome, debonair, gregarious Englishman, but not in a sexual way. She liked the way he talked and his energy, and they were becoming firm friends.

She had one of the best jobs in American television, jetting to Europe several times a year, taking in London, Cannes and occasionally Italy. She hobnobbed in New York with powerful oil magnates, made critical decisions which determined what millions of Americans watched each week, and was respected for her good taste and commitment to perfection.

But she had a darker side. She was a believer in the occult. Her black Mustang parked in the WGBH parking lot bore the licence plate WITCH. It was an interest that excited Jeremy, who loved anything outlandish or spiritual.

One of Jeremy's first TV jobs for *Piccadilly Circus* was to introduce Irish comedian Dave Allen to America.

'Dave takes risks,' Jeremy said, 'he kids about Catholicism and sex; makes satirical observations on anything and everything and even performs in sketches that combine the zaniness of *Monty Python's Flying Circus* and Marty Feldman.'

At that time the United States was awash with headlines about IRA bombs going off in England and people fearing for their lives because of the tense political situation in Northern Ireland. Suddenly Americans wanted to know about Allen, the funny Irishman whom they believed was busy easing the tensions with his outrageous brand of comedy. Allen, in his customary pose, performing from a stool while leisurely sipping a drink and smoking a cigarette, soon won them over.

Jeremy desperately wanted to bridge the gap between America and England in the same way that Alistair Cooke did hosting *Masterpiece Theatre* for the network. Strangely, he would one day be the star of *Masterpiece* himself, in the most successful TV detective series ever filmed.

'What Cooke did was to create a kind of island between the two countries,' he told American journalist Kay Gardella, sent along to interview him about the series. 'I cannot tell you how important his broadcasts about America are in England. He feeds us marvellously considered things about the States with deep, deep passion. I can only talk about myself and friends, but I can assure you that most of them listen to him every single week. The material he brings us is not just heavy news – but interesting anecdotes that serve almost as parables about contemporary happenings.'

As the conversation went on, Jeremy got into his stride, almost as if he were on stage. 'We don't know where we're going,' he said innocently about England. 'We've lost Ireland, we've lost Scotland. We're no longer the British Isles. Yet I'm so proud of my country, which is England, and we need you Americans desperately.' Sadly America didn't really need Jeremy. The gregarious, energetic and often over-enthusiastic actor was desperately trying to get a Green Card to allow him to live and work in the United States. But the authorities kept turning him down. Joan and WGBH managed to get him a temporary work permit but time was running out.

He had left for the wide open spaces of Canada and taken with him what he thought was a fairly watertight reputation – various West End hits, several seasons at the National Theatre, plenty of television and films such as *My Fair Lady*, *The Medusa Touch* with Richard Burton and *The Wild and the Willing* with John Hurt.

When he had first arrived in the country he had discovered that he loved the wide open spaces but loathed the extreme climate. The cold of the winter was fierce and the heat of the summer oppressive. He was lucky to land the role of the Captain in *Young Daniel Boone* for CBS TV because Jeremy Kemp had left to return to England. Suddenly, though, he found himself sitting in the foothills, eating avocado and thinking nice thoughts, waiting for more parts to come along.

He played Stratford, he read scripts, but he was lonely and took a series of male lovers while starring as Robert Browning in *Robert and Elizabeth* in Ottawa, Ontario and Toronto.

He waited vainly for the big parts to come along. Finally, forced by pride to do something because he had told lots of his friends at home that he was going to America to make it big, he relocated to Hollywood. He desperately wanted to be 'a mid-Atlantic star', an actor loved and admired on both sides of the pond like Audrey Hepburn, Elizabeth Taylor, Rex Harrison, Laurence Olivier and Deborah Kerr. But singing was out. He had now decided that if he was to be taken seriously as an actor he had to stop warbling on screen. The battle for stardom was on from the moment the taxi dropped him at his hotel in Beverly Hills.

First he went to an audition for *The Incredible Hulk*, the popular TV series starring Bill Bixby as the everyday guy who turned into a gigantic green monster, undertaking incredible feats for a good cause. The producers needed somebody to play an Englishman with a deep voice who was in cosmetics in Chicago. So he put on his blazer and went along with eighteen others to read. After the audition the casting director shook his hand and said: 'Welcome to the colonies, bud.'

Suddenly he found himself afloat in Tinsel Town at last. Directors in England began inviting him back home for roles. His fame was spreading. This was it – or was it?

Jeremy now found himself obsessed with Joan Sullivan. They would sit up into the early hours, drinking and talking about life after death and black magic, or fly to New York and dine at Yonah Schimmel's Knishes in Houston Street on the Lower East Side. They loved the thin pastry crusts baked around Yonah's potatoes, the smoked whitefish, pickled salmon and herring in sour cream with onion rings – with caviar, of course. They both adored dancing and would jive and rumba until dawn. Jeremy turned Joan into a kind of fantasy. She knew he was bisexual. But he loved her and was in love with being in love . . . and he was wonderful with her two children. The last thing on Joan's mind was marriage, but Jeremy still could not get a Green Card. His only chance was to marry an American. One night the two of them popped a bottle of champagne and toasted their forthcoming secret wedding. It was to be a marriage of convenience between two friends locked in a spiritual friendship, nothing more.

The following year Jeremy and Joan became man and wife at the home of a Justice of the Peace and they kept their secret from everyone. Jeremy bought a big new house in the Los Angeles hills and became an American resident. Being English in Hollywood he was offered, and accepted, parts playing anything from an Irish paddy in a remake of *Madame X* to a cool Brit in *Hart to Hart*. Then he took the lead role in the stage version of *Dracula*, breaking all box office records in California and Chicago. On TV, radio and in the press he described himself as a poor man's Frank Langella.

Next came a breathtaking appearance as Max de Winter in *Rebecca* for the BBC back in London. Many critics felt it was better than Olivier's portrayal for Hitchcock.

After a small part in *Battlestar Galactica* for Warner in America, Jeremy flew back to London to put on his aristocratic mask again as the Earl of Bristol in the BBC play *On Approval*.

Joan had always believed that the secret of a good marriage was healthy separations and theirs certainly had those. That year she spent a week with Jeremy in January. In February they got together when Mobil threw a party for *Masterpiece Theatre* and in April she flew to London to see him. Mostly he stayed in Los Angeles and she stayed in Boston. Joan rarely took holidays, preferring work to play. In many ways Jeremy found her bossy but he liked that. He would say to her: 'Darling, I'm so glad that we don't live together all year round.' He described their relationship as the perfect marriage even though they were two people whose first love in life was their careers. She became his confidante, his adviser. He would listen to her as he had to his mother. She understood the hell he went through as an actor.

Then, in 1981, Jeremy was back across the Atlantic again to play Dr Watson to Charlton Heston's Sherlock Holmes in *The Crucifer of Blood*. The honours went to him and he carried off the coveted Los Angeles Drama Critics Choice award for his performance.

This was Jeremy's first understanding of the relationship between Holmes and Watson. Watson wasn't the doddering plodder who followed behind the great detective after all. He had compassion, picked Holmes up when he was down and kept him straight. Jeremy wished he had a Watson in his life.

Suddenly he was looking at Holmes from Watson's side – and he began to learn that Holmes was the loneliest man in English literature. He felt that Holmes was a very private man, a tragic genius, while Watson had his friends and his surgery.

Jeremy didn't study the canon much for the part. The script was a *fait accompli*, based loosely on a Doyle story. It was not an authentic, faithful recreation. Even now, just as at Eton, Jeremy did not take much to Holmes, and the story didn't interest him that much either. He once even referred to his role as Watson as 'a bit like the cartoon character Snoopy'.

Paul Giovanni's play had started life at a small theatre in Buffalo early in 1978 and then moved to Broadway. It was a reworking of *The Sign of Four*, following the example set by Gillette's play, treating the story of a lethal curse as full-blooded melodrama with traditional thunder and lightning. It skilfully incorporated many of Holmes's celebrated maxims.

But it also added a modern twist, the playwright quoting Watson in the programme as having previously spared his readers 'the heart of this appalling story', for 'no event in my subsequent life could ever erase from my mind the pain and horror of this dreadful case. Now at last all can be revealed.' Though ingenious, the whole production had a belittling effect on Holmes and Watson. They were seen as an eccentric pair of English detectives who stumbled on clues quite by chance.

Jeremy returned to England to play a memorable Captain Ashburnham in *The Good Soldier* for Granada Television. Again he was hailed by the critics for his fine acting in the adaptation of Ford Madox Ford's complex novel.

Tarn had left Paris to live in Winchester again and weekends with her were now back on Jeremy's schedule. Her children adored him, but as they grew older they found him more bizarre.

'You can't go into the drawing room, Mother, it's flooded with Jeremy's tears,' her daughter announced one day, bursting into the kitchen.

Tarn wasn't surprised. Jeremy was always an inveterate weeper. He would shed buckets of tears over films on television, news stories, even a cricket match.

'He has to be my favourite person,' her daughter went on. 'I mean, to sit and cry like that over Charlton Heston in a chariot race.'

Jeremy was always popular with the youngsters, and with none more so than his cousin Martin Clunes.

Martin's father, classical actor Alec Clunes, who was Jeremy's uncle, had died when he was eight. They were extremely close and the death affected the boy deeply. To fill the hole that suddenly appeared in his life Martin turned to Jeremy for friendship and guidance. He was not disappointed. Jeremy became almost a second father, advising him and listening to his troubles. When Martin wanted to go on stage it was Jeremy who encouraged him and helped him to achieve his ambitions.

Martin trained for the stage when he was sixteen before going into weekly rep. Before he started, Jeremy offered to pay for an operation to have his ears pinned back. Martin, teased about his big ears at school, considered the idea for a while but in the end decided that they were the shape he was born with and that was the shape they should stay. They turned out to be his biggest assets, and less than 20 years later he was to be instantly recognisable in millions of homes across Britain as Gary in the smash-hit TV series *Men Behaving Badly*.

Jeremy's TV career was picking up again and in 1982 he played Prime Minister William Pitt the Younger in the BBC production *Number 10*. He remembered with pride how Premier Margaret Thatcher arrived at the studios one morning to meet him and they both stood on the doorstep of No. 10 on the specially created set of Downing Street. Next came Browning in *The Barretts of Wimpole Street* and King Arthur in *Morte d'Arthur* for the same station.

But there was one TV role to come that would change his life forever.

5 Becoming Sherlock Holmes

. . . A story for which the world is not yet prepared

Conan Doyle,
The Casebook of Sherlock Holmes

'DON'T BLOODY WELL DO IT!' Robert screamed down the telephone.

'But, darling, you bloody well managed it and came out the other side!' Jeremy laughed back.

'No, I just managed to get out from underneath and I was lucky it didn't kill me,' said Robert. 'You will have to go into such a pit to get into that man that you will self-destruct!'

Robert put down the telephone, knowing it was no use. His friend had made up his mind. He poured himself a large vodka and tonic to blot out the memory of his own disastrous time as Sherlock Holmes in the Billy Wilder movie that had made him so ill. And yet he was tougher than Jeremy. He was a rough-and-tumble working-class boy from Bristol, hard-drinking and hard-hitting. Jeremy was a silver-spoon softie, too sensitive, too inward. If he hadn't been able to handle it, how would Jeremy?

It was February 1982 and Jeremy had just been approached by Granada TV to play the Victorian supersleuth who had blighted the careers of a long line of actors.

Jeremy's agent, Jane Annakin, was worried too. She knew that Jeremy was very aware of what had happened to his friend and the toll the part had taken on other actors. She knew too how absorbed Jeremy became in a part. If he took the role of Holmes he would throw himself into it. He lived and breathed acting and this spilled over into his private life.

One hundred miles away, at the heart of the Granada TV empire, a bustling complex of office blocks, studios and never-ending corridors in Castleford, near Manchester, the seed of one man's dream had finally blossomed. For years producer Michael Cox had pledged that he would one day make a totally authentic and faithful adaptation of the best cases of Sherlock Holmes.

His quest had begun two years earlier in 1980 on the anniversary of Sir Arthur Conan Doyle's death. The 50-year copyright on the author's works had ended and they were now in the public domain. From his fifth-floor office, overlooking the legendary set of *Coronation Street*, Michael began to lay plans to fulfil his dream. He wanted the central characters to step right out of Sidney Paget's illustrations in the original *Strand* magazine which had featured the Conan Doyle stories. But he was hitting a brick wall. Granada executives thought his idea was corny. His only way forward was to prove his brainwave was a money spinner.

Paget had brought Doyle's gripping tales to life, capturing the moods, haunting looks and postures of Holmes. The drawings were recognised as the authoritative version of how the great detective looked, even though Conan Doyle himself was never entirely happy with the illustrator's interpretation of his character. Paget cunningly used his brother Walter as a model for the supersleuth because he had a long nose and eagle eyes. That nose was to become famous in sketches depicting 38 adventures, including *The Hound of the Baskervilles*. After Sidney's death, Walter even illustrated one of the stories himself.

On a grey, drizzly day in the autumn of 1981, Michael invited three people to dinner at a restaurant in London's Charlotte Street . . . Jeremy Brett, his son David, and Doreen Jones, Head of Casting for Granada TV. Jeremy, who was still living in Los Angeles, had flown back to Britain to look for work on the London stage, his dreams of making it big in Hollywood evaporating into the air like the smoke from Holmes's best clay pipe.

Michael already had the go-ahead for a Sherlock Holmes series provided he and Doreen could come up with some suitably charismatic casting. To their minds that meant a classical actor with a good voice who looked as though he had stepped out of a Sidney Paget illustration, and for Granada it meant an actor who would be acceptable to the American market so that the series could be sold to the Public Broadcasting Service in advance of production. Jeremy satisfied all the criteria – he had the looks, the intelligence, the presence and the physique – but that did not mean that he would automatically accept. However, Michael knew that the actor liked Granada. He had worked with them the previous year on *The Good Soldier*, so he knew what to expect of the company and of rehearsing in Manchester where his acting career had begun. This was a particularly good time for Granada. The company's international reputation was high because *Brideshead Revisited* had just been broadcast both in Britain and the United States and had launched a new decade of blue-chip television drama.

The evening went well with Jeremy at his outrageous best. Michael talked about his plans for the series which he promised would be faithful to Doyle and made to the same high standard as the other classic adaptations for which British TV was by now becoming famous. It seemed incredible to Jeremy that never before had Conan Doyle's stories been faithfully recreated on stage or screen. He was interested, enthusiastic even. But he did not commit himself. He wanted something on paper . . . dates and money and all the other things that actors always leave to their agents to sort out. David, meanwhile, was less than enthusiastic. He was polite but uncertain about the strain such a role would have on his father. He would be proved right. As the wine flowed, the four of them talked about everything else under the sun until the bill arrived and they drank a final toast to the Granada budget.

At that moment a damp and bedraggled young flower girl arrived at the table and asked if they would buy a pot of plastic blooms. With a wave of his hand Jeremy bought the entire stock and then entered into a lengthy conversation with her during which no one else could get a word in. When he discovered that she was a student trying to supplement a grant he appeared distressed and wanted to know if she had any warm, dry clothes to put on. The student, who had entered the restaurant feeling like Audrey Hepburn's Eliza Doolittle in *My Fair Lady*, eventually left feeling like Audrey Hepburn's princess in *War and Peace*.

As they drove home in the rain David turned to Jeremy and said: 'Dad, you don't really want to do this, do you – play Holmes, I mean?'

'No, I don't think so, I really don't,' he answered thoughtfully. 'After all, he's a bit of a hairy old chestnut. Everyone has done it. I don't think there is anything left to bring to the part.'

Days later Jeremy flew back to Canada where he was appearing as Prospero in *The Tempest* for his own company, Toronto Workshop Productions, formed out of his frustration with lack of Hollywood success. He also directed the play. Meanwhile Michael found himself beset by problems with copyright laws in the United States and the rest of the world, especially with a company named Mapleton Films, which claimed it owned the sole rights to the characters of Holmes and Watson. Michael pressed on undaunted. He brought in John Hawkesworth as a consultant on the project. John was one of the most respected names in television, both at home and in America. He was a first-class scriptwriter and had the advantage of being a top producer too, hailed as the man behind the successful TV series *Upstairs Downstairs*. John began his working life as a designer at London's Shepperton Studios with Victor Korda. One day Korda suffered an accident and John suddenly found himself art director on *The Third Man*. His career took off from there.

Michael couldn't believe his luck in getting him. He and John worked separately at first, making their own lists of the stories they thought should be used in the series. When they compared notes they realised they were on the same wavelength. But Michael still had his own firm ideas . . . and soon everyone on the set was to realise that, including Jeremy.

Next came the other parts. Who would play Watson? Who would play the great detective's arch-enemy, Moriarty, or Irene Adler, one of the two most important women in the life of the man who never really was?

Slowly, painstakingly, they came up with a list.

There was never a better bet. From the time Jeremy's name was mooted the only worry for the Granada team was: would he do it?

'He certainly has the look for the part,' an executive said at a meeting. 'Physically he is a very good equivalent of Paget's Holmes – the long nose, the slim physique.'

Like Michael and Doreen, the team were even more impressed with Jeremy's Shakespearian acting background. They felt he had the energy too. And he did. But no one realised that his energy was becoming a little more manic. And why should they? For them the most important thing was that he had the aura of aristocracy, elegance and poise of a Holmes the world was still desperately trying to understand. That is why he was never asked to undergo a test for the role – just like Hollywood actor Basil Rathbone, who for many Sherlockians was the definitive Victorian supersleuth. Rathbone was picked for the part during a dinner party in Hollywood in 1939, as the war clouds gathered over Europe. Top screenwriter George Markey turned to his host, Darryl F. Zanuck, the head of Twentieth Century-Fox, and said: 'You know, someone ought to film Conan Doyle's classic detective story, *The Adventures of Sherlock Holmes*.'

The idea instantly appealed to Zanuck. He downed a large martini, leaned back in his chair and replied: 'I like it, but who would play this strange Englishman?'

Markey didn't hesitate. 'How about Basil Rathbone?'

'And Watson?'

'How about Nigel Bruce?'

They proved to be inspired choices.

Michael knew he could not guarantee Jeremy success, nor could he offer anything to one of Britain's most mature and established stage performers other than months of exhausting work in a part that had defeated many actors, including his great friend Robert Stephens.

Everyone had told Michael that Jeremy was a perfectionist and, if he accepted the role, he would have to be fully prepared for the part in every detail. But Michael didn't realise at the time just how true this was. He would find out the hard way. And at that stage he didn't realise how frightened of the part Jeremy really was.

Meanwhile the long delay over copyright worked in

Granada's favour. For by 1983 Mapleton Films, which had made two movie-length TV episodes – *The Hound of the Baskervilles* and *The Sign of Four*, starring Ian Richardson as Holmes, had capitulated. The legal battle was over. There was more good news for the Granada team – Jeremy was back in Britain and had failed to raise any money for his new venture, a film version of *The Tempest*. By now, Michael and his research assistants had painstakingly combed Conan Doyle's legendary 56 short stories and four novels to create a sort of Bible on the master detective. Holmes was a complex character and such a document would be helpful to actors, directors, writers and the production crew on the new series. Conan Doyle had always acknowledged his debt to his teacher, Professor Joseph Bell at Edinburgh University, for providing the basis of one of Holmes's most famous traits – his skill in the art of deduction. Bell apparently had an eagle face and an eerie way of spotting details. It was this look and the body language that went with it which Michael was determined to capture. Jeremy was the ideal candidate.

From the detective's clothes and personal items to his eating and drinking habits, the 77-page Baker Street File, which was later to be Jeremy's dearest possession on the set, began to emerge.

Holmes would blow great clouds of cigarette smoke when he was triumphant. That fact found its way into the section headed 'Smoking', along with references to his pipe rack. As if referring to a dictionary, Jeremy would be able to look up detail after detail.

Holmes had an oily, black clay pipe and an old brier. He smoked shag – sometimes a whole ounce in one night. His long cherrywood pipe replaced his clay one when he was in an argumentative mood. His cigars were kept in a box and he would blow smoke rings from them. His 'before breakfast' pipe consisted of the plugs left over from his smokes of the day before, all carefully dried and collected in the corner of the mantelpiece at 221B Baker Street.

After each of the 1,200 references in the Bible there was a four-letter key, identifying which story the item came from.

Under the section on drugs, for example, Jeremy would turn to fact number 22 and learn that Holmes used cocaine regularly, alternating between the drowsiness induced by the drug and his own natural fierce energy. That item would be followed by the keyword SCAN – short for the story *A Scandal in Bohemia*.

One of the most interesting sections was mannerisms. Jeremy would follow the hints to the letter. Item 109 told how Holmes would pace the room with his head sunk upon his chest, his hands clasped behind him (SCAN). Number 112 revealed exactly how he would curl up in his chair with his knees drawn up to his hawk-like nose. His eyes would be closed, his black clay pipe thrust out like the beak of some strange bird as he pondered a problem (REDH) – *The Red-Headed League*.

The Baker Street file, however, shed no light on the theory that Holmes was addicted to cocaine, based on his repeated demand: 'Quick, Watson, the needle.' Nor was it very enlightening on the hypothesis that he was homosexual. Pro-gay theorists always pointed to Holmesian remarks such as 'Watson, the fair sex is your department', and the detective's observation that the doctor, his roommate, was his only friend and 'my boy'.

In many ways Jeremy would find the mannerisms of Holmes a reflection of his own character, the darker side of his own being. Holmes would sit with a weary, heavy-lidded expression that concealed his keen and eager nature; he would lean his chin on his hands and stare into the fire; he would laugh, sometimes heartily and for some time, often till limp and helpless. Jeremy would laugh, sing and shout aloud at restaurants, then, feeling limp, bored and reflective, suddenly leave in the middle of meals without explanation, returning home or to his hotel room, to sit weary and heavy-eyed for hours, staring into a fire or at a painting hanging on the wall.

Jeremy returned home from the library clutching a pile of books on the great detective who had earned his creator a knighthood. Could he do it, would he do it? He still didn't know. All he knew was that he needed adventure, he needed to work. First he had to understand Holmes, dig deep into him, see if he could 'become' the great sleuth. The only way to do that was through Conan Doyle. He had managed to 'become' Watson opposite Charlton Heston, but this was something entirely different. Although he had read one or two of the stories then, he had never become completely immersed in the fine detail of the detective's complicated character. There had been no need. This time it was different, though. If he was going to play Holmes he had to find out all he could about Conan Doyle too.

The author, he already knew from his days at Eton, had practised for eight years as a doctor in the residential suburb of Southsea, Portsmouth, before he charmed the world with his famous novels *The White Company* and *The Refugees* and then astonished it with *The Adventures of Sherlock Holmes*, the title of the planned Granada series. He was a physician with time on his hands who read detective stories and dreamed up the fictional Victorian supersleuth because in every book he read, the crimes appeared to be solved by flukes or the solutions were left unexplained. He knew that he could do better – and he did. But in the end his monstrous creation began to undermine him. He never planned or wanted to write so much on the dark character that was to make him world famous.

Jeremy started at the beginning. Edinburgh-born Conan Doyle was the son of artist Charles Doyle, grandson of famous satirist John Doyle and nephew of Dicky Doyle of *Punch* magazine. His early connection with literature came when he sat as a little boy on the knee of the immortal Thackeray.

Sherlock Holmes had first cast his elegant, caped shadow across the pages of crime fiction in 1887 in the novel *A Study in Scarlet*, followed by *The Sign of Four* in 1890. By then the public had come to believe that he was real. People in trouble turned up at Baker Street searching in vain for 221B. The building they saw did not relate to the fictional building they had read about and so they would walk up and down the street hoping to spot the house that Doyle had so vividly described. Surely Dr Watson, the chronicler, although renowned for his inaccuracy over dates, could not have made a mistake with the number of his famous colleague's house? In one story, Watson had described 221B as having a bow window at the front and so people began knocking on doors to ask residents if they knew of such a place.

Jeremy knew that a flood of letters still poured into 221B, an address occupied by the Abbey National Building Society. A secretary duly answered them all saying that Mr Holmes was away on business and could not take on any more cases. There were 80 societies honouring the memory of Sherlock Holmes in the United States alone. The largest, the Baker Street Irregulars, boasted 3,000 members.

Some people believed that Holmes was still pottering about in a netted helmet at his retirement home – a bee farm on the Sussex Downs. If that was true, Jeremy estimated that dear old Sherlock would be about 130 by now. He only hoped he would live that long.

Interestingly, Conan Doyle had originally come up with a rather exotic name for his great detective – Sherrinford Holmes – and his adventures would be told by Ormond Sacker. They were going to make their debut in a story called *A Tangled Skein*. But Conan Doyle finally rejected the names because they were too long and too obscure. The story became *A Study in Scarlet*.

Jeremy wanted to be the best living Sherlock Holmes the world had ever seen, but was afraid that the part of Holmes might bring his career to a grinding halt. The stage history of the great detective was littered with successes and failures. Holmes had transcended the pages of *Strand* magazine to feature in plays, films, television and radio. A host of talented actors had played the hawk-nosed detective in more than 150 films, ranging from silent-screen one-reelers to big-budget epics and made-for-TV movies. The earliest acknowledged play starring the intrepid detective was by a minor dramatist of the 1890s, Charles Rogers, whose only claim to fame was the success of his lurid melodrama *£1000 Reward*. Conan Doyle had in fact written his own play about Holmes which he submitted to the legendary actor-manager Herbert Beerbohm Tree, who tried to persuade him to rewrite scenes so that he could adapt the character to his own acting abilities and ego. Conan Doyle understandably declined and the play was abandoned. But in 1899 the script came into the hands of theatrical impresario Charles Frohman, who submitted it to stern-faced American actor and playwright William Gillette. The play was rewritten so thoroughly it was essentially new, and *Sherlock Holmes* opened in New York in November 1899 to ecstatic reviews. By September 1901 Gillette had brought the production to the Lyceum in London, with himself starring in the title role.

In 1921 the first serious British attempt to bring Holmes to the screen was undertaken by Stoll Picture Productions, which released a series of silent films entitled *The Adventures of Sherlock Holmes*. Conan Doyle, who saw some of them, was so impressed that he announced to the world: 'If Gillette was Sherlock Holmes to theatre audiences, then this man IS Holmes to cinemagoers!' The name of the star who played the legendary Victorian supersleuth was Anthony Edward Brett, a classical actor of the time. Lawyer's son Brett changed his name to Eille Norwood to placate his father who was angry that he didn't follow him into the legal profession after Cambridge, believing acting to be a lowly profession, full of homosexuals and ne'er-do-wells, not a career for the son of a successful man. Brett chose the Christian name Eille after an old girlfriend and Norwood from his father's address. Jeremy had a feeling of déjà vu.

Gillette's success with Sherlock Holmes continued, and as late as 1929, at the age of 76, he undertook a three-year tour of America with the play. He also made history when he became the first radio Holmes in 1930. In fact Gillette earned so much money from Conan Doyle's creation that he built a breathtaking multi-million-dollar castle along the banks of the Connecticut River where he would often stand looking down from the turrets in full Holmes regalia . . . the deerstalker, the cloak and the pipe.

Among other actors who had played the part were Clive Brook in the 1920s; Arthur Wontner and Louis Hector in the 1930s; Basil Rathbone in the 1940s; Alan Wheatley, Ronald Howard and Peter Cushing in the 1950s; Douglas Wilmer and Christopher Lee in the 1960s; and Stewart Granger and Roger

Moore in the 1970s. Not to mention John Barrymore, Frank Langella, Christopher Plummer, Tom Baker, Jeremy's friend Robert Stephens and Anthony Edward Brett, alias Eille Norwood, who had read all the Sherlock Holmes stories published at the time and had apparently vowed to make his character as close to the original as possible. In Jeremy's mind, that fact settled it for him. If he were to play Holmes he had to 'become'.

What fascinated him was Conan Doyle's obsession with spiritualism, which began around the same time as his world-famous creation. He would talk for hours with a patient of his named General Alfred Drayson, who professed to be an expert on the matter. Drayson, a well-known astronomer and mathematician, was a man after Conan Doyle's own heart who loved military history, writing and the card game whist. He was convinced that there was life after death following conversations he had with his dead brother through a medium. Spiritualism, Drayson insisted, was not only a fact – it could be proved.

During the last twelve years of his life, Conan Doyle wanted to be a missionary, to spread the good news of spiritualism to other people. 'Spiritualism is the basis for all religious improvement in the human race!' he said. 'When I talk on this subject I am not talking about what I believe, I am not talking about what I think, I am talking about what I know.'

Jeremy was now 47 years old and the mirror in his bathroom told him that he was beginning to look his age, although he was still a good-looking man. Men and women continued to find him attractive. He hadn't lost his figure but there were deep lines over his eyes which he thought gave him more character. Was this the time for a real character role?

A week later Jeremy flew to Barbados where a male friend kept a leather-bound set of Conan Doyle's complete works. He spent the entire holiday swimming, drinking and reading. When he returned to London he knew he had to do it, had to be the best Holmes the public had ever known. He couldn't stop himself now, even if he did feel he was revisiting the isolated world of his schooldays. Every night a train of thoughts sped through his mind . . . Holmes, Rathbone, Doyle.

The thoughts were fleeting and he tried to keep hold of them, especially the haunting words of his mother: 'I don't want you to do anything until you absolutely can't help it, or you are sure you want to do it!'

Within days he had signed the contract and had become the 117th actor to play the most famous detective in fictional history.

Michael Cox stared down from his office window at the set of *Coronation Street.* He knew that Holmes without Dr Watson was inconceivable. The success and durability of the Conan Doyle adventures were due to both men, who were inseparable. Without Watson, Holmes would probably have gone mad. With his all-consuming interest in crime he would have lost his mind without someone sensible by his side, someone he could impress, someone who would listen in awe, who would nag him to eat, remind him to dress properly, warn him of the dangers of cocaine. Someone very middle-class and at times a little boring, who would represent the man in the street. Somehow the vision of the great author in the early 1900s remained true in 1982. The majority of middle-class people in England were Dr Watsons. He was common ground. He had more in common with his creator than Holmes.

Equally, without Holmes, Watson would probably have died of boredom. As a retired army doctor on a small pension and with a boring practice in somewhere like Paddington, he would have cut a rather sad figure. Michael wanted an actor who could bring to the part an air of ordinariness with an added degree of charm, intelligence and wit. Someone who could get on with the ladies, something Holmes couldn't really be bothered with. That man was to be actor David Burke.

David had never worked with Jeremy before and didn't know anything about him personally. And like Jeremy, he wasn't sure about the Holmes and Watson saga being disinterred again. Nevertheless, the role was extremely well paid and he accepted it.

Jeremy Paul was rusticating somewhere in the country, when Michael Cox rang and invited him to join a team of writers to adapt the original Holmes stories for the small screen. The brief was to 'get back to Conan Doyle', to be as faithful as possible and set the record straight about the character of Watson. Spoofing was out.

Paul had also read the canon as a schoolboy but was no expert. The stories had registered but not deeply. It was a tremendous challenge and he accepted at once, particularly as his friend would be playing Holmes.

Paul started with *The Speckled Band*. The story was so beautifully structured for an hour's television that he scarcely had to tinker with it at all. Later stories were to prove tougher nuts. Several of them needed restructuring completely and took longer to write than a West End play. The scriptwriter slaved over his work because he felt there were thousands of Holmes devotees who could be grieved by the liberties he was having to take to fit the one-hour TV formula. After all, Sherlockians would spend hours discussing such matters as the depth to which a sprig of parsley might sink in butter on a hot day or the exact location of Watson's strangely transient war wound. Ask them for news of the giant rat of Sumatra and they would answer politely that it was a tale for which the world was not yet prepared. Such passionate enthusiasts made a tough audience. Paul had his work cut out. And so did Jeremy.

Slowly, painstakingly, over 200 sections of steel frame, strong enough to withstand the wind and rain of a north-west winter, were bolted together at the Granada TV studios. Designers huddled over copies of Victorian street maps, photographs and illustrations. Researchers studied old furniture catalogues from Harrods. Grey-green bricks were strewn across the bleak open space that was going to give birth to Baker Street, a mixture of three-storey houses and shops costing £250,000. The task had begun on a windswept January morning. Four months later, on a fine May afternoon, Jeremy walked along Baker Street in the shadow of the set's Victorian chimney pots. Before him was a furniture shop, a fruit shop, a wine merchant's, a tailor's, a bookshop, a jeweller's, a barber's, an estate agent and an undertaker's. The whole set felt as if it were inhabited by clip-clopping carriages, street urchins, fog and distressed gentlewomen. It was lit by gas lamps made by the firm that still supplied them for the kitchens at Buckingham Palace. At the far end there was a row of trees to indicate Regent's Park – and to obscure the view of Salford just beyond. Jeremy stood quietly watching as the production crew put together a brewer's dray and a milk pram. When he stepped back as a pair of flat carts, one laden with bales of hay, was pushed into position near the chestnut seller's stand he felt as if he were really living in the 1890s.

'Shouldn't the road be cobbled?' he asked the production crew.

'Believe it or not, Jeremy, Baker Street was tarmacadamed in 1890,' answered a researcher who had left no stone unturned in her quest for authenticity.

Or had she? Jeremy, standing with his friend Bamber Gascoigne, the legendary presenter of TV's *University Challenge*, was visibly impressed with the set. It was just so authentic with the horses and their droppings and the straw. 'You do realise though, Jeremy, that Regent's Park is at the wrong end?' said Bamber.

The famous Holmes apartments at 221B had been a problem, though. Everyone seemed to have their own ideas on where Conan Doyle intended them to be. Finally it was agreed by Michael Cox that they should be located on the left-hand side of the complex looking south, just a few doors up from the T-junction with York Street.

Meanwhile, inside Granada's recently renovated Victorian warehouse, work was under way on the interior of the apartments. Again great care was taken to make them look authentic. Michael and his team went all over Britain to find the right period furniture and fittings. Some people who agreed that their chairs and cushions might be used in the series asked for the first option to buy them back after the programmes were finished – in the hope that they would rise in value. The whole set brought to life the feeling of late nineteenth-century England – gaslight, horse-drawn cabs, dark streets and an intense feeling of dark criminality.

Jeremy was anxious to capture not just the darkness and cerebral power of Holmes but also the period. Day and night he would sit huddled over history books, trying to recapture the Sherlockian 1890s. They were a period of rising living standards, he learned. Workers were pressing for a twelve-hour day; the English weekend was coming to the fore with more working-class families going on trips to the seaside; team sports were being played in middle-class schools for the first time and Britain had gone bicycle crazy. Jeremy wondered if Holmes ever rode a bicycle and became obsessed with finding out.

Mass daily newspapers were becoming commonplace, featuring articles on leisure time and fashion, and there was better housing and more hygienic food for most people. The depression of the 1870s, which had brought new hardships and reminded workers of the uncertainty of their lot, encouraged a wider range of agitation, and now trade unionism was surfacing throughout western Europe. Groups such as dockers and miners were showing a growing ability to form national unions to press for monetary gains. Strike rates were increasing. German industrial output had surpassed Britain's, particularly in heavy industry. America had finally become a major industrial power and its agriculture also began to compete with Britain as steamships, canning and refrigeration altered the international trade in foodstuffs.

Satisfyingly for Holmes, the detection powers of the Metropolitan Police were not growing as fast as the economy. But the 'Peelers' had by now finally come to be respected. They had been set up under lawyer Sir Robert Peel in 1829. At first they had to weed out the drunks and the bullies who had been the main types of recruit in earlier attempts at policing cities. The public both ridiculed and fought with the new officers. But gradually the Peelers came to be trusted, remaining unarmed regardless of circumstance. By the time Holmes was cracking cases in Baker Street, they had learned to handle rioters without shedding blood and had the public on their side in the fight against crime. But still they couldn't beat the vast specialised knowledge of Holmes. Jeremy was impressed that Holmes could distinguish between 120 cigar ashes, 75 perfumes and 42 different impressions left by bicycle tyres. And he was way ahead of the forensic scientists in his study of fingerprints and the analysis of footprints.

This, then, was the world of Sherlock Holmes and his Dr Watson which Jeremy would take in his mind to the studios.

Production of the first Granada series, *The Adventures of Sherlock Holmes*, originally due to have commenced in September 1982, finally got under way in June 1983, with a target date of July 1984 set for completion. Jeremy plunged himself into every aspect of production. He had his copy of the original adventures, annotated and underlined during hours of reading and rereading. Where a line from the original had been changed or expanded, Jeremy fought tooth and nail for absolute fidelity. Sometimes he won, sometimes he did not. Nothing was taken for granted. In fact, sometimes Jeremy's passion irritated people. And so the rows began.

6 The Dark Side

A man should keep his little brain attic stocked with all the furniture that he is likely to use

Conan Doyle,
The Adventures of Sherlock Holmes

IT WAS A GRUELLING SCHEDULE. Jeremy was up at 3 a.m. to prepare himself for his role as Sherlock Holmes. His dyslexia meant that it took him hours to learn his script and then refer back to the Holmes stories. At 7 a.m. he would be polishing his magnifying glass, eating breakfast, smoking, making up with David Burke and rereading 26 pages of dialogue, going back all the time to the little red Bible of Holmes's mannerisms which he kept in his pocket. He plastered his face with white make-up and grew his hair longer so that he could gel it back across his skull to make his appearance more hawk-like. He lost a stone in weight to recreate the cadaverous Holmes of his imagination, weighing in at 12st 2lb, desperately trying to portray Holmes in black and white just like the Paget drawings. He was almost manic as he rushed about on the set, stopping here and there to ask the technicians about their problems, talking about their newborn babies, back pains or life with a sick mother-in-law. Everyone quickly became his family, from the scene-setters to the waiters in the nearby cafés – he knew them all by their first names.

The backroom boys became his instant fans. He was lavish in his praise of a job well done, whether a tricky camera movement, a beautifully chosen location or a striking piece of lighting. Sometimes he overdid it, but in the early days nobody cared. He would send flowers to men or women at the drop of a cue card.

'Jeremy, you mustn't keep doing that.'

'Well,' he would say, 'everybody loves flowers, don't they?'

Sometimes, though, as the months wore on, his early morning greetings weren't welcome.

'Darling, how bright and starry-eyed you look,' he would say to a make-up girl nursing the worst of hangovers.

'Oh, Jeremy, please give it a rest.'

The first story filmed in the series was *The Solitary Cyclist*, with location shooting in Manchester and the surrounding countryside. It centred around teacher Violet Smith, played by Barbara Wishere, who found that whenever she cycled to and from Chiltern Grange near Farnham to give music lessons to the daughter of a widower, she was followed by a mystery man on a bicycle.

'Welcome to your studio,' Jeremy told everyone as they arrived for the first day on the set. Then he didn't stop until he had put a seven-minute scene in the can. Cameramen and technicians were impressed. The industry was usually content with three or four minutes a day.

Jeremy couldn't help laughing at the improvisations of the production crew. They were supposed to be working in a soundproof environment inside the Victorian warehouse behind the main studio block. But there was so much building work going on around the Granada complex that they sometimes found it impossible to record. Then they came up with the answer. They sent a man around the perimeter on a bicycle, ringing a bell whenever they needed silence. And so the solitary cyclist heralded the birth of *The Solitary Cyclist.*

The episode was followed by *The Speckled Band*, *The Naval Treaty*, *A Scandal in Bohemia*, *The Dancing Men*, *The Crooked Man* and *The Blue Carbuncle.*

A host of well-known actors and actresses joined the series . . . Tenniel Evans, Norman Jones, Jeremy Kemp, Michael Carter, Brian Miller, Gayle Hunnicutt, Betsy Brantley, Alan Skilbeck, Rosalyn Landor. All were impressed with Jeremy's manic quest for perfection and authenticity.

He tackled each day with zest. In the heat of the chase he would leap over the furniture or jump on to the parapet of a bridge with no regard for his personal safety. But behind the scenes he didn't really believe he had become Holmes.

'I am a sponge, I squeeze the liquid out of myself and draw in the liquid of the person I am playing,' he would say. 'And yet I just cannot become HIM.'

Every night he chastised himself for making terrible mistakes. He felt he was miscast as Holmes. After all, he was a romantic, heroic actor and was terribly aware that he had to hide an awful lot of himself. He seemed brusque and too energetic before the cameras and his Holmes appeared more arrogant than he should be.

Some co-stars believed he was overacting the part and secretly Jeremy knew that he was.

During the highs and lows of filming *Sherlock Holmes*, Jeremy loved to laugh and have people laugh with him. He would smuggle a Polaroid camera into the studios and take pictures of people on the set during their unguarded moments, especially cameramen and sound technicians, then pin them on the walls for everyone to see.

His love of animals was evident to everyone. He was like an excited little boy every time his horse was needed on the set, rushing out the evening before to buy apples, sugar lumps and biscuits. Come rain or shine the next morning he would be at the stables before make-up time, feeding her and talking about his life at the Grange and Babs, the pony his father had bought him.

He would sit for hours with wardrobe designer Esther Dean, desperately trying to make sure his clothes were authentic. Esther had worked with Jeremy when he played Sheridan Owen in *The Ferryman* for Granada in 1974. She had won BAFTA awards for her costumes featured in the TV series *Hard Times* and *Jewel in the Crown*. Like Jeremy, she had not been convinced about making the Sherlock Holmes series. She too felt that the Victorian supersleuth had been overcooked. But once the production got under way, she realised that this was something different.

She and Jeremy would read the stories and study Paget's original drawings. The sketches were always their starting point. Jeremy was adamant about using the original illustrations because that is where he got his poses from. He would lean back in the chair, holding up a copy of *Strand* magazine, recreating the look, as Esther sketched and took notes. Slowly, painstakingly, they built up a wardrobe that went with the Paget artwork. Jeremy loved the scarves, but his favourite outfit in the beginning was a penguin frock-coat and top hat. He was to wear it until it was almost threadbare, just as he was to wear his own clothes all his life. Some people believed it to be actor's superstition. A pair of boots, a shirt or a hat would be thought of as lucky because the star had worn it during a stage play or filming and they had received good reviews. But with Jeremy it wasn't like that. He just became attached to the things he liked, felt good in.

At this time it was becoming apparent to everyone that Jeremy was scared of playing Holmes and it was getting to him. He was in many ways hiding behind his make-up – white powder and cream around his eyes and a deep violet colour under his chin. He had slipped into a strange, almost choked voice again and would hunch his shoulders forward to complete the look, twisting his wrists in the air until the scriptwriters and production crew had to take him aside.

'Where are you under there?' people asked on the set, sometimes joking, sometimes concerned.

Privately he would look into the mirror and admit to himself: 'Jeremy, dear, you look just like a gargoyle.'

All his life he had been told that the only way for an actor to stay sane was for him to leave his part behind at the end of the day. But he had started dreaming about Holmes and the dreams were turning into nightmares.

Everything was getting on top of him. Holmes was right-handed and Jeremy was left-handed. He tried long and hard to write a note with his right hand – but in the end he agreed to let a double do it. Holmes smoked a pipe. Jeremy hated them – they made him feel old, made him feel as if he looked old to others. His pipe-smoking brother Patrick gave him lessons and pouches of mellow tobacco. But it was all a struggle. Jeremy looked even more intense as he sucked in and blew out.

'Holmes is hollow like an edifice. You have to invent a life for him,' Robert told him.

He did.

In one episode he cried as Holmes. They weren't hollow tears – he admitted later they were real. Jeremy was good at crying all his life.

As he became even more tired and jaded the rows about the scripts, costumes and scenery grew more fierce.

'That's not correct!' he would suddenly say to the director. 'One moment, please.'

He would then walk across to an extra and adjust his hat . . . or her scarf. 'There, that's how they wore it in those days, darling.'

The director would patiently wait for him to return to his position.

'OK, sound, turnover!'

Jeremy would interrupt again, referring to his tatty Holmes Bible.

'No, this isn't right. In the book it says . . .'

Eventually, after around four or five false starts, the studio would manage a take.

On one occasion when this happened and everyone was breathing a sigh of relief, a throaty voice roared across the set. 'Oh my God, I had my bloody deerstalker on the wrong way round!'

On another occasion, over a restaurant lunch, Jeremy became so infuriated with a Granada scriptwriter who seemed to be deviating from the original, that he suddenly threw his plate of Dover sole into the air.

In the episode *The Crooked Man*, Jeremy had been irritated about discrepancies between the script and the true Conan Doyle story. His obsession was unstoppable. Michael Cox tried his best to reconcile the brooding, moody actor, explaining that rewrites were often necessary in the world of television and that it was sometimes impossible to transfer every detail of the Conan Doyle stories to the screen. Jeremy finally retreated but many people on the set believed that he had taken his argument too far. It was as if he was putting his own background into Holmes. The episode featured a military case brought to him by Watson, himself an ex-military man. But Jeremy felt that Holmes would have hated the military discipline, and so he acted out the episode in a bad-tempered way. Jeremy, it appeared, was putting his upbringing, his own self, into the part.

Finally he pleaded with Michael Cox to extend the rehearsal period to two weeks to allow more breathing space in which to get things right. It was a big upheaval in the Granada schedule but they agreed.

The disagreements would now take place during the first week and shooting in the second. Granada executives were happy. Jeremy was bringing great charm to the role and the cameras were catching a wide range of the Victorian supersleuth's moods through his facial and physical mannerisms. They knew they were on to a winner. Jeremy's lean, ascetic face and piercing eyes darting out under his swept-back hair were right out of *Strand* magazine. Even Rathbone had not captured the movements and the poses in the same way, they agreed. The indolent sweep of Jeremy's hand, his speech – sometimes languid, sometimes staccato – and a faraway, half-quizzical gaze gave the impression of a man who lived within himself, a man searching for something he had not yet found, much like the actor himself.

The series made its television debut on 24 April 1984 at 9 p.m. with the first story ever published in *The Strand* magazine, *A Scandal in Bohemia*. For Granada, this was an important decision. They wanted to win over the Sherlockians and the tales explored the strange, repressed sexual relationship with American adventuress Irene Adler, whom Holmes always referred to as 'The Woman'. The series ran until June 1984 and was to be shown in America the following year from March to April.

A Scandal in Bohemia had been perhaps the most testing piece for Jeremy to start with. It featured the two most important people in the life of Holmes – Adler, the New Jersey-born opera singer and adventuress with a soul of steel, who to his analytical and unemotional mind eclipsed the whole of her sex, and his loyal, dignified housekeeper, Mrs Hudson. As with most of his parts, Jeremy made up a little story about Holmes's relationship with the fair sex to help him reconstruct the past. For example, he pretended that when Holmes was at university he saw a girl across the quadrangle and lost his heart to her. But she never looked back at him and so he closed the door on his feelings about women. He swore to himself that he would never love anyone like that again. He just couldn't take the rejection. Jeremy didn't realise it then, but this was a mirror reflection of himself.

Irene was played by American actress Gayle Hunnicutt and Mrs Hudson by Rosie Williams, who was thrilled from the start to be reunited with Jeremy whom she had played opposite in their early days at Manchester's Library Theatre. She saw her part as 'a very firm and understanding lady with a maternal presence who had come down in the world'. Although she was to come through as a strong character in the series, she had in fact no more than 20 lines.

On screen Jeremy looked as if he was still on frosty terms with Holmes. But as the series progressed the Sherlockians began to sit up and take notice. They found Jeremy powerful – capricious, magical and magnetic. Was this man the real Holmes at last? While Basil Rathbone had sometimes been obliged to battle Nazis, the Granada project marked a satisfying return to the swirling fogs and clattering hansom cabs of Victorian England. David Stuart Davis, of the Northern Musgroves Society, commented later that Jeremy was 'brilliant, irritating, smug, rebellious and above all Doylean'. Jeremy adored the applause. He had given the TV series a true jolt. His prickly, occasionally off-putting performance, alive with every tic, twitch and pig-snort from his years on the stage, gave as much weight to Holmes's dark side as to his celebrated powers of deduction. He snapped at clients and had little use for social conventions. Even the word elementary seemed to get a vicious spin. There were dissenters, however, and some attacked him as a revisionist – but he was playing the game strictly according to Conan Doyle. After all, the author had written that Holmes was anything but lovable. Watson once described him as 'a brain without a heart, as deficient in human sympathy as he was pre-eminent in intelligence'.

Conan Doyle's daughter, Dame Jean Conan Doyle, said: 'I don't think my father meant Sherlock Holmes to be quite so rude, Jeremy.'

'I'm terribly sorry, I am just trying to find me!' he answered.

They were to become great friends.

Jeremy's portrayal seemed cold on the surface but he more than compensated for it by showing the heat of the detective's internal powers of deduction. The fevered excitement of Holmes on the scent as he portrayed it was an inspiring performance. He would hurl himself on the ground just to examine a flake of cigar ash. Slowly and yet confidently, as the years went by, Jeremy was to take liberties with the myth . . . and it would work. He didn't know it but he would in many ways displace the literary Holmes.

Jeremy's enigmatic half-smile on screen was winning the hardest of critics over. It strangely captured the idea that smiling was a weakness. They loved the almost manic glee with which he pounced on new clues. One reviewer wrote: 'Holmes seems to positively quiver with intelligence and his eyes are as sharp as his senses.'

And yet Jeremy knew he had to shake Holmes off. Sometimes he felt as if he had been playing opposite Jeremy Paul's wife in *Beauty and the Beast* again. He was the beast on set who had to turn into a prince off it, shaking off the black mourning clothes of the depressive detective and wearing bright, shiny colours to see his friends in. On would go the large bright green or navy cashmere sweater, white linen trousers and a warm, understanding, friendly smile that would deceive even the fiendish Dr Moriarty. The covert TV face – narrow, pensive, pinched with disdain for those less observant than *he* – would disappear under a tumble of ash-brown hair and wide, smiling green eyes. The only trace of Holmes in public was the hawk-like nose, still bold. Jeremy, built like a soccer forward at this time, radiated expansiveness and bonhomie. But underneath he was forever analysing himself.

'I feel like I have been playing a man who is the fox in my hunting days with my father,' he said. 'Holmes is one field ahead of me, maybe two fields. It is like a treasure hunt. Watson always said that Holmes was a mind without a heart. The trouble is I have tried to find his heart . . . perhaps to save myself.'

After filming the first series, Granada's Sherlock Holmes 'family' had taken a well-earned break. But while others jetted off to sunnier climes, Jeremy headed for the cameras again. First he flew to America to play Jacylyn Smith's father in the NBC TV movie *Florence Nightingale*. Then came a four-hour TV mini-series, *Deceptions*, filmed in England and Italy, starring Stefanie Powers in the dual role of identical twin sisters who traded places for a week. One was a bored New Jersey housewife, the other a European jet-setter. Jeremy played Bryan Foxworth, an evil, two-timing art dealer. The part was not a large one but it was, like Holmes, complex. Jeremy enjoyed it more, though, because Foxworth was enormously bright, alive, stylish and happy, unlike the morbid and calculating Holmes. But Foxworth was homosexual, which made him hard to play at this time. News of AIDS, like the disease itself, was spreading fast. Jeremy knew he had to take on the role with a sense of great responsibility. The gay community was facing a public backlash and the disease was not properly understood. People saw it as a plague and the doom merchants were predicting the end of civilisation. Once he would have been tempted to camp it up on screen; instead Jeremy played Foxworth with enormous panache and a huge zest for life. He found the deceitful side of the character thrilling. Foxworth was a lethal murderer, trafficking in drugs – a monster. In many ways he was an actor's perfect vehicle.

Another reason Jeremy had decided to take the part was his fondness for Stefanie, whom he had met when he undertook a guest role in her TV series *Hart to Hart*.

When he returned to the Granada set for the second series of *The Adventures of Sherlock Holmes*, Michael Cox handed over the reins as producer to June Wyndham Davies because of other work commitments. It had taken Michael some time finally to agree with Jeremy on his approach to the character, but they had become firm friends with a healthy respect for each other. There was a time, though, when Michael had doubts about Jeremy. He admitted to friends: 'I honestly believed that he didn't properly understand the part when he started!'

Jeremy always took particular pleasure in teasing Michael whenever he could. He loved dressing up, and *A Scandal in*

Bohemia had previously given him the ideal opportunity. When Michael turned up during rehearsals looking for him, Jeremy walked around the set made up as the drunken groom. As Michael asked cameramen where the star was, Jeremy appeared right beside him – and still wasn't recognised. It was only when he jumped for joy that Michael realised the joke. When they came to film the scene it was Jeremy's idea to remove the drunken-groom disguise on camera. Everyone reluctantly agreed, fearing the worst. They all knew that if anything went wrong they were faced with an hour's delay in putting the make-up back on again. But Jeremy, professional in every respect, managed to carry it off without a hitch, even though the crew were startled by an uncanny pause. Jeremy had suddenly stopped and stared into a mirror at himself. Minutes later he carried on and everyone quietly sighed with relief.

In the end Michael began to realise that the actor had to have his say. As the productions progressed Jeremy became so agitated about keeping to the canon that he threatened to quit unless everyone followed his advice. He finally rested much easier several series later when his producer put a copy of a favourite review by the Sherlock Holmes Society of London on his dressing table, with a note calling it the ultimate accolade. As he sat reading it, Jeremy recalled what his friend Alistair Cooke had once told him: 'The three most memorable men of the twentieth century are Winston Churchill, Adolf Hitler and Sherlock Holmes.' It was a thrilling yet daunting thought. He was Sherlock Holmes now. He had to live up to Alistair's exciting expectation of him.

One evening Peter Ecclesley, Granada's Head of Drama, invited June Wyndham Davies to dinner at the Midland Hotel with a special guest – Joan Sullivan.

June had heard all about Joan and her work for WGBH in Boston. It was a lovely meal and the wine flowed. The two women hit it off immediately and June was full of the studio rumours that had been circulating that day.

'Did you hear that Jeremy has got married?' she asked. 'Who on earth can it be?'

'Don't you know?' Peter answered.

'No.'

'It's me,' said Joan.

At last the secret was out.

Jeremy had by now accepted himself in his heart as being bisexual, but he was madly in love with Joan and madly in love with the thought of being in love. Their friendship had blossomed into romance and now they were happy to tell the world of their relationship. When they were in New York together they would dance the night away and Jeremy knew he had found a woman in a million.

'She is wild and wonderful,' he told Robert and Tarn. 'We have a once-in-a-lifetime love. She is an incredible person, the best woman a man could have. It is the kind of relationship where I start a sentence and she finishes it. Sometimes you can see behind someone's eyes and feel as if you have known them all your life. That is how it is with us.'

But their separations were long ones. They were two workaholics living apart and sometimes coming together.

Joan's passion for black magic did not hinder her career. As executive producer of *Masterpiece Theatre*, she had become something of an American institution and had twelve Emmys to her credit. 'I look for that quality of great drama that appeals to everyone, that reaches out to people,' she said. Since 1973, she had led *Masterpiece Theatre* through financial crises, production problems, union hassles and occasional public controversies.

She screened hundreds of hours of programmes a year from the BBC, Thames and other British producers, and was renowned for bringing *I, Claudius* to the American screen.

Her favourite job was producing the wraparounds for the series – opening and closing essays written and delivered each week by aristocratic host Alistair Cooke. Joan and Jeremy had nothing but praise for Alistair. They adored his 'exquisitely' honed pieces which framed each show.

Once Joan, who had a British accent, was stung by persistent criticism that *Masterpiece Theatre* was too British. She responded by pointing out that Alistair, the quintessential English gentleman, was now an American citizen.

'He is very Americanised,' she said. 'His manners are British, but he is American in his wit and perspective. Did you know that he is one of only three Americans ever knighted by the Queen?'

But Joan was mindful of the cultural differences between England and America. Not every British production 'travelled well'. Accents sometimes posed a problem, especially a thick Scottish dialect or rapid East End speech. Different attitudes towards sexual taboos also influenced her choice of series. Once she turned down a popular British series that examined the personal life of Peter Pan author James Barrie, who was attracted to young boys.

'My English friends loved it,' she said. 'But I told them that I didn't think Americans would be as captivated by the passionate, darker side of Barrie. Our Mickey Mouse was their Peter Pan and I preferred my Peter Pan as Mary Martin flying through the air.'

Joan always steered clear of British material which she found sexually exploitative of women, which Jeremy would gently tease her about.

'I find too many British plays sexist,' she told him. 'Did you know I went to one of your musicals called *Privates on Parade* thinking it was a fun production about soldiers! Instead it was about a randy bunch of men who saw women as pieces of meat!'

'Darling, you mustn't take things so seriously,' Jeremy chided.

Joan firmly believed that there was a voyeuristic streak in British drama. She rejected another series about a boys' school because it featured whole scenes about sexual escapades.

Jeremy admired her professionalism. While one of her most sensitive responsibilities involved her role as a censor, trying to balance Britain's greater tolerance for explicit sex and violence against what she saw as America's ingrained conservatism, she did try and break new ground as much as she could. The numerous orgy scenes in *I, Claudius*, for example, were among the most graphic shown on American television. On the other hand she cut five minutes out of the thirteen-part series because they were either too gruesome or violent. The largest incision she ever made was to throw out thirteen of the first 26 original episodes of *Upstairs Downstairs*, reasoning that the plots were repetitious and the performances not strong enough.

Joan was a tough, no-nonsense, discerning editor, good at administration. But she was often the butt of American jokes. Asked how it was that a woman who took her tea with milk, was married to an Englishman and made her living by importing British programmes happened to drive a 1978 Mustang, she replied: 'I believe in supporting the American economy!'

Somehow Jeremy always had the niggling feeling that he was asked to play Holmes because of Joan's recommendation. If he had known this for a fact it would have crucified him. Michael Cox assured him that it was because he looked so much like the original Sidney Paget drawings. But Jeremy never totally believed him. He knew that Joan had been in on the casting meetings before the leading actor was chosen.

Jeremy could smell the gas lights as he slowly walked across the worn carpet and past the armchair. He rubbed his tired eyes and stared back for a moment at the slipper on the floor, the bullet-mark initials on the wall, the violin and the pipes. He entered the bedroom and eased himself on to the bed, pulling his penguin coat tightly around him, trying to focus for a moment on a spot on the ceiling before fading away into the welcome sleep of tired and anxious men. It was lunchtime on the set. But Jeremy didn't want to go to the Winnebago today. He felt at home in Baker Street, the womb of Conan Doyle's creation. From now on Jeremy would often find rest and refuge in the apartments of 221B, faithfully recreated in the Victorian warehouse. It reminded him in a way of his rooms at Eton.

By now June Wyndham Davies was moving more and more out of the Granada set and was using real Victorian houses wherever she could find them. The production team went out to the streets and parks of Manchester but in the end they had to go further afield – to Liverpool, because in Manchester the buildings were mostly red brick and not authentic enough. Shooting some of the scenes was troublesome. Shop signs and scaffolding had to be covered up, or the cameras had to steer clear of traffic lights and twentieth-century telephone boxes. Even the municipal sports hall in Warrington was used for interior shots, with equipment hidden from view.

Wherever Jeremy went his fans would find him – especially women. He had a way with them, made them feel important, special, as if he were interested in no one else on the planet. The men didn't flock to him so much, initially finding him a bit of a luvvy. But when they got to know him they adored him. He was their friend for life too.

While filming the Sherlock Holmes series Jeremy, Joan and her two children borrowed the top flat of Philip Kingsley's Mayfair home for a while. Philip had now taken up residence in New York where he had started a clinic. But even though Jeremy's new family had a London base, he spent most of the time near the studio in his beloved Midland Hotel while Joan commuted across the Atlantic.

This was the most successful period for the series. Jeremy had stretched the great detective's uncanny, cerebral powers in dozens of tales of skulduggery and mystery. Both Jeremy and Holmes were tested to their limits of physical and mental endurance. As the series went on Jeremy's style came fully into its own. In a short space of time he had effectively eclipsed memories of all the other Baker Street virtuosi, including even such hardy favourites as Basil Rathbone's splendidly lean, staccato version of the thirties and forties. Jeremy seemed to have the instinct to dare to go that bit further. He brought to the screen a mixture of passion and coldness, fire and ice. One critic said that his style was kitsch and high camp, intermingled with a shuddering sense of danger. Whatever the mixture, it was a recipe for success.

Television audiences seemed fascinated by his brooding concentration and disturbing on-screen hint of formidable power barely in check. His Holmes was a fragile, brittle, reasoning machine, not as briskly self-assured as Rathbone. Jeremy wore his loneliness and alienation openly enough for Watson and the viewers to recognise them for what they were, cloaking them with an air of aloof superiority that was frequently cold, inflexible and cruel. Such a portrayal had won over even the biggest cynics. But the press wasn't satisfied. They were looking for flaws.

As the success of the series continued, more than 3,000 letters from around the globe arrived at the Granada TV studios every week. The Société Sherlock Holmes de France petitioned the French Government to award Jeremy the Légion d'Honneur, and fans of the world-famous detective in America and Japan pursued the actor for lecture tours.

Jeremy had become the idol of nearly 500 Holmes clubs worldwide. In Britain alone there were more than 50,000 members of the Sherlock Holmes Society, and there would have been more if they hadn't closed their books. No one in their view captured the greatest fictional amateur detective of them all quite like Jeremy.

During this time the boy from the Grange and Eton remained a man of great warmth and generosity of spirit, just like his mother Bunny. It was as if he were haunted by her goodness. He cared deeply for his friends and colleagues and always acted spontaneously. If he was in an antiques shop and spotted something he thought a friend might like, he would just buy it for them, no matter what the cost . . . Victorian cufflinks, a French clock, an Elizabethan brooch. To this day Philip Kingsley still has the wonderful gold cufflinks Jeremy bought him on a whim.

But the dark shadow that threatened to eclipse his good nature was growing. His workload was pushing him to the limit of his physical stamina and he still felt he had not mastered the role, even though others disagreed. At every shoot he felt he was not good enough. He would shout on the set if another actor misinterpreted his lines, or stop speaking in the middle of shooting to refer yet again to the tattered Bible of Holmesian mannerisms in his pocket. He hated people being on the set who had no place there to his mind. On one occasion, Peter Haining, author of the book on the series, arrived in the studio and tried to make himself scarce. Jeremy looked over at the dark area behind the camera, knowing someone was there, and just glared. When he realised it was Peter he seemed to accept him. But barely.

Peter then watched as Jeremy walked over to his designated spot, looked down and very slowly began to lift his head as the change came over him – from a caustic Brett into a chilling Holmes. It was like watching Jekyll and Hyde. Some small-part actors were so in awe of the man who had become Holmes that they forgot their lines, which only made matters worse.

Although Jeremy didn't know it then, both his mind and body were ailing. He had begun to feel unwell.

'The truth is that I am risking everything to find the actor within me and I am doubtful it is really there,' he admitted to Joan. 'I honestly believe that Conan Doyle's Holmes is such a complex and brilliant creation that nobody, no matter how good, can capture him completely. He should be read – not acted.'

Suddenly it all began to go wrong. Jeremy had tried too hard to become Holmes, spending all his free time drumming the lines into his head, reading the originals, hibernating in his hotel room, living away from home and friends and family. Life was becoming very bleak.

While other actors disappeared to the canteen for lunch Jeremy would sit alone in the set's Victorian sitting room, thinking about Holmes, fretting about him. By now he had gone far behind the lines of the script. He was looking at every nuance; every word that Holmes spoke had a double meaning. He began to refer to the dark Victorian supersleuth who had taken over his life as 'You Know Who' or 'HIM'.

He was obsessed with bringing even more passion to the role. But he was speaking with the passion of two people. He would switch without realising it from referring to himself to referring to You Know Who.

'When I gloat, or You Know Who gloats because he has defeated an opponent or a temper flares when people are not listening to you or don't understand what it is you are saying, then there is real passion,' he told an American radio interviewer.

'There is passion underneath You Know Who's brusqueness and rudeness that makes him real. What I am talking about is an inner life. I am talking about becoming. Watson describes You Know Who as a mind without a heart, which is hard to play. Hard to become. So what I have done is invent an inner life. I even know what You Know Who's nanny looked like, for example. She was covered in starch. She probably scrubbed You Know Who but never kissed him. I don't think HE saw his mother until he was about eight years old. Maybe he caught a touch of the fragrance of her scent and the fragrance of her dress. I suppose his college days were fairly complicated. He was probably quite isolated. He probably saw a girl across the quadrangle but she never looked at him so he closed the door. And he became a brilliant fencer, of course. A master of boxing and many more tiny details which you have to make up to fill the kind of well Conan Doyle so brilliantly left out. Doyle's works are better read because he built this extraordinary edifice and if you are going to try to climb it, it is much better read. And that is the truth.

'If you are going to be rash enough to try and bring him into life by the visual arts I would rather listen to him than see him. Seeing is limiting, you know. You do develop a body language. Whenever he thinks, he makes a pyramid with his fingers and puts them up. He has rather eccentric hand gestures. It is all Doyle. Funny, there is one moment when Doyle says, "Holmes wriggles in his seat and roars with laughter." You see, sadly, I never even thought of Holmes laughing.'

The second series of six adventures started with *The Copper Beeches*, starring Natasha Richardson, daughter of Vanessa Redgrave, as Violet Hunter, governess to Mr Jephro Rocastle's small son. She had called in the great detective because she was at her 'wit's end'. The fact that Rocastle, played by Joss Ackland, had made Violet cut off her flowing chestnut hair before taking up the post intrigued Holmes no end.

Next came *The Greek Interpreter*, featuring Charles Gray and Victoria Harwood, *The Norwood Builder*, with Rosalie Crutchley and Colin Jeavons as Lestrade, *The Resident Patient*, starring Patrick Newell, *The Red-Headed League*, with Eric Porter as the dastardly Moriarty, and finally *The Final Problem*.

* * *

It was one of the most breathtaking stunts ever seen on British TV. Holmes's spectacular fall in the grip of his arch-enemy Moriarty down the Reichenbach Falls in the Swiss Alps would be the climax to *The Adventures of Sherlock Holmes.*

Conan Doyle had wisely taken temporary exile in Switzerland when his story *The Final Problem* was published in *The Strand* magazine in December 1893. About 20,000 readers cancelled their subscriptions with immediate effect when it appeared, and young men in the City wore black silk and hat bands. Even women went into mourning.

'You beast!' began one of the thousands of letters dashed off to the great writer, who was widely accused of murder most foul.

The truth was that Conan Doyle had tired of his detective. The writer had diverse interests – medicine, science, theosophy and the occult – and he wanted to pursue other endeavours and put Holmes to rest once and for all.

The Granada version was to be a superb finale to the second series. Eric Porter was in outstanding form as the Napoleon of crime, Moriarty, and the climactic duel between him and Holmes at the Reichenbach Falls was to be shot for the very first time at the actual location. While filming in Switzerland, the production team were also working on scenes to be included in the third series, *The Return of Sherlock Holmes*, already being planned. Much to Jeremy's chagrin, Michael Cox announced at a press conference: 'Just as Conan Doyle was forced to by public pressure to bring back Holmes after his disappearance at Reichenbach, so we have decided to go ahead and make seven more stories for the viewers.' The only change would be a new Dr Watson.

Jeremy had moved into a chalet near the Sherlock Holmes hotel close to the falls for the shooting. The fierce water quite unnerved both himself and Eric Porter. They had to film their struggle about eight feet from the edge of the 430-foot drop. Every time Jeremy looked down at the plunging white wall of water he felt sick, and to make matters worse his feet kept slipping on the mud and grass that were soaked in spray. The trouble was that his favourite old Holmes boots just would not grip. Finally Esther came up with the solution – a new pair, which Granada insisted he wore because of their insurance cover. Happily for Jeremy and Eric the actual plunge was enacted by two plucky stuntmen – Alf Joint and Marc Boyle.

But that didn't make Jeremy feel much better. Before the stunt, a dummy figure was dropped down the falls by the film crew as a test. Jeremy hated heights and any form of violence, and so he stayed in the hotel while the rest of the cast watched in horror as the figure smashed into the cliff, lost its head and disappeared into the torrent.

Since his nightmare days as a young boy fighting for his life in the grip of rheumatic fever after the diving competition at Eton, Jeremy had always been respectful of the power of water. The strength and the beauty of this manifestation of nature captured his imagination. Somehow he felt threatened by it . . . and yet he loved it. When he first saw the falls, he suddenly felt very small, and a feeling of euphoria swept over him. It was a difficult feeling to explain to others, and he did not bother. No one would really understand it, and he believed that perhaps this was what set him apart from the world.

How clean the water looked. How pure. Not really like him and his life and his sexuality. Not like the murky waters of the Thames in his sad days at Eton. Jeremy still felt strangely ashamed of his own bisexuality. He often wondered how he might have turned out had it not been for his experience in the coal shed as a young boy. Perhaps he would not have felt like he did about men. There was no doubt now that he found them sexually attractive and good company. Indeed, there were many like him in the acting profession; it was almost the norm. But he didn't like others knowing about his sexuality. It still didn't sit comfortably with him.

Aided by engineer Dave Bickers, a former world champion motorcross rider, Alf and Marc were suspended by lengths of thin steel cable fixed to harnesses under their clothes and run from a specially built winch on a platform at the top of the falls. Then, just far enough away from the cameras so that their features could not be recognised, they were thrown spiralling and twisting down the precipice at over 30 miles an hour.

Everyone was praying for their safety, and so was Jeremy . . . from his hotel room. He just could not bear to watch.

When it was all over the telephone rang. Minutes later he appeared with the champagne. The stuntmen had been paid £2,500 each . . . but Jeremy wouldn't have done it for a million pounds, he admitted.

It was in *The Final Problem* that Jeremy provoked the Sherlockians. In spite of his loyalty to Conan Doyle, he had allowed himself one liberty. Viewers were to see Holmes relaxing on a Swiss hillside, smoking a familiar curved-stem calabash pipe. Although the calabash had become a familiar totem, Holmes never actually smoked one in any of the original stories. Jeremy knew that perfectly well and had decided for once to tease the true disciples of the canon.

'It's my little hello to Rathbone,' he told a cameraman, 'and anyway Holmes might have picked one of these up in Switzerland.'

Jeremy put the telephone down and surveyed the small room – the wooden cupboard, the dressing table under the mirror, the trouser press, the courtesy bar, still locked. He was looking but not seeing.

Just minutes earlier Joan had told him that the tests were positive. She had cancer of the pancreas. He wondered for a moment about what the pancreas did. He could understand the lungs, the liver, the bowel, but the pancreas? Could you live without it?

He felt comfortable in the airless, dusty little womb of the room. He could be left alone with his thoughts there. But sadly it couldn't last forever. There was the party that night, the farewell party. He would act it out, wear colourful clothes, bright green or yellow perhaps, go through the motions . . . the entrance, the laughter, the bows, the exit and curtain-down. No one would see his desperate sadness, because if they did they wouldn't understand it. Only he understood. No one had the depth of understanding that he did. He thought of the flat in Clapham that they had just bought, the wild times in New York and Hollywood, the dancing, the stability that she had given him. He broke down and cried.

Hours later Jeremy stoically toasted the cast with champagne at the farewell party in the hotel and popped some of the balloons he had blown up with the production crew earlier that fateful day. The next morning he flew to Joan's side. He knew now that he didn't want to play Holmes any more.

'But, darling, you must,' she said. 'You've signed the contract and anyway you know I'm a fighter. I'll beat this – then we can go on as we were before.'

But the die was cast and for Jeremy it was yet another turning point in his life, one that would have disastrous effects. *The Final Problem* was yet to come.

'Jeremy, surely you're not going to audition for the part. You're established now!' said Tarn on the phone.

'I must be with Joan, it's the only way,' he replied.

'But it's ridiculous. Rex Harrison knows you and so does Lynn Redgrave. There's no need. And anyway, is this part really for you?'

Jeremy was adamant. 'I don't care. At least I will have the distinction of being the oldest juvenile lead on Broadway.'

He was so desperate to work in New York, so that he could be near Joan while she had chemotherapy treatment, that he didn't care what people thought.

And so Jeremy auditioned for the part of Willie Tatham, the romantic lead in the revival of Frederick Lonsdale's drawing-room comedy *Aren't We All*, with Rex, Lynn and Claudette Colbert on Broadway. There was no doubt in the producer's mind that Jeremy was the man, especially as Rex had politely suggested that he should get the part. But the play wasn't opening for some time and Jeremy still needed work in America as he and Joan began their desperate battle against the disease that was threatening her life and his stability.

Then he had a lucky break. He signed up as behind-the-scenes narrator of Martha Graham's new ballet *Song*. Some nights he performed live, but on evenings he was on stage at his old haunt, the Brooks Atkinson, a recording of his voice was played.

Jeremy adored Martha, now 91, and what she stood for. It

was hard to believe that the woman they called the 'Mother of Dance' did not dance professionally until she was 21. For 60 years she had been as vibrant and ruthlessly perfectionist off stage as on. She had developed a revolutionary technique of movement that had been copied by dance companies all over the world. He remembered reading a newspaper interview in which she said: 'I know that I'm vain and arrogant. All artists are vain . . . I want to be vain. It is essential and I try to teach the girls in my company to be vain. It's essential not just for the artist, but for everybody to treasure themselves, to honour themselves and to look well . . .'

Jeremy had always applied those words to himself. He had seen Martha on stage several times during the late fifties and early sixties and found that she was never afraid of controversy, creating gripping depictions of lust, greed, jealousy and love. Her virgins, goddesses and madwomen disturbed and mesmerised audiences with raw emotion as they whirled across bare stages in bare feet.

Martha's company had enjoyed a successful summer season at the Royal Opera House, Covent Garden, in 1979, and she had been showered with recognition and honours including the American Medal of Freedom and the National Medal of Arts.

In the early hours one morning, when Jeremy returned to the hotel he and Joan were sharing, she woke up to find him stroking her forehead.

'You know, darling, if one day I am asked to name the four most important things I have done as an actor, I would certainly mention *Song*,' he said. 'It is one of the greatest joys of my life to kneel at the altar of Martha. I think she is as important to the United States as the Chrysler Building!'

7 Releasing the Spirit

Whatever you do, don't go on the stage

George Bernard Shaw

THEY WERE QUIET on the way back from hospital, and that night in bed she apologised to him for being so weak and ill. Then slowly, gently, she began touching him, and fearfully he touched her and held her, afraid of harming her. It was as if his own life were slipping gently away. Suddenly he cried and clung to her, and then hated himself for it. He wanted to be brave and strong and manly, but instead he felt like the little boy back at Eton. 'God, please don't take her away,' he prayed, and begged for a miracle. Maybe the chemotherapy would work. Jeremy was struggling to maintain the power of positive thought he had used so often before walking on stage. It was difficult. The first time he walked into the treatment room and saw the tubes and wires, he fainted.

Joan wished she could be well for him again and tried to make him promise that if anything happened to her he would get on with his life.

He wouldn't listen.

'Nothing will ever happen to you,' he vowed.

Then she said a strange thing.

'I don't want to be buried, but I know that I must be.'

'Hush, you're not going to die.'

'No, listen to me. If anything happens I know that is my family's wish. They have all been buried. But you must free my spirit somehow. Promise?'

'I won't let you die, the chemotherapy is working and . . .'

'Promise!' She gripped his arm.

'Promise.'

Jeremy wondered if something of the Cherokee Indian in her was calling out to him. She did believe deeply in the power of the spirit.

His beloved Joannie seemed suddenly to have grown older over the last few weeks. She cried as she fingered another clump of dislodged hair. He tried to reassure her.

'It's only because of the chemotherapy,' he said. 'You're rubbing your hair against the pillow. That even makes my hair fall out, darling.'

She knew he was lying. But Jeremy was always the Florence Nightingale.

He was becoming a well-known face among the New York media set ... the gossip columnists and the show business writers. Again, bright colours were his trademark, especially a gold V-necked sweatshirt which he told everyone he wore to help him get over the gloominess of playing Holmes for 20 months. He also had similar shirts in bright blue, orange and red. A pair of sunglasses was forever perched on the top of his wavy dark hair, and his chain-smoking habit was legendary. He was never seen without his shoulder bag in which he kept his letters from home, some from his 82-year-old godmother, who had been charting his fame.

Jeremy was popular with American audiences and some critics were hailing him as the new Jeremy Irons. At 49 he was showing his versatility. Millions of Americans had seen him on TV as Holmes in Joan's *Mystery* series, funded by Mobil Oil, as Jacylyn Smith's father in the NBC movie *Florence Nightingale*, and as Bryan Foxworth in the four-hour TV mini-series *Deceptions*, starring Stefanie Powers.

This, then, was a good time to be back in America, even though his stay was tinged with sadness. He and Joan flew backwards and forwards from New York to London, on to Boston and back to New York, seeking alternative medical opinions on treatment for her crippling disease. Slowly Joan became more upbeat, more positive about her condition. She had lost weight and a lot of her strength, but everyone felt the chemotherapy was working. Jeremy willed himself to be positive and threw himself into his role as Willie Tatham in the revival of Frederick Lonsdale's 1923 comedy *Aren't We All* at the Brooks Atkinson. He regarded Rex Harrison as a master of laughter and told everyone that 82-year-old Claudette Colbert had 'absolutely the best legs in town'. He was spellbound by the fame of the legendary actress who had worked alongside such stars as Clark Gable, Charles Boyer, Cary Grant, Fred Astaire and Greta Garbo.

Jeremy found her unyieldingly professional, even at 82, and was amazed when Rex Harrison told him that she still hated her left profile being featured. As a Hollywood movie star in the early 1930s, if the situation absolutely demanded a shot from that perspective she would have the scenery reversed so that her left side could pass as her right.

Claudette's last role on the big screen was as Troy Donaghue's mother in *Parrish* in 1961 but then, as the film parts dried up, she went back to the stage.

'I was on the screen for thirty years,' she said, 'and never did get used to getting up at five in the morning. In the theatre you stay up late and you sleep in the morning. It's a delicious life.'

The actress, who claimed she was 'born with sex appeal', had returned to the London stage for the first time in 57 years with *Aren't We All* which had a successful run at the Haymarket Theatre in 1985. Jeremy would sit talking to her backstage day after day during breaks in rehearsals.

True to form, he had worked out a complicated history for his character Willie. As he saw it, Willie served in World War I and lost most of his contemporaries to the casualty lists. He based most of the part on his own father, carrying his medals around in his favourite shoulder bag ready for the opening night.

A few days before the curtain rose Jeremy presented Joan with a hairnet to wear in bed.

'There, your hair won't be on the pillow any more,' he said. The next morning, when she woke up, he had left a fabulous dark wig for her at the foot of the bed.

That evening he returned home to find her resplendent. She had dressed with dignity and decorum in a flowing black skirt of fine silk and a softly pleated white silk blouse. Sapphire and diamond earrings winked in her ears and their sparkle was echoed in her matching bracelet. Her perfume was expensive and he guessed correctly that it was Chanel No. 5. She put some music on and they danced and then he cried. It was all so wrong and unfair, and as he cried he began to believe his life was over. The thought of losing her was too much to bear. He wanted to take her back to London and be safe there. The fact that one day he might be truly alone again filled him with a sense of terror, as if an iron fist were clutching at his throat, taking his breath away. He was filled with a pain he could hardly cope with. Joan had never seen him as he was now, often unshaven, his beard spreading like heavy grime below his fine cheekbones. It came as a shock. His eyes were shadowed, his clothing, normally bright and stylish, often rumpled. He seemed tortured, broken.

Aren't We All was a soaraway success. From the moment the curtain went up on Monday, 29 April 1985, the critics adored it. Rex Harrison stole the show as Lord Grenham, closely followed by Claudette Colbert as Lady Frinton. It compared wonderfully with the original New York production of 1923 at the Gaiety Theatre, featuring a cast that included the legendary hard-drinking Leslie Howard and Mabel Terry Lewis. It was so successful then that it ran for 284 performances.

When the curtain came down the critics rushed for the telephones and Jeremy, with his usual bonhomie, rushed for the champagne. He had already ordered a bottle of the best bubbly to be delivered to Rex's dressing room . . . and of course flowers for the ladies of the cast.

Director Clifford Williams had taken New York's glitzy Rainbow Room for a star-studded party that night.

It was a wonderful balmy spring evening and the place was full of peach blossom. Joan looked radiant, wearing silver and scarlet and the glorious wig Jeremy had given her. It was an exact facsimile of her own hair and it suited her perfectly. She and Jeremy danced the night away as the notices flooded in. The critics had fallen at his feet and one had mentioned him eleven times in his review. When Joannie was too tired to carry on, Jeremy snatched a bottle of champagne and, with his arm around her waist, almost carried her to the taxi.

The next few months seemed to speed by. Joannie was admitted to Massachussetts General Hospital where treatment was being stepped up, and Jeremy found a 'guardian angel' in the shape of WGBH president Henry Becton. He visited her every day and rang Jeremy on Broadway to tell him how she was. Jeremy was torn. He wanted to be by Joan's side, but the play had to go on. One night he was so agitated that he left a 45-minute message on Henry's answering machine, ringing back time and again to add more thoughts.

Then, early one evening, Joan sneezed down the telephone.

'Bless you, angel,' said Jeremy.

He was about to go on stage, and they had been talking about taking a trip into the country when she felt strong enough.

'I'll ring you tonight. What you need is a hot whisky, my darling. Nothing better for a cold, my father always said.'

Three days later, on 4 July, Independence Day, Jeremy's beloved Joannie died, after watching the firework display through the window of her hospital room. Her immune system had not been able to fight the cold and it took her from him.

He staggered on with the play . . . but the lights had gone out in his life.

Jeremy stood watching Joannie's coffin being lowered into the grave at the private family service. It was a dry, windy day in Marblehead, Boston on Monday, 8 July 1985.

There had been tremendous tributes to her across America.

'She was *Masterpiece Theatre*,' said Alistair Cooke at the service, and WGBH president Henry Becton told of Joan's good taste and judgement in choosing television programmes for the public.

Under Joan's guidance, *Masterpiece Theatre* had won thirteen Emmy awards, two Peabody awards and a Christopher award. *Mystery* had won an Edgar Allan Poe Award from the Mystery Writers of America and Joan had twice received the Corporation of Public Broadcasting Award for exceptional achievement in local programming. She was also honoured with the Matrix Award for Broadcasting by Women in Communications and held two honorary doctorates – from Salem State College in Massachusetts and from her alma mater,

Grinnell College in Iowa, where she earned her bachelor's degree. America had nicknamed her Miss Television.

Jeremy felt the kiss of the wind on his face and imagined it was Joannie's lips as he cut the string that held 100 blue and red balloons. They fluttered off into the sky like a flock of starlings.

'Goodbye darling Joannie,' he said, watching them fly high and free. As he had promised, he had released her spirit.

Joan had been the source of his confidence. He hadn't wanted to play Holmes any more, even less so now. There was no point. If only he could get out of the contract. Somehow, he didn't know how, he struggled through the last performances of *Aren't We All*. Rex and Lynn Redgrave did all they could to comfort him, taking him out to dinner, ringing up at all hours to see how he was.

Then, on 21 July, seventeen days after Joan's death, the curtain came down for the last time and Jeremy booked a flight back to England. In all, he had appeared in 96 performances.

Filming of the third Granada series, *The Return of Sherlock Holmes*, was due to start in September . . . with a difference. There was to be a new Dr Watson.

Actor Edward Hardwicke was taking over the role because David Burke had signed up with the Royal Shakespeare Company. He was anxious to spend more time with his two-year-old son Tom and actress wife Anna Calder-Marsha. Anna, knowing of her husband's concern for Jeremy, had secretly recommended Edward for the role of Watson because she believed he was ideally suited for the part.

David had found common ground with Watson and always believed the doctor had more empathy with his creator than Holmes had. To prove his point he would recall how he had met an elderly man who had, in his youth, been Conan Doyle's gardener. The old man told how one day the writer's house was burgled but nothing serious was stolen, just a few sentimental items. When he found out, Conan Doyle threw himself onto his hands and knees, checking flowerbeds and inspecting doors and windows with a magnifying glass. Two hours later, when the police arrived, he was still hard at it, but hadn't found any clues. He seemed disappointed that the police had already arrested the thief without his help. Conan Doyle had tried to be Holmes but had ended up a Watson.

At first, after waving David goodbye from the platform of Manchester station, Jeremy was worried. The success of Holmes's confidant and chronicler on screen was crucial to his role. The mainstay of the Sherlock Holmes stories was their deep friendship. They were an odd couple but they complemented each other.

Edward Hardwicke, however, proved to be the perfect choice as the new on-screen Dr Watson.

Someone else was equally pleased: Sherry Rose-Bond, co-founder of the Philadelphia-based Clients of Sherlock Holmes Society.

Sherry immediately informed members, who met five times a year, that Edward was the son of legendary Hollywood actor Sir Cedric Hardwicke. Even better, Edward grew up in Los Angeles where his father's best friend was fellow English thespian Nigel Bruce, whose portrayal of a bumbling Dr Watson was immortalised in fourteen films starring Basil Rathbone.

'There are connections everywhere,' Sherry excitedly told the world. 'The more you dig, the more you find – just like Holmes.'

Along with her husband, Sherry was always digging. Jeremy learned that the couple lived in a Mount Airy house where an entire room was turned over to Holmes memorabilia – first editions, photographs and souvenirs (including a brick from Baker Street and a bottle of water from the Artesian well beneath 221B).

Edward, a Londoner, spent most of his early childhood in Hollywood with his father, Sir Cedric, the scholarly looking, high-domed Englishman with an imposing, booming voice who played Sherlock Holmes on the radio and was a lifelong friend of actor Nigel Bruce from their early days in repertory. It was in London that George Bernard Shaw gave Sir Cedric's young, impressionable son some meaningful advice. 'Whatever you do, don't go on the stage, Edward.' The Irish dramatist's thoughts were among a plethora of comments written on the pages of

Edward's most treasured possession – *A Book of Good Advice*, which Jeremy would later be enthralled by.

When Edward was a toddler his father used to carry the book around with him. He would ask the wisest and wittiest men of the time to write a little piece in it. They all did. There were remarks by authors such as H. G. Wells and J. M. Barrie. One day his father even met Albert Einstein. Einstein's words were typically offbeat. 'Never accept foreign advice without proof. Ultimately rely only on your own judgement.'

But Edward was more impressed with car magnate Henry Ford, who wrote simply: 'Learn by doing.' And he was touched by Walt Disney's drawing of Jiminy Cricket with the words: 'Let your conscience be your guide.'

When Edward's father, a former medical student and army officer, arrived in Hollywood, the first person to meet him was Nigel Bruce. Edward was nine and would stand watching his father and Nigel playing bridge every weekend and fall asleep in the armchair listening to them gossiping about the colony of English actors who were living in Tinsel Town at the time. The English were as thick as thieves, playing polo and cricket and cards. Then one evening there was a knock at the front door – Basil Rathbone arrived to play cards too.

Edward's own acting career started in Hollywood when he played a small role in *A Guy Named Joe* starring Spencer Tracy. Later he returned to England to train at the Royal Acadamy of Dramatic Art. In 1962 he appeared in Peter Ustinov's *Photo Finish* at the Saville Theatre in London and in 1964 joined the National Theatre in its first season, appearing in *Othello* and *The Royal Hunt of the Sun*. He remained with the company almost continuously until 1971 and knew Jeremy well, although he had never acted with him.

His film credits included *The Day of the Jackal* and on TV he played in *Colditz*, *Some Mothers Do Have 'Em* and *The Brothers*.

By now Jeremy had a firm picture of Watson in his mind. He believed he was a strong man, a man of rhythm and regular habits. He had a job, a regular one, had been in the army, moved among men and had many friends. He was a member of some of the best clubs in London and came into contact with people through his surgery. He also had a wife. Holmes, on the other hand, was exactly the opposite and only had one friend – Watson.

Somehow Watson had seen Holmes's need. Holmes fell apart when he did not work. He shot up, straight to the vein, the seven per cent solution. He smoked too much. He scraped on his violin, not very well. He practised chemistry – nearly blowing people to pieces if he was not careful – so was a problem child as well as a brilliant, if impossible, friend. Watson also realised that Holmes just could not bring himself to say 'Thank you' or 'Good night'. Or 'Help'. But what he did occasionally say could be rather sweet. In *A Scandal in Bohemia* he told Watson: 'You see, I did remember you were coming; here are your cigars.' Little things like that meant a lot to the good doctor and Jeremy worked hard at these lines to capture such poignant moments. He wanted to show how much Holmes really needed and cared about Watson without actually saying it.

Edward had a similar view of the relationship. He spent weeks watching every Holmes and Watson film he could find before rehearsing the scenes. And just like Jeremy's his desk at home was covered with stories from the canon. Edward felt that Holmes and Watson were like characters in a Shakespeare play – they changed slightly depending on the age in which they were read. Watson was by no means a stupid man, but the main difficulty Edward found in playing him was that, as he narrated the stories, there was an awful lot of him missing on film. Happily the actor found a vast well of humour in the role, which pleased Jeremy no end, as Holmes didn't seem to have any. Where detection was concerned, however, Watson was in awe of the great detective and Edward managed to capture that look of complete admiration, respect and amazement brilliantly. At other times he viewed him with wry amusement. Jeremy and Edward both agreed from the start that Watson was the person who knew the real world. Holmes may constantly have accused him of romanticising the stories, but if the supersleuth had written them he would never have become so famous.

As a newcomer to the series, Edward at first felt governed by what had gone before. But right from the start he knew that Jeremy had discovered a wonderful way of playing Holmes. It was almost as if he were playing tennis with a very good player.

'He just holds up his racket in the right place and when the ball comes it goes right back over the net,' he said. But Edward and the production team were very aware that Jeremy was grieving. He would suddenly talk about his beloved Joannie as if she were still with him and he would be seeing her soon. The TV crew and Granada executives were used to Jeremy's eccentric streak ... but Edward was learning about it for the first time.

The third series of cases which formed *The Return of Sherlock Holmes* opened with the appearance of the great detective in London after his supposed death at the Reichenbach Falls. John Hawkesworth's adaptation of the famous story *The Empty House* featured Edward's debut as Watson, although he had actually first gone before the cameras in *The Abbey Grange*, which was the first episode to be filmed in the autumn of 1985. It was a perfect start because Watson had little to do or say in the story, which gave Edward the chance to get used to his new role.

Edward was taking the part extremely seriously. He wore a wig in the style of Watson's hair and, to increase his height, inserted wooden platforms in his shoes.

In *The Abbey Grange* there was a chase across a muddy field and Jeremy streaked across it, leaving Edward in hot pursuit. But the wooden platforms weren't designed for running and poor Watson slipped and stumbled everywhere.

'Oh, Edward, for goodness sake, take out the platforms and I'll act the rest of the episode with my knees bent,' said Jeremy.

As always the new series featured a host of well-known stars. In *The Abbey Grange* Anne Louise Lambert played Lady Mary Brackenstall, the beautiful Australian woman married to an unpleasant English lord, alias Conrad Phillips. The episode was shot at Dunham Massey, Altrincham, Tabley House in Knutsford, Cheshire, and Adlington Hall. When Lord Brackenstall was found brutally murdered, Holmes was soon on the scene along with Inspector Hopkins, played by Paul Williamson. The programme also featured Oliver Tobias as Captain Crocker and Zulema Dene as Theresa Wright.

Next followed Jeremy Paul's adaptation of *The Musgrave Ritual*, starring Michael Culver as Reginald Musgrave, an aristocrat who called in the great detective to get to the bottom of the strange events occurring on his estate at Hurlestone – in particular the goings-on in the manor house, which was believed to be the oldest inhabited building in the country; *The Second Stain* featured Patricia Hodge as Lady Hilda Trelawny Hope, wife of a government minister caught up in the case of a mysterious murder at Westminster; and *The Man with the Twisted Lip* starred Clive Francis in the dual roles of Neville St Claire, who mysteriously disappeared, and Hugh Boone, the unmasked beggar.

The last two episodes to be shown were *The Priory School*, Edward Hardwicke's favourite, with Christopher Benjamin as Doctor Thorneycroft Huxtable, and *The Six Napoleons*, a story described by Holmes as 'absolutely original' in the history of crime. It concerned a series of burglaries in which it seemed the criminal's sole purpose was to destroy busts of Napoleon. Holmes was put on the trail by the first victim of these strange offences, Morse Hudson, played by Gerald Campion, forever remembered as the television Billy Bunter. But an even stranger robbery served to deepen the mystery. For after a similar entry into the home of Mr Horace Harker of the Central News Agency, played by comedian Eric Sykes, the body of an unknown man with his throat cut was found in the grounds not far from the remains of yet another bust of the emperor.

Throughout the series, everyone agreed that Jeremy was playing the role of Holmes differently. But the producers thought his new approach suited the part. The truth was that he was becoming even more isolated and was acting on autopilot. His manic episodes were getting worse.

Esther Dean put down the telephone. She was shattered. Her mother, whom she lived with in London, had died of a heart attack. She walked slowly back to the dinner table where Edward Hardwicke and Jeremy were sitting.

'I'm sorry, I must go, my mother has died,' she said.
Jeremy and Edward drove her back from the restaurant.
'What about the rest of your family, will you tell them?' Jeremy asked.
'Yes, when I've got myself together I'll tell my brother,' Esther replied.
Jeremy was thoughtful for a moment, then he said quietly: 'It doesn't matter about getting yourself together or putting off bad news. I'll never forget doing that to David once.'
Jeremy recalled the time when David was at school and his beloved Nanny Gertie died. He and Anna didn't know how to break the news to him. So they took him out for the day and gave him a wonderful time. Later that evening they sat him down and told him that Nanny had passed away.
He was crestfallen.
'I wish you'd told me straight away. I was enjoying myself all day. I would rather have known about Nanny!' he cried.
'I've always regretted doing that,' Jeremy said. 'That's why you should never put anything off, Esther.'
She turned and looked out of the window at the rain. How right he was.

The day was cold but it was sunny and the light was clear throwing a shaft of white through the gap in the bedroom curtains. Jeremy had been aimlessly staring at the spot it had struck on the wallpaper for the last hour. He had woken at dawn, lying still, thinking about life, about Joan, about Holmes.
He looked around the room, at the clothes strewn on the floor, the mess on the mantelpiece, the scattered books and magazines, the dust. Holmes would have been proud. The detective's thought process was neat and methodical but his habits were entirely the opposite. He kept his cigars in a coal scuttle, his tobacco in the toe-end of a Persian slipper, and his unanswered correspondence transfixed by a jack-knife thrust into the centre of his wooden mantelpiece.
Jeremy picked up the tattered script from the bedside table and went to the bathroom, turning on the taps and pouring in bubble bath. Steam rose in white clouds.

He let himself gingerly into the bath, clutching the script and a pencil, and slid down under the suds. Little splashes of water dotted the typed cover page and he rubbed them off with the back of his hand, wondering what Holmes would say. The Victorian sleuth had a horror of destroying documents.

The new script was a testament to this. *The Musgrave Ritual* was to become one of Jeremy's favourites. It would also win Jeremy Paul the Edgar Allan Poe Award from the Mystery Writers of America. As depicted in the story, Holmes's life paralleled his own, with outbursts of passionate energy followed by periods of lethargy, during which he would lie about with his violin and his books, hardly moving except to walk slowly from the sofa to the table. Month after month his papers would accumulate until every corner of the room was stacked with bundles of manuscripts that were never to be destroyed.

Jeremy didn't play the violin but he did drag himself from sofa to bed now, and the mail he never opened accumulated on his doormat. In *The Ritual*, Jeremy Paul had presented Holmes as a bored and reluctant guest at Hurlestone Manor. Jeremy lay pondering the idea, and then it came to him in a blinding flash. Holmes was on cocaine again. He would play the part wearing a travelling rug round his shoulders – and giggle irrationally. He threw the script and pencil on the floor and soaped his arms, stroking the suds away with a slimy sponge, musing on the day ahead. When the water grew cold he eased himself out of the bath and rubbed himself down with a towel, stopping for a moment to look into the mirror. 'You are but a brass rubbing of Holmes,' he said to himself, wrapping his bath robe around him.

Now Jeremy would walk home from a restaurant completely oblivious to everyone around him. He had entered a silent world but there was no silence in his head. It was racing with a hundred thoughts, darting from subject to subject. But instead of the colourful mental pictures that had characterised earlier spells of rapid thinking, his mind was drenched in terrifying sounds and frightening visions. He was walking through a nightmare but he was not asleep. It never occurred to him that he was ill. Eventually the rapid thoughts would go away by themselves, but only for long enough to regroup and mobilise for another attack that would come without warning.

It was a beautiful bright and hot day. They had all returned from the beach and Tarn was fixing cold drinks on the patio of the house she had rented in Ibiza. Jeremy was still struggling with Joan's death and she had been pleased to take him away with the family. Jeremy loved Ibiza, its uninhibited atmosphere, the 'behave as you please' lifestyle.

'Small is beautiful, just like Dudley Moore,' he would say of the tiny 200-square-mile island in the Spanish Balearics, home of the sometimes outrageous pace-setters. He loved the North African air of it and the mix of Arab architecture. That afternoon, though, he seemed to be acting wildly. His voice sounded thin and the day before the youngsters had found him sitting meditating surrounded by candles. It was a wonderful holiday and Tarn was glad Jeremy had been able to come, but he clearly wasn't himself. Of course, he was always odd, but this was something else.

The youngsters were beginning to laugh at him, poke fun at him. It was starting to irritate Tarn. Jeremy and the children had always been so close. Her daughter and her friends arrived on the patio, giggling.

'What's the joke?' she asked.

'It's Jeremy,' they said.

'What's he doing now?'

'Come and look.'

Tarn went down to the garden and stood quietly, watching her friend. He was pirouetting across the lawn, jumping and spinning, waving his arms in the air.

'He told us he was performing a dance to the sun,' they whispered.

Tarn was beginning to believe that Jeremy was on drugs. But it wasn't true. The demon thoughts were taking over.

During the next few months his friends and family began to set up a pattern, telephoning each other when they noticed that things were getting worse, that his behaviour was even stranger.

A phrase spoken over the telephone, such as 'I'm terribly anxious about something', would start the wheels turning and one of them would soon be by his side.

Then one fateful weekend Jeremy moved into the penthouse apartment he had bought in Clapham for Joan and started to unpack and hang the pictures.

She had seen it just once before leaving for medical treatment in America, and being there again brought back painful memories for Jeremy. He and Joan had climbed out onto the roof and stood admiring the view, which she adored. The house, based on the Tuileries with its towers, was built in 1864 by James Knowles, who also created the Grosvenor House Hotel. Their new home was one of the gatehouses on the road to Crystal Palace and Victoria and Albert had often passed it.

Joan was typically American and had wanted to know all about the history of the area. As they sipped orange juice, enjoying the view, he had explained that Clapham was once known as Clopeham, a small village until the seventeenth century when the Great Plague and Great Fire of London led to many more people moving out of the city and living there. Samuel Pepys had once lived on the north side of the common, as had Sir Charles Barry and Captain Cook. Joan was enthralled.

Jeremy hung a mirror in the bathroom and stood back to look at it. It seemed to be following his every move. If he moved left it followed him. If he moved right it did the same. To comfort himself he began to talk to it, but once he started he could not stop. Overwhelming confusion was taking over the strange clarity he had been used to in the past. He went into the bedroom and lay on the bed, getting up a few seconds later to go back to the mirror. It was still following his every move so he remonstrated with it and began to unpack ornaments wrapped in old newspapers. Every page seemed to have coded references about him. One seemed to be from Zeus, the God of Fire. He threw the scraps of paper on the floor and picked up some books. One was his well-fingered favourite, *The Teachings of Buddha.* He frantically flicked through the pages, desperately looking for the paragraph he needed.

'Where is it? Where the bloody hell is it?' he screamed. He was manic, almost tearing the pages to find what he wanted. Suddenly he stopped and read aloud:

'Once upon a time a man looked into the reverse side of a mirror and, not seeing his face and head, he became insane. How unnecessary it is for a man to become insane merely because he carelessly looks into the reverse side of a mirror!'

Jeremy raced back into the bathroom, snatched the mirror from the wall and turned it over to stare at the other side.

Suddenly the whole world dissolved into pink and white.

'God, you need spectacles, what the hell are you bloody well doing?' he shouted, and the mirror smashed to the floor.

Slowly his mind cleared a little. At least, it seemed to him that it had but he couldn't be sure. Perhaps his mind was lying to him. Perhaps it was Moriarty up to his old tricks. The thought made him perspire and he could almost hear his heart thudding against his chest.

That night he greeted a group of friends at a restaurant. As usual he bought every table a bottle of champagne in a spontaneous gesture. All the guests were delighted, except the friends on his own table. Jeremy nevertheless believed he was in dazzling form. He felt he was the centre of attention and couldn't stop talking.

The truth was that even the restaurant manager felt uncomfortable with him.

The next morning, after a sleepless night, he remembered nothing of his frenetic behaviour, only that he felt inexplicably afraid. He found himself having an exasperating dialogue with God, who had come through the penthouse window riding on a beam of light. He tried to tell his family and friends when they arrived uninvited. He shouted at them to go away but they didn't.

On the way to the hospital in the ambulance he sang to the audience. He had counted just sixteen of them, or was it six? Or two? What did it matter? His thoughts were coming so fast that he couldn't remember the beginning of a sentence he had half begun or the words of the song he kept trying to sing. Fragments of ideas, images and sentences raced around his mind like shooting stars before imploding into black holes. There was no notion of time as a million other shooting stars were born, shone, raced by and died. From the moment he walked into the Maudsley Psychiatric Hospital in south London, quite peaceably, wearing his familiar white trousers and pink shirt, he became acutely aware of most appalling pain all around him.

'My God, I must help these people!' he said aloud before being sedated. His pink and white world went suddenly black.

Jeremy stayed in the Maudsley for eight weeks. His friends and David were worried. All the stories they had heard about psychiatric wards haunted them.

During that time Jeremy realised that his son really needed him to be well again. David was distraught. He felt it was his duty to rescue his father, even though he hadn't grown up with him. When he saw the tears in David's eyes one morning as he lay in his hospital bed, he willed himself to recover, willed himself through the blackness, willed himself to have positive thoughts. David gave him the courage he so desperately needed to find. 'If my son needs me then I can never let this happen again,' he vowed to himself.

As a young boy David had loved the eccentricities of his father, whom he greatly admired. He expressed himself in his paintings and essays at school and became a bit of a loner . . . as he was now.

Family friends and Jeremy's colleagues were forever ringing him up, asking him to control or help his father, and he was embarrassed about that. But he would always drop everything and fly off to some distant place where his father was creating mayhem.

Then things would quieten down and they would go their own separate ways again. But David always tried to keep the link and he would send his father his paintings which took pride of place in Jeremy's Clapham home.

In a way, as much as they loved each other, David grew up without a real father and never became close to Joan Sullivan's children Rebecca and Caleb.

Slowly Jeremy began to turn the corner. One evening, face

down on his bed, he punched the pillow and shouted: 'I will never, never, never risk my mental health again just to be a bloody actor. Damn you, Holmes!'

Jeremy hated the Maudsley and began to call it the Snake Pit. He joked that it was like the prison in the movie *Midnight Express*. All around him was the pitiful reality of the sights and sounds and smells of insanity. He was so drugged that he couldn't even tell the doctors that he felt sane.

He didn't know it then but his family and friends believed he would be 'sectioned' (forcibly committed). David was determined not to let that happen. If it did, he feared the fact would be stamped in his passport and follow his father for the rest of his life. Anna Massey would drive David to the hospital but never go in. Edward Hardwicke went to visit him though and found the hospital a depressing place – even though the doctors were among the finest in the world. He took Jeremy some 'silly bits of food' and found his new friend very subdued. Jeremy admitted that they had 'balanced him and subdued him' and he feared he would never act properly again. Eventually David and Granada managed to get him out.

Tarn and David took him to Greyshott Health Farm in Hampshire, but he still needed help. Finally Anna Massey recommended London's Chelsea and Westminster Hospital and a top psychiatrist there. It proved to be the saving of him. But even then his personality took over. He tried to manage everybody, sorting out visiting times for patients to see their families and checking the staff rotas.

Now, for the first time, everyone was beginning to realise how desperate and how ill Jeremy had really been. As he recovered, his family and close friends struggled to come to terms with his breakdown and understand it. They began to recall the signs they now knew to be obvious symptoms of manic depression – getting high and excited, talking all the time, sometimes not making sense. He hardly ever seemed to need any sleep. Sometimes he said unpleasant things or had sudden rages. At other times he would go on a spending spree, buying everyone presents or ornaments for the house. Things would never be quite the same again.

8 Challenging the Depression

Where there is no imagination there is no horror

Conan Doyle, *A Study in Scarlet*

'I'M SORRY, would you mind explaining that again,' Jeremy asked. He lay on the bed, trying to understand what the doctor meant, how his words would affect his life, would affect what he still had to do ... be an award-winning actor, win a BAFTA.

'Lithium is a simple salt but, as with so many medicines, no one really knows how it works. In fact there are conflicting facts about its effects on brain amines,' said the doctor, flicking through his notes.

Jeremy felt as if he were in a scene from a stage play.

'And what does that mean to me, my life, my acting? Isn't this the dreaded Elvis Presley drug? Didn't he get fat?'

The doctor smiled sympathetically and went on.

'Lithium is mostly used as a prophylactic drug, protecting against recurrent mania, manic depression and, to a lesser extent, recurrent depression. For some manic depressives it has completely changed their lives, providing sustained relief from periodic suffering. There is a famous case of a man who had a regular forty-eight-hour cycle of mania-depression, mania-depression, and so on. He was given lithium for two-and-a-half years and had no further manic or depressive episodes. At the end of the two-and-a-half years, without him knowing it, a placebo was exchanged for the lithium – and his forty-eight-hour cycle resumed.'

Jeremy kept asking question after question. He didn't like the idea that he might have to take drugs for the rest of his life.

'Who is the drug really suitable for?'

'Although lithium has been phenomenally successful it should be used only if the episodes of mania and depression are definitely recurrent, like yours are. But it does have side effects.'

'Such as?'

'Minor side effects include increased thirst and urination, initial loss of appetite, a fine tremor in the fingers which gets worse on drinking alcohol. Headaches and weight gain, nausea and loose stools. Conditions can worsen to severe thirst and excessive urination, vomiting and diarrhoea. There is a lack of co-ordination, slurred speech and of course drowsiness.'

'And they are the minor side effects? What are the bad ones?'

'In severe cases there is a ringing in the ears and blurred vision. Overdoses can cause damage to the kidneys.'

Jeremy took his huge 'Mickey Finns' like a good boy and they seemed to stabilise him. He became better each day. When the time was right Granada stepped in and put him into the Charters convalescent home for a two-week stay. At last he was getting back into normal life.

Part of Jeremy's healing process involved learning the history of his condition.

He began to realise that he had been ill for some time, perhaps all his life. He was a classic case of manic depression, with excessive changes of mood, swinging from extreme depression to great elation and hyperactivity, occasionally totally losing touch with reality. There were of course periods of complete stability, but they had been getting fewer and further between.

Slowly, painstakingly, he came to terms with his illness. Mercifully mania had at least some grace in partially obliterating memories. He couldn't remember his behaviour; there were only other people's recollections of it. But that was hard to bear. He dreaded facing his family and friends in the future. Who knew what? What did he really do? Were they too polite to tell him?

He remembered the doctor's words: 'Victims, such as yourself, will have spells of tremendous energy. There will be an inability or unwillingness to sleep, a rapid flow of ideas, often penetrating, imaginative and perceptive, but as the mood increases with less and less reality and coherence.' Jeremy wondered how he could live with himself knowing all this.

For two weeks he lay in his bed in the Charters clinic reading the brochures doctors and friends had given him. Perhaps after all, as the pamphlets said, he needed a carer, someone who could monitor him . . . but who? He had become so isolated now. He had many friends in and out of the acting world, but they had their own lives to get on with. His family, David and Patrick and the rest of them did too. Who could it be?

He realised from everything he had heard and read that there were many ways of influencing his own mood swings. The most important thing was to catch the strange, angry, azure-blue spells early. The doctors had told him: 'You must catch the mood swing at its birth.'

Jeremy couldn't wait to leave his walled-up existence and get back to the outside world. He hoped he was cured, although he really knew he wasn't. The doctors had hinted that he would never be cured. His only hope was to live with his condition, look for the signs of a manic onslaught and deal with it. But he had to get out, play again, rebuild his life, his confidence.

Dawn broke in the room and all seemed right with the world. He had sat quietly watching the sunlight burst through the window like the sunbeam that had shone on him through the stained-glass window of the Eton chapel. He had busily packed his bags at 4 a.m., cleaning his teeth and carefully twisting the cap back on the toothpaste tube before putting it into his blue travel bag. June Wyndham Davis and David would be picking him up. Suddenly there was a knock on the door and two journalists burst in. They had tricked the reception desk into believing that they were members of the Huggins family.

'Mr Brett, is it true that you have AIDS?' one of them shouted as the other one clicked away with a camera. Jeremy flew at them and there was a scuffle. The camera fell to the ground and smashed as the clinic staff arrived. The two journalists were thrown out. The incident put Jeremy back several weeks. He retreated into himself, believing that if the world was like that outside he would rather stay in. From that day on Granada banned the newspaper from the set.

Finally Jeremy was discharged and there to meet him, like a good Watson, was his friend Edward Hardwicke, who drove him back to Clapham. Slowly, over the next few days, Jeremy finished unpacking and tried to understand what had caused his breakdown. Was it really Joan? Or was it Holmes? Whatever it was he knew now that there was one person who would get him through – the dark master of disguise himself. He had to get on the train to Manchester and walk into the Granada studios again. He had to pick up the gauntlet. He had to break the spell Holmes had over him. His father had always told him to get back on the horse no matter how hurt or frightened he was after a fall. Holmes was his horse.

Within two months Jeremy was back in front of the cameras to film a two-hour Conan Doyle special, *The Sign of Four*, with Edward, John Thaw and Jenny Seagrove. Granada was spending £1 million on the production to celebrate the 100th anniversary of the first publication of a Sherlock Holmes story, *A Study in Scarlet*. Conan Doyle had finished it in April 1886 and it appeared in *Beeton's Christmas Annual* in 1887, for which he was paid the princely fee of £25. Other prospective publishers had turned him away, telling him: 'The market is already flooded with cheap fiction!'

If Jeremy had not recovered, Granada would have dropped all plans for the lavish production. But from the moment he walked back on to the set he knew that continuing with the role was the only way forward.

'My God, I've cracked it, I am better,' he told Edward.

This time he was different again. In the beginning he had been robust, always bounding everywhere, just like Holmes. But now the drugs were slowing him down and he was putting on weight. He was playing a lonely, tortured man, despite the fact that he had been outgoing and gregarious all his life. Now he seemed to slip into the role more easily. He would shut himself away in his hotel room and get his meals sent up. No one would see him. There were no more parties, no more champagne-for-all binges.

Problems always arose in location shooting for the series. This was especially so in *The Sign of Four*, in which Holmes and Watson searched for clues in a mysterious treasure trove of pearls and some even more mysterious deaths centred around the beautiful Mary Morstan, played by Jenny Seagrove. Using 35-millimetre film for the first time, the episode was made on location in Manchester, Liverpool, Yorkshire, Malta and London, with the finale of Holmes in pursuit of the villainous Jonathan Small, played by John Thaw, shot on the River Thames. The Thames was a problem from the start. The sound recordist found it difficult to shut out the sounds of drills, aeroplanes and motor boats. Jeremy and the crew used the new glass and concrete Tower Hotel opposite the Tower of London for their base but had to trek off to quiet moorings at lunchtime and in the late afternoon to record much of the soundtrack which would later be superimposed on the action shots.

The Thames posed other problems too. Granada surveyed the river from Kew to Greenwich six or seven times, to find that only about 150 yards remained as they were in Holmes's day. Wharves had fallen derelict or had been demolished and modern flats had been built. Even when they found a suitable location they would return the next day to find a crane had gone up overnight, ruining the skyline.

Finally the Thames was recreated – on the peaceful River Yare in Norfolk.

With 20 one-hour films under his hat and *The Sign of Four* finished, Jeremy planned to make six more one-hour episodes for Granada, including a two-hour version of *The Hound of the Baskervilles*, and then hang up his deerstalker, put away his black frock-coat and retire from the series for good. He knew that by then he wouldn't be able to go on as Holmes and he would have to learn to live again, even though it would probably mean a return to the doublet and hose. In a way he quite relished the thought.

'I think I will go and do something romantic,' he told everyone. 'Get this henna out of my hair. Let it grow a little bit and do something like Browning or Byron.'

As he spoke his face would come alive. 'I know I can't get into the twentieth century. I can't get into modern dress. I've tried and tried. The nearest I managed was as Max de Winter in *Rebecca* for the BBC in 1978; and then I only made it to the 1930s. The trouble is I'm from a bygone age. If I put my hands in my pockets I nearly fall over because I've been in tights all my life!'

The Hound of the Baskervilles was another lavish two-hour adaptation of the most famous of all Sherlock Holmes cases. Granada had to build a huge set representing the Grimpen Mire in the studios. Yorkshire and Staffordshire locations were also used to represent the wilds of Dartmoor for the Victorian detective's dangerous mission to track down the huge demonic hound that was the curse of the Baskerville family. Again the TV company stayed amazingly faithful to the master. Even confronted by the difficult hiatus in the middle of the story when Holmes drops out for two chapters, they resisted the temptation to rewrite, except for fleeting off-stage appearances to reassure the uninitiated that he was still around.

Kristoffer Tabori played Sir Henry Baskerville, the latest in the family line, and an eleven-stone, two-year-old Great Dane named Khan was his co-star.

Jeremy, as always, found the animal lovable and Khan adored him, especially when Holmes went down on all fours off the set to rub his nose against him.

'How can this great luvvy possibly scare the viewers?' Jeremy asked the production crew. When they produced a ferocious robot head with flashing teeth and piercing eyes that would be used in the close-ups, he was convinced.

As always he and Edward Hardwicke had studied and restudied their roles and the background to the story. They learned that the first distant baying of the hound came on a cold Sunday evening in March 1901. Conan Doyle was convalescing in an hotel on the Norfolk coast. A fire crackled in the grate and the wind howled off the North Sea like the moaning of Black Shuck, a spectre said to haunt that part of the coast in the form of a gigantic dog. With Conan Doyle was his great friend Fletcher Robinson.

Thoughts of Black Shuck led Fletcher to recall a legend from his native Devon. Conan Doyle was fascinated, and so was Jeremy.

Fletcher told of a house named Brook Manor, near

Buckfastleigh, on the edge of Dartmoor. In the seventeenth century it was owned by an evil squire named Richard Cabell. One night, in a jealous rage, Cabell attacked his wife and beat her so cruelly that she fled across the moor with only her faithful hound for company. Cabell rushed out in pursuit, ran her to ground and killed her. Her loyal hound flew at him and tore his throat out before it too died of knife wounds. From that day, said Fletcher, the monstrous hound appeared to each new generation of the Cabell family. Conan Doyle sat entranced. And so did Jeremy as he delved deeper and deeper into the story.

Conan Doyle, of course, knew a bestseller when he saw one. Within a month he was writing from Rowe's Duchy Hotel, Princetown, in the shadow of Dartmoor jail. Today it is the prison officer's mess.

At that time Dartmoor held more than 1,000 prisoners, all controlled by the cat-o'-nine-tails. From his hotel window Conan Doyle would watch the convicts being led out to break stone in the quarries. In *The Hound of the Baskervilles* he called his escaped murderer Selden, a cheeky joke, because that was the name of one of the toughest warders in the history of the prison.

'Robinson and I are exploring the Moor over our new Sherlock Holmes book. I think it will work out splendidly, indeed I have already done nearly half of it. Holmes is at his very best!' Conan Doyle wrote back home.

He borrowed the name Baskerville from Fletcher's coachman. Brook Manor became, with the addition of a couple of towers, Baskerville Hall. Grimspound and Fox Tor Mire became the terrible Grimpen Mire and the moor itself added the brooding presence that gave the book its haunting atmosphere.

For Jeremy, the filming brought back disturbing memories. When he was a child his mother and father would drive him across the moor on the way to family holidays in Cornwall. He could remember the fear he felt in the car, the bleakness of the sinister brick walls of the prison. He could smell the supernatural then, and he could smell it now.

Jeremy loved the story . . . the element of the lamb to the

slaughter in the shape of young Baskerville returning to his inheritance. The threat to him ran right through the story and no one had any idea whether it was human or animal, metaphysical or supernatural. Was the Hound of the Baskervilles real? Even Holmes left his options open. Jeremy liked that.

One weekend Jeremy decided to climb the hill to Buckfastleigh churchyard following in Conan Doyle's footsteps. Below him on one side lay the ancient Buckfast Abbey, away on the other stretched the dun-coloured moor. He tried to enter the church but it was locked, so he walked around it until he found a gardener tending the graves.

'Excuse me, but can you tell me where Richard Cabell is buried?' he asked.

The gardener looked blank for a moment, then said: 'Ah, you mean the haunted tomb?'

He pointed to a small building beside the South Porch. In it, behind metal railings, stood a crumbling gravestone. Richard Cabell was apparently buried there in 1677 – or was it Richard Capel? Legend, it seemed, could not even agree on his name. Jeremy stood looking at the railings, smiling to himself.

'Whoever you are, you are at peace now . . . not like me,' he said.

He looked at the overcast sky. It was thickening, great splodges of cloud shifting from grey to black, bulging and spreading. The wind blew against his face and it was as if Cabell were warning him. Or perhaps it was Joannie. He looked back at the grave.

Some stories said Cabell sold his soul to the Devil, others that he stole young girls from the local villages, or that he was a huntsman who rode with a pack of hell hounds. Jeremy wondered what the truth was. Whatever he had done it was bad enough for the villagers to have placed a massive slab of granite on his coffin in order to keep his spirit in place. Ghostly hounds were said to howl around his grave and local children dared each other to put a finger into the keyhole for Cabell to gnaw at.

Jeremy drove on. Three miles from Buckfastleigh, in a coomb below the moor, lay Brook Manor, a shiny tower at the end of a long narrow drive. By now the afternoon light had worsened, shifting to a false twilight. He had it in mind to knock on the door.

He walked up the long, winding path and smiled at the footprints of a large dog embedded in the damp green banks around the grounds.

'They're wolfhounds,' the manor's new owners told him. The young couple bred them. Jeremy was immediately taken with Paddy, a hound the size of a donkey, as it nuzzled up to him. Then he realised he was a day late. The previous night, 5 July, was the anniversary of Richard Cabell's death, and his ghost was supposed to ride out along the drive with his hounds from hell. Jeremy wondered if he had missed anything, but the owners explained that the calendar had changed since the seventeenth century – perhaps legend had the wrong night.

Later, Jeremy could almost feel Cabell's presence as he stood gazing down on the chilling grey stones of the giant Dartmoor prison. He was glad he had made the trip.

Two miles south of Princetown were the derelict tin mines of Whiteworks, where the moor was pitted with shafts and littered with the ruins of miners' cottages. Beyond, in a depression in the hills, lay Fox Tor Mire, where runaway prisoners and wild ponies would be swallowed in the oozing mud. In his mind's eye Jeremy could see Conan Doyle standing there accompanied by the coachman Baskerville, knowing he had the last elements of his story.

Standing in the same spot, Jeremy shuddered. He was surveying the Grimpen Mire, where everything ended. How brilliant Conan Doyle had been to keep the hound bounding through the story at every moment, gleaming and salivating.

Jeremy was in awe of the vast gloom. The hound could be anywhere. No wonder Holmes was so fearful for Watson's safety.

The press milled around the bar after the preview, nibbling nuts from saucers and downing beer and champagne. Granada TV had just shown them *The Hound of the Baskervilles* and there were as many different reactions as there were notebooks and pens. Jeremy was working the reporters hard as usual, and a shower of 'darlings' poured from his lips.

For two hours they had watched him impersonating a high-browed, keen-eyed, dark-minded Sherlock Holmes. Now he mingled with them in a blue jacket over a white shirt, white trousers and white shoes, looking as if he were on his way to an afternoon at Wimbledon. He acknowledged for the umpteenth time that it was daunting to follow in the shadows of so many other actors who had played Holmes. 'I'm just bending the willow that little bit,' he crooned in his caressing thespian tones.

Assuring another reporter of his full co-operation, he murmured to everyone: 'I shall just spread myself around you like a meat paste, darlings, and you can lap up the bits you like.'

Ten minutes later he had gone.

The critics weren't friendly to Jeremy. They hounded *The Hound of the Baskervilles.*

He read the reviews at home: 'Doyle's most famous Holmes novel, as one might have expected from the Manchester team, was executed with loving care in every department, especially in the excellent casting, with one surprising exception: the hound itself,' said one.

'All we saw was a flash of green phosphorus; Sir Henry's last and near-fatal walk went almost for nothing. Maybe they had casting problems . . .'

'I'm slightly worried about Jeremy Brett, though. After playing Holmes in 24 short-story adaptations and two of the full-length novels, he has absorbed every character nuance of fiction's most celebrated detective until the least mannerism, holding his long, thin hands together, has become second nature. Unfortunately he has also become, how shall I put it? More substantial. Holmes retained his lean, hungry look to the end. Should Mr Brett, in the interests of art and an impersonation that has delighted millions, go on a diet?'

Jeremy was crestfallen. He could hardly bear to take another lithium tablet – but he had to.

He stopped in Clapham High Street and looked at his reflection in the rain-spattered window. First he scowled at himself, then he laughed. People were walking by but that didn't matter. The glistening wet pavements were a black mirror. He could see his blackness looking back at him and he smiled at it. Suddenly he spun around and waved his arms in the air, admiring his reflection. The streetlights shimmered in the puddles. It seemed to him that there was nothing alive now. It was 2 a.m. and the small shops and offices were closed. A distant traffic light winked at him in amber. He looked over his shoulder. The High Road was nearly deserted. Nothing moved but the dribbling rain. Perhaps *he* was there, watching, lurking.

Jeremy rolled his shoulders back, straightened his spine and crossed to the other side of the road opposite the tube station. He would follow a devious route home. *He* wouldn't follow him then. Jeremy could give *him* the slip. Or could he? He could see his house now, its castle-like tower. But he would keep walking, staring ahead, because *he* would be following in disguise.

Suddenly he saw an old woman, or was it really an old woman? A red bus came in the opposite direction and Jeremy darted across the road, slipping behind it, round the common. Quickly now. He felt the keys to his sanctuary in his pocket. Soon he would be home safe. Or would Holmes be there already?

He sat staring at his hands for a moment.

'So you see I lost my darling Joannie, a wonderful, generous, kind person. When she died a little bit of me died too,' he said thoughtfully.

Linda sat quietly in the dressing room, clutching the photograph he had given her of him as Holmes, not really knowing what to say.

'I did not give up hope until the moment she passed away,' he went on. 'There are success stories and there are miracles and one always thinks you are the one who is going to get away with it, beat the odds. Right up to the very last minute there are cases, of course, where people do. And I always thought Joannie would come through.'

He stopped again and smiled at her. It was a kind smile, she thought, although deeply sad.

'What is extraordinary to me is that the human spirit is so strong, that one doesn't give up hope until really the very end,' he said, waving his hand every now and then to make a point. 'The hardest thing about being left behind is that you have to pick up the pieces. You try and carry on as normally as possible, but very often it is not possible, so one has to give oneself a lot of space, a lot of sitting still and a lot of praying, to come to terms with all the resentment one sometimes feels, like I did. There is a feeling of intense anger that it should be done to the person that you love so much. All these mixed-up feelings have to be released and let go and that takes time. Anyone who has been through it knows that it isn't a comfortable journey. I don't think one ever gets over it. One just gets used to it. So he or she must be prepared to cry and let it all out, not be too brave. Bravery is fine on some occasions, but sometimes it can be quite a dangerous thing. The stiff upper lip is not always best.'

Jeremy smiled easily at her again as he stretched his long legs out before him. It was good talking to her – she was so full of life, young, alive and caring. She seemed so excited about seeing him, so excited about her planned run around Britain. He envied her that excitement. Somehow it seemed real, not forced like his sometimes was. Her life was filled with challenges to be met, and fresh beginnings. A lot of the excitement in his life seemed to be behind him.

It was 12 September 1988, and Linda Pritchard was meeting Jeremy for the first time in his dressing room at the Richmond Theatre in Surrey, where he was starring in the play *The Secret of Sherlock Holmes* with Edward Hardwicke. From that moment on Linda and Jeremy would become firm friends.

Earlier that year she had started to make plans to turn a distant dream into reality, a dream that her family and friends thought impossible – a 5,000-mile run around the coast of Britain to raise money for cancer research. It was a huge undertaking and some of the problems seemed insurmountable. She needed money for accommodation and food and for a back-up car and driver. Linda, a south London bus driver who lived with her parents, had hardly anything.

'I just know that someone, somewhere will help,' she told her mother. 'I have a feeling deep inside me. Call it intuition.'

One evening Linda arrived home after a twelve-mile training run looking forward to a hot bath. For some reason she couldn't explain, she went straight to the television set and switched it on. For the next hour she was mesmerised by Jeremy's portrayal of the sinister sleuth Sherlock Holmes. She had never seen the series before and had never had any interest in Conan Doyle's fictional detective. But it wasn't Holmes who kept her spellbound, it was Jeremy.

'There is something strangely familiar about him, I can't explain it,' she told her mother. 'I just feel I am going to have the most wonderful adventure and my life is going to change forever. It is as if I have lived all my life to reach this moment. I have a sixth sense about him.'

Within days Linda had written to Jeremy at the Richmond Theatre asking him if he could help her in her bid to raise money to beat the scourge of cancer. She also requested a signed photograph of him to take on her run. She could hardly believe her luck when Jeremy replied agreeing to help and inviting her to his dressing room after the play.

That night after the show they had talked about his life, his work and the tragic death from pancreatic cancer of his beloved Joannie. Linda was touched by Jeremy's words about her and vowed to remember them always.

The run, called 'Keep Hope Alive', kicked off on 12 April the following year from Greenwich, London. Jeremy helped Linda by getting her publicity for a back-up driver and vehicle, raising money for running shoes and sponsoring her with £2,000 he had received when he won the Pipe Smoker of the Year award at the Savoy Hotel earlier that year.

The round-Britain event took over six months to complete. Linda visited cancer wards and hospices, meeting patients, doctors and nurses. It was a long, hard slog and during the journey she ran into problems that tested her resolve to the limit. She injured her ankle, her back-up driver fell ill, the weather conditions were atrocious, and she had trouble finding accommodation, often having to sleep rough in the car. But Jeremy kept her going by telephoning her at different stopovers.

Once, when she was at her lowest ebb, he rang to tell her: 'Sometimes our hopes and dreams do not go the way we planned but we must never let despair overcome us. We have to try, we have to care, we must never give up when we still have something left to give. Remember, Linda, nothing is really over until the moment we stop trying. You will succeed in the end, of that I am sure.'

And as Jeremy predicted, the run was a huge success, raising over £50,000 for cancer research.

When her dream was realised Linda returned to her job driving a London bus and wondered whether her friendship with Jeremy was over. In her heart she felt that he lived in the magical, glitzy world of theatre and television and she existed in the humdrum everyday world.

By this time *The Secret of Sherlock Holmes* had transferred to the Wyndham Theatre in London.

The script, by Jeremy Paul, offered a new slant on the Holmes–Watson partnership, showing the as-yet-unknown Victorian sleuth and the Afghan battle-scarred doctor as two lonely bachelors pooling their resources to take a lease on 221B Baker Street. They were good for each other. Holmes curbed Watson's rash spending and improved his friend's powers of observation. Meanwhile Watson filled in some of Holmes's general knowledge gaps, such as his total ignorance of politics and astronomy, and saved him from succumbing to his black fits and drug habits. He also appointed himself as his friend's official biographer. Privately the actor in Jeremy thought they were rather like Neil Simon's odd couple, setting up house together.

The germ of the script came from some of Jeremy's darkest moments when he had sat alone in his flat in Clapham, brooding about Holmes. He had dug so deep into the part that he had taken a tape recorder and talked for some eight hours into it. He asked himself why the man had become so strange, so distant, so dark. Why he was so isolated. He talked about Holmes's childhood, about his friendship with Watson. He looked for the cracks in the marble that made the great detective human and revealed his own little inventions that he used to keep his performance alive. It was good therapy because somewhere deep inside himself he still saw Holmes as a destructive force, but through the tape he was able to exorcise some of those feelings. The microphone was an outlet. Jeremy's friends knew that he could no longer take off Holmes's dark frock-coat at the end of the day, and in a way he realised it too. He had lost the battle of leaving the part behind in the studio and instead took the obsession home. He had broken down once – would he break down again? Everyone was worried about him – the studio, his family, Robert. The Granada production crew tried to tell him that school was over at the end of shooting each Friday night but he just wanted to be there again before term began and so he hung around, sometimes not going back to his hotel until dark. He had become Sherlock Holmes. There seemed little else in his life.

Jeremy Paul was enthralled by the tapes because by now, like Watson, the writer had become a chronicler, a sort of latterday Boswell, faithfully recalling the exploits of an elusive and beguiling hero.

The idea of writing the play had first come to the scriptwriter the previous year. Jeremy had reminded him that it was the centenary of Conan Doyle's creation and they ought to do something about it – a celebratory evening in a theatre or a reading from the canon. But they both agreed that such projects could prove heavy-going and boring.

They laughed at some of the plans already under way in America for the centenary. One TV network was planning a movie called *The Return of Sherlock Holmes* which was to star Michael Pennington as Holmes and Margaret Colin as Watson's great-granddaughter who discovers, and thaws, the great detective's frozen body in contemporary Boston. There was even talk of the movie being made into a series. It was the latest example of a burgeoning trend in films and books . . . taking the Holmes character and creating new fictions and mysteries in various times and places. Such ideas ranged from Julian Symons's *The Three Pipe Problem* and Nicholas Meyer's *The Seven Percent Solution*, with Holmes encountering Sigmund Freud, to a strange paperback quickie that had the supersleuth working alongside Tarzan.

The centenary challenge, however, triggered off something that had been burrowing away in Jeremy Paul's subconscious for a long time. While working on the adaptations of the Conan Doyle stories for TV, he had found himself more and more fascinated by their beginnings and endings. They revealed extraordinary details of the Victorian friendship between two men with no sexual overtones at all. Just friendship, uncomplicated in its nature, something that perhaps the fast-moving world of the 1980s had lost sight of. Added to this was Conan Doyle's sharp insight into the social and moral climate of his times. So often these openings had to be skimmed in the television versions in order to move quickly into the narrative of the case. Yet here was a record of real life that included everything from what Holmes and Watson had for breakfast to what they did on a rainy afternoon in Baker Street. As the idea began to form in his mind, Paul began to read the beginnings again, starting with *The Musgrave Ritual*, Jeremy's favourite. The story opened with Watson admitting that Holmes was one of the most untidy men who ever drove a fellow lodger to distraction. He said: 'Not that I am in the least conventional in that respect myself. The rough and tumble work in Afghanistan, coming on the top of a natural Bohemianism of disposition, has made me rather more lax than befits a medical man. But with me there is a limit and when I find a man who keeps his cigars in the coal-scuttle, his tobacco in the toe end of a Persian slipper and his unanswered correspondence transfixed by a jack-knife into the very centre of his wooden mantelpiece, then I begin to give myself virtuous airs. I have always held too, that pistol practice should distinctly be an open air pastime and when Holmes, in one of his queer humours, sits in an armchair, with his hair-trigger and a hundred Boxer cartridges, and proceeds to adorn the opposite wall with a patriotic V.R. done in bullet pocks, I feel strongly that neither the atmosphere nor the appearance of our room is improved by it.

'Our chambers are always full of chemicals and of criminal relics, which have a way of wandering into unlikely positions, and of turning up in the butter-dish or in even less desirable places.'

The words were a gold mine and Paul decided there and then to write a play about Holmes and Watson, based on Conan Doyle's own little descriptions of their life together. It would be a glimpse into the tortured soul of the world's most famous detective, aided by notes from the tortured soul of the famous actor who played him. But as Holmes adventures went, this production would be a quiet one, with no crimes, clues or imperilled clients. In previous stage incarnations, Holmes had faced demonic hounds, poisonous swamp adders and any number of Professor Moriarty's evil schemes. But not in this one. Paul was anxious to make it a psychological study.

Entranced by the idea but a little wary, Jeremy commissioned it and the writer plunged headlong down what he knew was a thorny and well-trodden path. But he didn't care. He became something of a magpie, plundering the canon for bits of this story and that, discovering along the way Conan Doyle's marvellous ear for theatrical language and humour. And of course, the scriptwriter had another bonus – he could constantly tap into the tapes of his actor friend's own knowledge. Jeremy had delved so deeply into the part that he had even filled in the gaps, including the mystery of Holmes's unrecorded childhood and his inner feelings about The Woman, Irene Adler. The tapes, which fused Jeremy and Holmes, proved invaluable as Paul worked out the past and the relationship Holmes had with his brother. Were, for example, Holmes and Watson abandoned to Victorian nannies as babies and boys? What really made them both tick? In the tapes Jeremy seemed to have weaved a bit of Holmes into his own childhood, or perhaps a bit of his own childhood into Holmes.

If this was to be a play about friendship before and after *The Final Problem*, there was one mystery to solve, however. How could any man allow his closest friend to believe he was dead for three whole years? Watson had arrived at the Reichenbach Falls in *The Final Problem* only to find Holmes's silver cigarette case and a last note from his friend. It was a kind of treachery. That was the enigma and the key to Holmes's complex personality. If only Paul could unravel that.

Eventually he did. Surely Holmes had suffered a nervous

breakdown. He just had to get away from being himself! But where had he been all that time? The answer came to Paul in a flash of Sherlockian inspiration. Holmes had been to Tibet to find spiritual peace and sanctuary.

The lines began to tumble from his keyboard on to the paper.

HOLMES: I amused myself by visiting Lhasa. I spent some days with the Holy Lama.

WATSON: Was that instructive?

HOLMES: It was . . . illuminating. You may have read of the remarkable explorations of a Norwegian named Sigerson, but I'm sure it never occurred to you that you were receiving news of your friend.

WATSON: Sigerson?

HOLMES: Sigerson.

WATSON: I remember now . . . that was the name I used in my advertisements. (Holmes gives Watson a very sharp look, then recovers. Nothing Watson does from now on will surprise him.) Where did you go after Tibet?

HOLMES: I passed through Persia, looked in at Mecca . . .

WATSON: (amazed) Mecca? You looked in at Mecca?

HOLMES: I then paid a short, but interesting, visit to the Khalifa at Khartoum, the results of which I have communicated to the Foreign Office. But to return to you, Watson . . .

Paul's mind raced on to the 'secret' of Holmes and Moriarty. His idea was that Moriarty never existed, except in the dark chasms of Holmes's own mind. Such an idea must surely have been explored many times, if only as a hypothesis. He checked with a Sherlockian friend who reassured him that he was on relatively new ground. It had once been proffered humorously by A. G. Macdonell in *Punch* magazine in the 1930s but was never followed up. The truth was that Watson had never seen Sherlock Holmes and Moriarty together. That was good enough. The fun was in stirring up a debate. An enthusiast could always put the secret through its supreme and ultimate test by measuring it against the evidence in the canon.

One other element was important to the writer, something he remembered from Michael Cox's first briefing – to do justice to Watson's character. He was a brave soldier who had seen the horrors of war, a general practitioner who understood the complex psychology of human beings, and a man whom his friend described as 'the one fixed point in a changing world'. Jeremy Paul needed Watson to have his day, to play Holmes at his own game and not be found wanting.

9 A Different Holmes Again

What of the bow?
The bow was made in England,
Of true wood, of yew wood,
The wood of English bows

Conan Doyle, *The White Company*

IT WAS A LONG, hot summer. Jeremy Paul had been slaving away for six weeks giving birth to his brainwave.

'Darling, how is it going?' Jeremy asked him excitedly.

'It's fine, I'll have it finished by Friday,' Paul blurted out. It was Wednesday already and he had no idea how the play would even end. Why on earth had he said that?

'Marvellous. I'll be round at teatime.'

Paul put the phone down. Bloody hell, he thought to himself. What have I done? But as he sat down at the typewriter again he realised that the truth was he really needed a deadline. No one had given him a date for completion and he was drifting a little. Now he had set one for himself.

At 5 o'clock on Friday morning he was still hammering away at the computer keyboard. At 4 o'clock that afternoon Jeremy was on the doorstep with a bottle of champagne and two punnets of strawberries.

'I won't be long,' the frantic playwright shouted to his wife Patricia from the top of the stairs.

Ten minutes after the sound of a popping champagne cork, the final page fell on to the study floor.

They all went into the garden in the sunshine. Jeremy was spellbound. Slipping into his Sherlockian mode he walked around and read aloud, waving his hand in the air here and there to emphasise his words.

'Watson retired behind a book. Holmes comes furtively to the front of the stage and speaks privately of his innermost thoughts.' He paused and then adopted his best, deepest Holmesian voice. 'If it wasn't for Watson, I would have been dead within two years. A man needs a companion, he cannot sit alone . . . With his silent reproaches, his hurt look, Watson controlled my addiction. And our walks, our conversations . . . the sheer breadth and enthusiasm of his mind on any manner of subjects kept me sane when the black fits were upon me. There never was a better friend. And I treated him abominably.'

Jeremy was quiet for a moment. The writer was worried that the play's crisis, which found Holmes himself stretched to breaking point, might strike uncomfortably close to the bone for his actor friend. But then Jeremy suddenly said: 'Right, what are you doing on Monday?'

'Actually I was going to . . . to play cricket,' Paul answered.

'Nonsense, dear heart, we must start rehearsing. I shall fix it. We will get a West End theatre and do it, air it!'

'But who will direct it?'

'You will!'

With that the actor disappeared into the early evening air clutching the script.

The following Monday morning Paul turned up at the Granada rehearsal room at the Oval. His friend had paid for everything. They rehearsed for six weeks, and the scriptwriter began to realise that for Jeremy this was a way of filling in his summer. He just could not let go of the Holmes role.

'Don't you want to go on holiday?' he asked him.

'No, I must do this!' Jeremy replied. Then Paul realised that there was another demon buried deep within the actor. He had not appeared on the English stage for several years. It was a hurdle he had to get over. He wanted to find his stage confidence again. He had been ill, but now he was well and he was asking himself if he could still do it.

Watson was played at rehearsals by a handsome young man still at drama school. It was impossible at such short notice to get Edward Hardwicke, but he would come later.

Jeremy had the wonderful idea that the director's chair should be vacated in rehearsal so that actors could pass through it in turn. Sometimes he would direct and Paul would play Holmes, sometimes the young Watson would direct, and so on. Once Robert Stephens even came in and took the chair.

One evening after rehearsals Paul went to see his widowed mother, who had been ill for some time.

'I'm afraid she's not terribly well, she may only last six months,' the doctor told him.

His mother, former stage actress Joan Haythorne, who was noted during her career for her impeccable timing, was worried about her bills, and Paul did his best to sort out her paperwork before leaving. Early the next day he was driving up Richmond Hill on his way to rehearsals at the Oval when a lorry pulled out in front of him and scraped the side of his car. Somehow he felt it was a bad omen.

Later that day he was called to the phone in the middle of rehearsing a scene with Jeremy.

'I'm sorry, Mr Paul, but I'm afraid your mother died in the night,' the doctor said. Paul was numb. He returned to the rehearsal room and blurted out to Jeremy: 'My mum has just died and I don't know what to do.'

The actor gave him a long, silent hug. 'You must go home,' he said, patting the scriptwriter on the back.

'No, no, I think I would like to rehearse for a bit. I'll tell everyone when they can go home, if that's all right. I'll tell them in half an hour, or an hour, or more than an hour.'

They all agreed to continue and Paul sat in the director's chair issuing sharp instructions – don't do this; don't do that; smile when Watson says that; frown when Holmes speaks. After an hour he stood up and said: 'I think I'll go now.'

Sherlock Holmes walked across to him and put his arm around his shoulders. 'That was a great act of courage,' he said.

One week later the play opened for a celebrity night at the Mayfair Theatre.

'Mother always did have impeccable timing,' the distressed scriptwriter said to Jeremy. 'If she had died a few days later we would have had to call everything off.'

Jeremy had invited the whole of theatreland to view the deeply psychological play. The Mayfair was packed. Paul was playing Moriarty and Conan Doyle. It was a nerve-racking experience for the playwright who was sure his knees were visibly shaking during his opening dialogue. And he was almost speechless as he watched his actor friend give a performance that bore no relation to the rehearsals whatsoever. But the audience thought he was electrifying.

Paul also had to mimic the chugging of a train. It was Jeremy's favourite scene and his eyes sparkled with laughter at the perspiring playwright 'choo, chooing' away in the wings. He had only himself to blame. It was his own stage direction.

Then came Paul's star moment. He had to walk across the back of the stage as the shadow of Moriarty. Jeremy, sensing it was his only possible moment for a stage whisper, breezed by him and said quietly: 'No shoes!'

'What?'

'No shoes, Moriarty!'

Paul looked down at his feet, struggling to think what he meant. Then he realised that to play a shadowy, moving Moriarty, who actually existed only in the mind of Holmes, an actor on stage had to glide silently. It would have killed everything for the audience to have heard the plodding of the ghostly figure's shoes. Moriarty's feet, after all, were never seen, as all Sherlockians knew.

The play opened at the Richmond Theatre with Edward Hardwicke in his familiar role as Dr Watson. Before rehearsing for the part Edward had intended several times to phone to tell Jeremy that he just couldn't do it. He hadn't been on the stage for several years and the idea of a two-handed play was daunting to say the least. In the end he never made the call because he knew that Jeremy would not listen to him.

Jeremy and Edward were the only two actors in the production directed by Patrick Garland. Patrick had begun his career in the theatre as an actor with the Bristol Old Vic after leaving Oxford University in 1959. But directing was always his ambition and he had gone on to direct Alan Bennett's *Forty Years On* starring John Gielgud and the author. The following year he masterminded Paul Gallico's *The Snow Goose*, which won a Golden Globe award, and later he oversaw the film of *The Doll's House*, which was nominated at the Cannes festival in 1974. In 1980 Patrick was appointed artistic director of the Chichester festival, a position he held for four years, during

With Joan Plowright, Robin Phillips and Mia Farrow at the Greenwich Theatre, 1972

Inside Greenwich Theatre, 1973. Joan Plowright as Rebecca West and Jeremy Brett as John Rosmer in Ibsen's *Rosmersholm*

With John Alderton in Sheridan's sparkling comedy *The Rivals*

As Mr Nightingale in the 1977 BBC series *Supernatural*

Robert Stephens in the role he warned Brett about, from Billy Wilder's *The Private Life of Sherlock Holmes*

A Scandal in Bohemia. The very first episode of *The Adventures of Sherlock Holmes*. Jeremy Brett and David Burke embark on an extraordinary adventure

With the next Watson - Edward Hardwicke in *The Master of Blackmail*

At the famous Baker Street residence

Obsessive and depressive, Holmes's personality fascinated and frightened Brett

Holmes takes a quiet moment with his pipe before he confronts . . .

. . .*The Final Problem*. The crucial episode screened on 22 February 1990

Edward Hardwicke listens patiently on the set of *The Secret of Sherlock Holmes* at the Richmond Theatre, London, 1988

Jeremy rehearses through recurring bouts of ill health, 1991

Vith Linda, early in their riendship

Mad Dogs and Englishmen, 1994

'If God has a theatre in heaven, Jeremy will have auditioned by now'

which time eight of his productions transferred to London, including *Kipling* with Alec McCowen. Jeremy told everyone he was lucky to get him.

Holmes and Watson were in their element as soon as the curtain rose to display 221B Baker Street in the first half. All the familiar paraphernalia was prominently positioned around the stage – the chemical apparatus, the long-stemmed pipe and newspapers of the day. After an initial glimpse of Holmes moodily sawing away at his fiddle, Watson strode to the front loaded up with books and took the audience past several milestones in his friendship with the great sleuth. From the first meeting in *A Study in Scarlet* to Irene Adler and the *Scandal in Bohemia*, everything was briefly recalled, including the supposedly final climactic tussle with Moriarty at the Reichenbach Falls.

Here Watson's brave character was illuminated in the words of Holmes.

> HOLMES: Watson, tell the truth! Or as much of it as your gullible public can digest. We shall not skirt round your gallant contribution to that disastrous war.
>
> WATSON: My part in it was insignificant.
>
> HOLMES: Appointed an Assistant Surgeon to the Fifth Northumberland Fusiliers, you arrived in Bombay to find the second Afghan War had broken out. You made your way through the passes, deep into enemy country. Reached Candahar by a miracle. Took up your duties. You were despatched to join the Berkshires just in time for the fatal battle of Maiwand. There you were struck on the shoulder by a Jezail bullet, which shattered the bone and grazed the subclavian artery. You would have fallen into the hands of the murderous Ghazis, but for the devotion and courage shown by your orderly . . . what was his name?
>
> WATSON: Murray.
>
> HOLMES: Murray, yes . . . who threw you across a pack horse and brought you safely to the British lines.

The 'secret' in the play's title – that Moriarty was a persona assumed by Holmes in order to get the upper hand over the underworld – came in the second half. The great detective had faked his plunge into the Reichenbach Falls and then taken himself off for three years to Tibet for a period of enlightenment. The concept was similar to that of Jekyll and Hyde, or even Beauty and the Beast. Good and evil needed to exist together. There could be no evil without good and vice versa. Moriarty didn't exist. Holmes invented him as an adversary as clever as he was. The part was tailor-made for Jeremy.

But many critics panned the plot while apparently admiring the acting. Irvine Wardle said in *The Times*: 'Looking lonely on Patrick Garland's stage, despite the apparition of a stuffed Moriarty and the descent of an Alpine storm on the buttoned leather furniture, the partners are extremely well played. Jeremy Brett works from a centre of brooding melancholy, startlingly offset by cackles of Mephistophelian laughter and bursts of mischief. As he uses his arms, he reminds you simultaneously of the violin bow and the cocaine needle. Edward Hardwicke elevates Watson from docile stooge to combative equal and prize student sleuth. They would be excellent value if they had a story to tell.'

The unanimous verdict was that this was a play for the most devoted Holmes fans only. But whatever the critics felt, the audiences loved it.

At the end of the first night the whole crew went out for a meal. At the restaurant Jeremy was his usual exuberant and flamboyant self, laughing, joking and singing. He was, as always, assiduously host-like, fussing over the arrangement of the tables and chairs, even attending to the emotional needs of the waitresses. And then suddenly, in the middle of the party, he simply got up and left. When at the end of the evening, the rest of the crew asked for their bills they were told by the waiter that Jeremy had paid for them all on the way out.

That night he was spotted by a lighting technician walking slowly home, all the way to Clapham from the West End with a piece of paper in his hand. Later he admitted it was one of his favourite possessions – a letter from Dame Jean Conan Doyle. It said: 'You are the Holmes of my childhood.' It was, for Jeremy, the final accolade. The following evening he accompanied all the front-of-house staff to the same restaurant – and did the same thing all over again. He left early and paid the bill for all of them on the way out.

Behind the scenes at the theatre, however, wardrobe designer Esther Dean was having enormous problems. Jeremy, true to form, would wear only his old tried-and-trusted clothes, particularly his favourite Holmes boots. They were tatty and old and Esther had trouble prising him out of them. But they were like a good-luck charm to him now, and he felt comfortable in them. His black frock-coat too was worn and rather undistinguished.

Finally a member of the audience sent him a letter.

'Is Sherlock Holmes so poor that he can't afford new boots and a coat?'

Jeremy laughed but never relented.

One evening Philip Kingsley went to see the play. Once again it was a packed house and afterwards Jeremy and Edward met him backstage. 'Darlings, we must all go to dinner,' Jeremy announced with a wave of his hand.

An hour later they were ushered out of the stage door and through a crowd of 150 women, mostly middle-aged, some of them trying to thrust their phone numbers into Jeremy's hand. He was polite as always.

'How do you stand all this?' Philip asked.

'Sorry, dear heart, it's a bit thin on the ground this evening actually!'

Meanwhile plans were under way to take the production to New York. This was Jeremy's real dream – to star on the Broadway boards again in the part that had now made him world famous. To visit his old haunts, luxuriate in the memory of Joan, dine at their favourite restaurants, relive America. He would at last be a Rex Harrison or an Audrey Hepburn . . . a true mid-Atlantic star. To this end he had invited author Daniel Stashower along for an interview at the Wyndham. Daniel was a winner of the Raymond Chandler Fulbright Fellowship in Detective and Crime Fiction Writing and wanted to do a piece for the well-read international magazine *Armchair Detective*. But Jeremy's teasing ways were irrepressible as usual.

Stage superstition had it that it was bad luck to speak of Shakespeare's Macbeth in a theatre. Over the course of two evenings, Jeremy took great delight in trying to coax the offending name out of the author.

'That was the year,' he would say, his voice falling to a dark whisper, 'that I toured with . . . that Scottish play . . . er . . .?'

Daniel had spent enough time around actors to know that if he rose to the bait and answered 'You mean *Macbeth*?' the traditional forfeit would require him to do something like run into the hall, turn three times and spit on the floor to ward off bad luck. Or maybe even worse. And so he cleverly kept his mouth shut.

When the interviews were finally over, Daniel had a drink to unwind and an hour later walked slowly and thoughtfully towards the stage door. Suddenly he stopped at the sound of Jeremy's laughter echoing through the wings and turned. A member of the production team was spitting into a fire bucket. Jeremy had won at last. At that moment Edward Hardwicke and Jeremy exchanged a 'high five' clap.

As he walked home through the London winter drizzle, Daniel reflected on his strange encounter. At their first meeting Jeremy had sat in his dressing room, running a handful of pink styling gel through his hair. 'Sometimes I feel that I cannot play this man,' he said, staring at himself in the mirror. '*He* is like quicksilver, just ahead of my consciousness. I cannot reach him. I think I am nearly there and *he* slips away. *He* dazzles me.'

He leant nearer the mirror and started to line his face with a charcoal pencil. With short quick strokes he exaggerated the sharpness of his brows and highlighted the sharp edges of his nose and chin. Then he picked up a black make-up pencil and darkened the hollows beneath his eyes.

'*He* is such a giant,' he said, stopping for a moment and staring at Daniel's reflection in the mirror. 'Such a genius, such a bore, such an . . . an isolated, damaged penguin – I hate him!'

Then he suddenly swung round in his chair, displaying the familiar face of Holmes. 'Every time I nearly get there he escapes me again!' he said, staring hard at the journalist.

Several evenings later, Jeremy wasn't quite so friendly.

'But, Jeremy, what do you make of the theory that Holmes was a manic depressive?' As soon as Jean Upton asked the question over the phone she knew it was a bad idea.

Her idol suddenly yelled something unintelligible down the line and banged the receiver down.

The road to that fateful telephone call, a few days after *The Secret of Sherlock Holmes* was premiered, began one summer afternoon in 1987. That day members of the Sherlock Holmes Society had been invited to Granada Television's studios in Manchester to visit the set of 221B for the preview of *The Sign of Four*.

When Jean, a member who lived in America, was told of the forthcoming visit she jumped at the chance to fly to England and meet her idol Jeremy. Her father's funeral had taken place a few days earlier and this was the perfect opportunity to get away from it all. It was her first attendance at a Society event, so no one was quite sure what she looked like. There was only one answer. The Sherlockians asked Jean to wear a deerstalker so that they could recognise her at London's Euston station, from where they would all catch the train to Manchester. Jean tucked one into her flight bag but just couldn't bring herself to wear it. Instead she travelled to Manchester alone, and after a short trek through the city managed to find herself in the midst of nearly 100 fellow Sherlockians who immediately made her feel welcome. Her group was escorted to a reception for an introductory speech and refreshments. Then, in the company of Michael Cox, June Wyndham Davies and Rosalie Williams, they were led to the interior 'mock-up' of 221B. Jean was at the head of the queue in deep conversation with June when she was ushered through the doorway of the set along with an army of photographers and reporters. There to meet them was Jeremy in his familiar Holmes black coat, arms flaying, the complete thespian as always. In the mêlée someone mentioned that Jean had travelled over from America for the occasion. Reporters swarmed around her. This was an angle, a peg to the story – a woman who had flown 2,000 miles to meet a British actor because the land of McDonald's and Disney loved a legendary fictional English detective. One tabloid newspaper photographer shouted: 'Does anyone have a deerstalker?'

'I have one in my bag,' Jean said helpfully and innocently.

Within seconds the hat she had brought across the Atlantic was on her head and she was posing next to Jeremy as the flashbulbs popped. Then Jeremy and Jean were led away from the main set by PR executives for more pictures and a non-stop series of interviews. Suddenly Jean found herself pressed into a corner. The journalists needed more details of the woman who had travelled thousands of miles just because of Sherlock Holmes. Jean explained that the trip was a much-needed break to enable her to recover from the death of her father. But one question led to another and she was struggling with the answers.

'How much was the price of your air ticket? How much will your stay in England cost? Are English hotels more expensive than American? Hasn't TV detective Columbo made Sherlock Holmes seem old hat? Why do Americans love English history?'

The long flight and depression over her father began to take their toll. Jean's voice started to crack. Suddenly, like a hurricane, someone stormed through the press pack. She felt a hand on her neck and before she knew it she was being marched away. 'Gentlemen, that is enough!' Jeremy announced with a sharp wave of his hand, as if playing Hamlet. Then he swept her away to a quiet corner. Jean broke down and cried before pulling herself together and thanking him. Jeremy stood staring at her for a moment in amazement. Then he flung his arms around her, giving her a reassuring squeeze that almost popped the lenses out of her wire-rimmed glasses, before returning to the fray and signing autographs.

Later, back at her hotel, Jean vowed she would never forget Jeremy's kindness. She felt he had understood her grieving; after all, he was still grieving for his beloved Joan.

The following year Jean returned to England to see the opening night of *The Secret of Sherlock Holmes* at the Wyndham Theatre. She was riveted from the moment the curtain went up. Later she ventured backstage where she had been invited to meet Edward Hardwicke through her Sherlockian connections. After seeing him in his dressing room she got caught up in a stream of people moving about backstage. Suddenly she realised that she was standing outside Jeremy's dressing room. Jeremy had nicknamed it his Green Room because the door was always open and people could just wander in for a glass of champagne or a cup of tea and tell him their troubles. Anyone was welcome, from the doorman to a visiting dignatary. Jean appeared at the door and someone handed her a glass of wine. Before she knew it she was being greeted by Michael Cox and Dame Jean Conan Doyle. She was swept off her feet. It was the highlight of her visit to England and she went away with a handful of photographs of Jeremy with the great author's daughter and the promise of a telephone interview with the man who became Sherlock Holmes a few days later. This was a great opportunity for her to take back news for a series of Sherlockian meetings taking place in the autumn.

Jean duly rang and Jeremy was in fine form. They chatted happily for ten minutes and he told her how pleased he was about the play, especially as it included the dramatisation of Holmes and Watson's first meeting as chronicled in *A Study in Scarlet*. He was ebullient and energetic, full of hope. It was difficult to interrupt him. He spoke of the influence of TV on the stories and how the series would be largely responsible for bringing Sherlock Holmes into the twenty-first century. Certain elements of the play brought out the darker side of Holmes's schizophrenic personality, he said. Then there was silence. This was Jean's chance. She quietly enquired if Jeremy was familiar with the theory that Holmes was a manic depressive. As soon as the words left her lips she knew it had been a bad idea. She was heartbroken when Jeremy slammed down the phone. Her idol hated her.

She hardly slept that night, worrying about seeing Jeremy at their arranged meeting the following evening. She was almost resolved not to go, expecting to be snubbed or shouted at. She was instead lifted off her feet in a rib-crushing bear hug. They chatted as he signed autographs for people and parted affectionately. No reference was made to the phone call that had gone so badly wrong.

Jeremy settled himself into the armchair in his drawing room, balancing the plate on his knee and staring at the rather forlorn-looking lettuce leaf. How he yearned for pasta, cheese or chicken legs. But he had to lose weight. He rested his head against the chair and closed his eyes for a moment as the radio music introduced the Gloria Hunniford programme. Her guest was actress Prunella Scales, and Jeremy had been looking forward to listening to her.

Five minutes later he sat bolt upright and the plate fell to the floor as Prunella choked with emotion. The programme had been interrupted by the news that Sir Laurence Olivier had died after a long illness. Jeremy broke down and sobbed.

That evening he sat quietly at his bureau, reading every note the doyen of the English theatre had ever written to him, knowing that no one would ever replace him.

'I want a big parson's nose, darling, are these all you have?'

The shop assistant leant over the freezer and rummaged through the plastic bags of chicken pieces.

'I'm afraid that's it, sir,' she said, 'but that looks about the biggest.' She pointed to the bag in the actor's hand.

Jeremy was cooking Linda a meal that evening and knew that her favourite piece of the chicken was the parson's nose. He was determined to find the best one.

Their friendship was now closer than ever. Since her run to raise money for cancer they had met at least once a week in Clapham, sometimes at a small café called Tea Time where they would sit and talk for hours. On one occasion they were the first customers to arrive in the morning and the last to leave in the afternoon.

'You know, darling, when I used to cook a meal for Penelope Keith at my house 'Ness' in the 1980s it was always chicken. In fact she got so sick of it that she once arrived, smelt the aroma of stock wafting out from the kitchen, and said, "Oh no, Jeremy, not that again!" '

Linda laughed. It was so nice to see him happy. He could be very quiet sometimes . . . well, reflective anyway. Other times he wouldn't stop talking for hours.

That evening he talked about the past, his childhood at the Grange. He was sad that he didn't practice archery any more. He had been proud as a young man to be one of the Woodmen of Arden, the historic archery club at Meriden, near his home. His father and all four of his sons were members. They shot with longbows and wore glamorous outfits – Lincoln green, cut-away tail-coats, buff waistcoats with gold buttons, white slacks, white shoes and New Zealand-style hats that turned up at the sides.

It was funny, Linda thought. Jeremy's favourite clothes now seemed to be green cashmere sweaters and white trousers.

He told how the club was originally formed in 1758 by the Earl of Aylesford, who was its captain. The joining fee was one guinea and candidates had to be elected by two-thirds of the membership. They would shoot against the Queen's Bodyguard for Scotland or the Royal Company of Archers. Jeremy had loved the longbow almost as much as he had loved horses. His father particularly liked the spirit of the club. When the woodmen walked off to their targets to collect their arrows, a glass of port would be waiting for them in the shadow of the bullseye. His mother had a special lightweight bow and when he was growing up he used her hand-me-downs.

'But you have to concentrate. Archery is a skill and a very physical sport. My brother John shot two of his teeth out once because he simply forgot to take the pipe out of his mouth. And Michael winged a lovely old fellow named Nunky while he was walking in the woods near the targets. Nunky told him to think nothing of it as he carefully removed the arrow from the sleeve of his coat.'

Linda laughed.

'I must have been four or five when my father gave me my first lesson,' Jeremy recalled. 'My parents joined the club first, then my brothers Michael, Patrick and John became members. Finally, I followed in their footsteps when I was twenty-one. On my first day I wore Michael's tail-coat. It had to be taken out a bit because he was narrower in the shoulders. I felt so gauche.'

He told her how he had been nervous that first day, standing in the company of some of the finest archers in the country. But the warden told him to buck up and he did. He had been practising like mad for the occasion. Finally he took aim at 100 yards and let the arrow go. It wobbled in the air for a moment and to everyone's amazement landed smack in the middle of the target.

'Not only was it a great start but I was also made Master Forester on my first day – a title which carried with it the honour of sitting at the high table.'

Jeremy recalled just how demanding the social side of archery could be. That day the lunch had run to twelve toasts, and he recollected staggering out afterwards full of venison and summer pudding, cheeks pink from the port and his nose still twitching from his first pinch of snuff. He went quiet for a moment, lost in his thoughts and memories.

'Sorry, I'm going on about myself again,' he said. And then went on again.

Later that night Linda lay awake on the spare bed upstairs, having agreed to stay because it was late and the wine had flowed. She could hear Jeremy pacing the lounge as he normally did. Slowly and quietly she came down the stairs and found him staring at a picture of his first wife, Anna Massey. When he saw her he started talking, again recalling the Woodmen of Arden. Archery seemed to be playing on his mind. Strange how the wheel came full circle. In the Granada production of *The Problem of Thor Bridge*, Holmes had received longbow instructions from wealthy magnate J. Neil Gibson, alias Anna's brother Daniel Massey.

'Ah, the jigsaw of life's rich pattern,' Jeremy said quietly.

He walked into the loo and looked at his longbow. He kept it there with his arrows because they had to be near running water. It was vital for them. Sometimes he ran a bath and hung them above it on a rack to let them soak up the steam. He loved his central heating system but his bows and arrows hated it.

That morning, as daylight broke, a quivering arrow flew

across the common and fell close to the huge cushion at the foot of the tree. Moments later another arrow sped through the air. The old man walking his dog stopped for a moment and wondered whether it was safe to go on. Then he watched as the solitary figure of bowman Jeremy Brett walked slowly across the field, picked up his arrows and the cushion and went home.

By the time the fifth Granada series, *The Casebook of Sherlock Holmes*, was screened, the adaptations were receiving scathing criticism, perhaps not so much for the performances as for the improbable screenplays, which teetered on the edge of pastiche. Jeremy had always been a perfectionist. It was largely his personal interest (some would say his interference), arguing for seemingly minor details of dialogue, costuming, and direction, which had made the first four series ring so true to the original Conan Doyle stories. His recurring bouts of ill-health were now evident not only in his physical appearance but also in the lack of authenticity of the episodes. The fight seemed to have gone out of him, and his loss of influence was clear to Sherlockians. He was noticeably heavier, and was under fire from his fans and the press. But they had no understanding of the medication he needed, the side effects of which caused fluid retention. Neither diet nor exercise could alter that.

And yet he had many friends, among them the cameramen on the series. When the power of the trade unions was finally broken and companies felt free to run things as they saw fit, Jeremy went to the Granada management and pleaded with them to consider the effect of repeated fourteen-hour days and six-day weeks on the private lives of their employees. They listened to him politely, nodded their heads, and one of the executives at the meeting even asked for his autograph. They all parted the best of friends – but the schedules were never reduced.

The difference in Jeremy slowly became more noticeable as the series developed on screen during 1991.

The first episode to be shown in February was *The Disappearance of Lady Frances Carfax*, with Holmes wrestling with the puzzle of the mysterious wanderings about Europe of the beautiful lady herself, played by Cheryl Campbell. A week later came Jeremy Paul's adaptation of *The Problem of Thor Bridge*, reuniting Jeremy with the Massey family in the shape of Daniel, who played archer and wealthy magnate J. Neil Gibson. Holmes was investigating the death of Gibson's wife and the subsequent suspicion thrown upon the couple's governess, Grace Dunbar, played by Catherine Russell, whom the wealthy landowner loved and believed to be innocent. The case also introduced Holmes's Baker Street helpmate Billy, played by Dean Magri.

True to style, Jeremy was agitated about every detail in the script and the filming. Actors and technicians on the set couldn't help but notice that he was portraying a different Holmes again. But then even Holmes had to age and lose his energy and agility, didn't he?

The first two episodes were followed by *The Boscombe Valley Mystery*, dramatised by John Hawkesworth and starring Peter Vaughan as an old Australian highway robber of the 1830s. Bromley Cross Quarry near Bolton doubled as the Australian outback for a flashback recalling the ambush of a gold wagon in the story of Holmes's investigation into a brutal murder in Cheshire.

Next came *The Illustrious Client*, dramatised by Robin Chapman and featuring Anthony Valentine as Baron Gunner, an unscrupulous man described by Holmes as 'the Austrian murderer'. He had so beguiled the beautiful Violet Merville, played by Abigail Cruttenden, that she could see nothing sinister in his plans to marry her. But a family friend, Colonel Sir James Damery, alias David Langton, understandably worried about her future, recruited the aid of the Baker Street sleuth to thwart the Baron's plans and bring him to justice for all his crimes. It was a case that produced a murderous attack on Holmes.

Shoscombe Old Place, dramatised by Gary Hopkins, followed. The episode featured Robin Ellis as Sir Robert Norberton, nicknamed the 'daredevil rider', who was desperately trying to avoid financial ruin by secretly preparing a horse he hoped would win the Championship Stakes. But his plans began to founder with the dramatic discovery of a corpse and the reappearance of his old enemy – his chief creditor, a money-lending rascal he had once horsewhipped at Newmarket.

Last in the series was *The Creeping Man*, starring Jeremy's lifelong friend Charles Kay as Professor Presbury, who dismissed his daughter's claims of waking to find a strange figure at her bedroom window as a bad dream. Her fiancé, Jack Bennett, thought otherwise and sent for Holmes.

Jeremy looked at himself in the mirror. In *A Study in Scarlet*, Conan Doyle had described Holmes as being over six feet in height and so excessively lean that he seemed to be considerably taller. His eyes were sharp and piercing, except during intervals of torpor, and his thin, hawk-like nose gave his whole expression an air of alertness and decision. His chin had the prominence and squareness that marked a man of determination. How different Jeremy looked to Conan Doyle's vision. The trouble with Holmes, he thought, was that there was something endearing about the devil. But he wasn't really like him, was he? He had worked hard all these years to find some sympathy with the awful man – and now he had perhaps grown to love him.

'Do you believe in ghosts, Peter?' he asked.

They were sitting in the studio caravan parked in Manchester High Street as everyday life went on around them. Jeremy picked up a strawberry, staring at it for a moment, twisting it around in his fingers before popping it into his mouth.

'In fact I do,' Peter Haining replied.

They had strolled out of the studios and walked down the street to the Winnebego for lunch. Jeremy was in his full Holmes regalia, waving to astonished passers-by and asking how they were. Peter, who was updating his book on the Holmes television series, was used to Jeremy's eccentricities and took the strange journey in his stride.

'Mmmm. But have you seen a ghost?' he asked, leaning back in his chair.

'No, but my Elizabethan house in Suffolk is supposed to be

haunted. Every June there is a strong smell of smoke in every room. My wife and I wondered what it was when we first moved in. Then the local villagers told us that a former owner of the place died in a blaze many years ago.'

Peter, who had written a best-selling book about ghosts, went on to explain about his experiences with people who had encountered spirits. He had researched spiritualism, visited haunted castles and studied Victorian photographs of Indian spirits and ectoplasm. But Jeremy wasn't really listening. He seemed miles away. They sat in silence for a moment and Peter fidgeted in his chair.

'Conan Doyle believed in life after death, you know,' Jeremy suddenly announced.

'So I believe,' said Peter.

'He was a great friend of the escapologist Houdini and was convinced the little Hungarian had supernatural powers. You see, the Great Escaper and You Know Who's creator had a joint quest – to discover if there was life after death. Doyle really believed that Houdini dematerialised to effect his escapes.'

'And do you believe in life after death, Jeremy?'

'Yes, yes, dear heart, I do.'

Peter was riveted by Jeremy's total absorption in his role as Holmes. He called the set his home, the place where he now did much of his thinking. He described it as his 'womb'.

That evening Peter had dinner with Edward and Jeremy at the Midland Hotel. As usual Jeremy became absorbed in the problems of the waiters and insisted on paying for everything. His love of poetry and quotation was evident to all the other guests. If something came into his mind he would just recite it aloud. As they left, he burst into loud laughter, pointing to a sign with the manager's name on it – 'Mr Moriarty!'

By now Jeremy had been playing Doyle's ascetic supersleuth for so long he was becoming almost as set in his habits as Holmes himself. Peter noticed how he seemed to adopt a Paget pose as he sat in a chair, legs crossed, his eyes distant.

The strain of recreating the character on screen for all these years had obviously got to him. He hadn't realised until recently what an effort it was trying to be clever and quotable to the press three times in one day. He bitterly regretted the interviews he had set up over the next few weeks. The press seemed so much more intrusive now, looking for a chink in his armour, a sign he was failing. Why else would they come? They had enough quotes from him – they only had to check the cuttings. He recalled with embarrassment one occasion when he had jokingly threatened a writer that unless she wrote something nice about him he would slap her face.

The problem was that his story had been told so many times before and he was becoming bored with it. He was the definitive Sherlock Holmes on TV; he had a war-hero father; his mother was a Quaker; he was a well-known Shakespearian actor who always wanted to be an Albert Finney; he suffered a nervous breakdown not long after his second wife died, etc, etc, etc. No, he did not know that Laurence Olivier was having an affair with Sarah Miles in the 1960s; no, he did not sleep with Robert Stephens.

He was still accustomed to spending his weekends in luxurious solitude. Granada were taking good care of him at the Holiday Inn Crown Plaza, alias the Midland Hotel, in Manchester. Every Saturday morning he strolled to the hotel's leisure centre for a swim, sitting afterwards on the terrace with a pot of coffee and the morning newspapers. Often he would send a cheque to an editor for a deserving cause, something or someone he felt desperately sad about. Then he would stroll around the city centre, wrestling with details of the Holmes scene to be filmed the following Monday. Sometimes he would visit an art gallery or an antiques shop, now and then buying a present for somebody before returning to eat a light lunch, musing over the script and joking with the waitresses. At 3 p.m. he would be back in his room for a lie-down and a little doze if he could manage it. Later he would emerge for a leisurely dinner in the hotel's French restaurant.

'You must get awfully bored with me,' he would tell the waiters after ordering the same simple menu of melon filled with raspberries followed by poached salmon.

Sundays were spent reading the morning newspapers and

studying his script again. He couldn't wait to be back in the studio the following morning. Life then would have meaning, even if he was feeling more tired these days and his temper seemed to flare more easily. On the odd occasion when he did return to London on Friday nights, the most strenuous thing he did was to practise the piano, but he didn't play with any pleasure. He loved music but as he hadn't played consistently over the years any talent he might have had had drifted away.

Back at his beloved Clapham penthouse, once owned by the composer Edward Grieg, he devoted a lot of energy to walking across the common, down the high street and back home, daydreaming of old times and times ahead, of old friends and new ones. He thought about Robert a lot. The wiry old fox had been dragging himself through a tangled thicket of affairs, as he always had – from actress Margaret Leighton to 'Carmen Rollers', his nickname for a sexy dentist's receptionist.

Jeremy didn't do so much entertaining now. People didn't seem to just drop by like they used to. But he had it in mind to throw dinner parties again. One winter's morning he went out and bought a beautiful and rather expensive round table made by an artist and craftswoman friend. It occupied pride of place in his apartment and he would often stand admiring it. He felt that King Arthur was right to choose such a shape for his knights so they could all face each other. But his dream did not turn into reality. None the less, it gave him pleasure to visualise dinner parties when the nights became lighter and guests could enjoy the wonderful rooftop view of London from his window.

Jeremy loved his turreted flat. His collection of ornaments was treasured for their sentimental value. His father's military commendation for service in World War I, signed by Lord Kitchener, took pride of place on the fireplace. On his desk was a treasured first-night good-luck note from Laurence Olivier and an autographed photograph of Gladys Cooper by Cecil Beaton. Paintings by and of his family were strewn across the walls, his son David's pictures taking pride of place. Even the furniture had meaning for him – his mother's sewing chair stood proudly in the lounge, along with other items from the Grange. Relics from his first marriage to Anna Massey were scattered throughout the rooms – a tiny ballerina inside a walnut shell, a large childhood portrait of her, a bargello cushion she once needlepointed.

His favourite piece of furniture was the headboard on his bed. It featured an erotic painting of a man and woman. It had started life as the surround for a fireplace and Jeremy was going to have it covered with fabric. But a little-known Argentinian artist offered to paint it for him in 1973. The man was Luis Frangello, who later became one of the most respected painters in the world. Now it was worth a small fortune.

From his rooftop window, he could see the Clapham schools that Holmes had observed from the train.

'Lighthouses, Watson. Beacons of the future . . . out of which will spring a wiser, better England.'

10 Borrowed Time

Of all ruins that of a noble mind is the most deplorable

Conan Doyle, *His Last Bow*

THE FIGURES DARTED ABOUT the common.'Try over there!' shouted a man with a torch, pointing the beam at the line of old oak trees.

'No, can't see anything,' the woman replied.

They walked on and were joined by two other shadowy figures.

'Let's fan out,' one of them said, and they spread out in a line, walking slowly into the darkness.

The common was ringed by brightly lit roads but there was no moon to speak of that night and the centre was black, like the mind of the man they were searching for.

'Over there!' one of them shouted.

When they arrived at his side the woman made a choking sound and burst into tears.

Jeremy's feet were bare and torn. His hands were bleeding and it looked as if he hadn't shaved for a week. He was on his hands and knees and deep in conversation with someone, they didn't know who.

Linda put the phone down. The news was unbearable. Jeremy had suffered another nervous breakdown and was ill in hospital with manic depression. From that moment on she knew that her life would become a battle against Sherlock Holmes's ill-health.

She didn't know anything about manic depression but vowed to learn everything she could.

Seeing Jeremy in his hospital bed was a depressing sight. The drugs he was being given were producing short-term side effects similar to the symptoms of Parkinson's disease. His speech was slurred and when he eased himself out of the bed he would shuffle across the room like an old man. Because of the cocktail of Haloperidol and lithium he was being given he couldn't think straight. The drugs were not curative but would eventually, it was hoped, alleviate the course of his manic depressive illness. They would help to restore his mood to a state nearer normal without altering his personality. It was explained to Linda that the drugs were no longer used as chemical strait jackets to keep patients quiet and sedated. They were used to improve the quality of life for the sufferer. Nevertheless she left the hospital in despair. It did not take her long to discover that there appeared to be a severe lack of understanding about Jeremy's condition, even on the part of some doctors. One even had the idea that anyone who suffered from manic depression had brought it upon themselves and should simply pull themselves together. This angered her. She began to phone experts and sufferers and laid her hands on every book she could find on the subject. She soon learned that manic depressives were often deep, fascinating and sympathetic people because they had experienced a wide range of feelings. The mood swings they suffered were often creative. Their visions when they were on a high could be transferred to canvas if they were frustrated artists, or they could write with great vigour and clarity. Caring for a manic depressive was a difficult route to travel. Linda realised it would challenge her intensely and test her own strengths and values.

She would have to deal with someone who had three distinct personalities – stable, manic and depressed. She decided that one of the first things to do was to help supervise Jeremy's medication, because she had read that sufferers could be careless in complying with their dosage levels.

After Jeremy left hospital, he and Linda would spend the evenings together having dinner at one of the restaurants around Clapham Common, or cooking quietly at home. Jeremy loved to watch television. They both enjoyed nature programmes and sport. Jeremy's favourite was horse events and Linda's was football, but the type of programme that always took preference above all others for Jeremy was opera. He adored it.

If there was nothing interesting on the box they would spend their time puzzling over crosswords. Linda had introduced them to him when he was having difficulty coping with the rapid flow of ideas that sped through his mind during his manic depressive episodes.

They would often meet in their favourite green-and-cream-walled café, Tea Time, minutes' walk from his home. Jeremy had become even more claustrophobic and would sit at the same table in the corner facing the door so that he could see an escape route. But Linda soon discovered to her cost that trying to help him regain his confidence was the hardest battle she had ever faced in her life. Just walking to the bus stop took enormous courage for him. He felt ashamed that he had not been able to control his mind all his life.

'The worst thing is that I have never been able to read the signs, Lindy,' he said as they walked home together one afternoon. By now Linda could sense the signs.

He would become obsessive, constantly eating the same things. Slowly, painfully, she learned that a carer should not try to control or dominate a manic depressive on a high. The best course, she discovered, was to try to persuade Jeremy that it was his idea not to eat, say, olive oil any more. That was the way forward, and slowly it began to work.

By now Jeremy realised that there was no definite conclusion to manic depression. Someone could inherit a genetic predisposition to the illness which could be triggered by major stress events like the death of a partner or a financial crisis, or hormonal changes such as those experienced during adolescence or for childbirth. The fact that after such a traumatic experience the area of the brain responsible for moods suddenly activated itself and caused changes in feelings and behaviour was strangely comforting. It wasn't his fault. It was an inherited thing. Was it from his mother's Cadbury line . . . or his father's? He was stuck with it, but the world must see it wasn't something he could be responsible for. Did his brothers have it? Did his son? Did it begin in the shed all those years ago when the coal boy came to call?

He knew that he was a textbook case and he had to get to know himself, his real self. Everything the doctors had told him and everything he had read fitted the pattern: manic depressives had tremendous activity and energy levels; an inability or unwillingness to sleep; a rapid flow of ideas, often penetrating, imaginative and perceptive, but as the mood intensified decreasingly coherent. He also realised that the rapid speech and movement that so often came across on screen in his role as Sherlock Holmes, and even back in his days on stage at the National Theatre, were part of the syndrome. As were his talking to strangers, his lengthy telephone calls, his excitability, his sometimes incoherent state, his inflated self-esteem, his impulsive decision-making, his irrational spending of money and his involvement in questionable endeavours, his lack of inhibition and vulnerability to sexual liaisons, his irritability and impatience, deluded thinking, hallucinations, both visual and auditory, and his intense insights and powerful perception of a reality not normally experienced by others.

He also knew that, in the mild form of mania, the energy and insight that he had gained had resulted in highly productive periods of creativity.

As he got better, Jeremy felt as if yet again he had been given another chance. First he had nearly died of rheumatic fever, then he was almost put away for life in a mental hospital.

'Suddenly I realise how wondrous borrowed time can be, darling,' he said as June Wyndham Davies drove him back to his home from a restaurant one evening. 'It's a very special, very azure-blue time. You know, one sad aspect of being ill is that a part of you feels like a leper – you're damaged goods. I feel that all my friends will be watching every move I make. If I scratch my ear too quickly, they will wonder if it signals a problem.'

Jeremy believed there was a thin line between what was considered zany and what people would now think was mad. Suddenly he found himself constantly checking himself, pulling back from a chance remark or a moment of wild fun. He felt pigeonholed as weak and neurotic.

For the next six months June and the Granada executives tried to reassure him, but it was no use; he felt his friendships were deeply damaged.

Most of it was his own fault. He just didn't want to be with people to whom he had been close because it reminded him that he had been ill. He believed that they had been through hell coming to see him in hospital for ten weeks and that they wouldn't be able to bear the idea that some day he might be ill again. And, of course, neither could he. People seemed to his mind terribly nervous about his health, and that, in turn, made him nervous too. But he was slowly rebuilding his confidence and self-esteem. He felt a little prouder of himself. But around him were the bitter reminders of his ill-health . . . medicine to take, resent, take, resent and forget – but always to take; crumpled receipts discovered in pockets – a reminder of an extravagant night at a restaurant or an expensive present bought on a whim for a friend.

He announced to the world: 'I'm thrilled to be healthy again and I know it is a relief to my family and friends. It is such a good feeling to know you are not going to embarrass or let them down any more. I'll never do that to them again – it is too rude, too vulgar, too bad-mannered. These things do happen and they happened to me, but I don't want to burden those close to me any more by being ill. And I won't.'

The truth was he was wondering who he really was underneath the wild, impulsive, chaotic, energetic and sometimes crazy Jeremy Huggins. Was he really dark and quietly calculating like Holmes? In the worst stage of his manic attacks, did the black side of this fictional man he had become manifest itself? He tried not to think about it too hard.

As a thank-you for taking care of him after he had come out of hospital Jeremy invited Linda to be with him at the preview of the two-hour Granada special *The Eligible Bachelor*. But he warned that one or two scenes could be a bit upsetting for them both, although he didn't know for sure what the finished version of the film would be like after editing.

The fifth special co-starred Simon Williams as Lord Robert St Simon, the scion of an aristocratic British family whose wife-to-be, American heiress Henriette Doran, played by Paris Jefferson, disappeared on the morning of their wedding. As Holmes probed deeper into the case he found that the clean-cut Lord Robert was actually a man full of dark secrets.

The screenplay, by T. R. Bowen, featured 93-year-old actress Mary Ellis as Lady Florence, and for her the Granada special evoked memories of the first stage Sherlock Holmes, William Gillette, whom she had met as a young girl in 1912.

The Eligible Bachelor was taken from Conan Doyle's story *The Noble Bachelor*. It found Holmes adrift in infernal territory. Without a compass he floundered and was torn apart by nightmares in which he struggled once more at the Reichenbach Falls with his old adversary Professor Moriarty. Other images, just as powerful, appeared in his dreams to torment him. Torrents of water cascaded through a great house; a beautiful chair had its red upholstery ripped to shreds; Holmes was trapped in a quagmire and a creature, caked in mud and open-mouthed in a silent scream, crawled towards him. When Holmes abandoned sleep and walked London's fog-bound streets, women brawled and even laughter became sinister. A mysterious veiled lady almost collided with him and theatre billboards proclaimed ghosts.

Linda sat in excited anticipation at the idea of seeing Jeremy once more as Sherlock Holmes. She felt a sense of nervousness coming from him as he moved uncomfortably in his seat. When the opening scene began, she realised why he was on edge and why he had warned her about the film. A woman was seen being drugged and forcibly taken, screaming and fighting, to a mental institute. Then the camera panned to show Holmes and Watson arriving outside the walls of the asylum in a horse and carriage. Next came a close-up shot showing Holmes in deep thought, with the sounds of cackled laughter coming from the deranged woman. Watson then turned to Holmes and said: 'The misery there must be behind those walls.' Holmes looked distant and replied: 'There is no escape from the terrors of the mind.'

Linda shuddered with horror and wondered what Jeremy was thinking at that moment. As the film continued, his body tensed next to her and she put her hand on his and gently stroked the back of his taut fingers, which were gripping the seat. His tension eased. But she wondered at the irony of it all. Jeremy had made the film only weeks before he ended up back in hospital. She found herself asking why fate had decided that he should make a film with such distressing and fearful scenes when he was already distressed and in fear for his own well-being. Then a scene with Mrs Hudson had her fighting back the tears.

Holmes's housekeeper sat at the bottom of the stairs leading to his study and cried over his state of health, which was something Linda had done with Jeremy so many times.

During the remainder of the film Jeremy and Linda sat in silence, each of them concerned about how the other felt. When the credits finally rolled, Linda's anxiety was quickly sensed by Jeremy.

'All is well now, my darling,' he whispered to her. 'We mustn't dwell too much on the past. We both went through a very difficult time together, but what's important is that we got through it and we're both better and wiser people because of it.' He gently squeezed her hand and she in turn hugged him and congratulated him for completing a difficult film under such circumstances.

During the sixth Granada series, *The Memoirs of Sherlock Holmes*, viewers and critics began to believe that Jeremy was on drink or drugs. The truth, which was being kept a closely guarded secret at Granada, was that doses of his lithium medication were difficult to handle and the drug was affecting the valves of his heart. Every day seemed longer than the last now. Everyone in the crew thought that there couldn't be any more pain . . . but there was. His suffering seemed endless.

Linda now appeared on the set with him, checking that he was taking his drug cocktail at the right time. He called her his nurse and would become quite agitated if he didn't know where she was. Some people resented her and made it plain, nicknaming her 'The Nurse'. But Jeremy was the star and that was the end of it. As hard as he tried, Jeremy just couldn't get his weight down. He was retaining pints and pints of water. One day on location a doctor was sent for and drained thirteen pints from his thorax. June Wyndham Davies could hardly bear to watch. She knew from his puffy eyes that he was crying a lot.

He was tired and having trouble with his lines. He would sit in the Winnebego, psyching himself up to go on the set, to stand up.

'I am trying, I am bloody well trying to shake *him* off, but Holmes seems to haunt me these days,' he confided to Linda.

The lithium and steroids were having a devastating effect. He was getting so big that Esther Dean had to prise him out of his old frock-coat – but he still refused to wear a new one. Different trousers had to be used each day as his weight fluctuated. When he arrived on the set in his favourite green cashmere sweater and white trousers, he had to be prised out of those too. The only thing that seemed to fit him was Holmes's trilby hat, which had by now become his favourite piece of costume wear.

The lithium was dulling his senses, shortening his concentration span. Reading was a struggle and he was having difficulty with his co-ordination in everything from walking to raising a cup of coffee to his lips.

He didn't drive any more. It had been drummed into him that it was as much an offence to drive whilst under the influence of drugs as it was under the influence of alcohol. And he particularly had to avoid alcohol now because the drowsiness induced by many of the drugs he was taking was enhanced by booze. Reaction time would slow almost to a stop and there would be a loss of mental concentration.

Jeremy began to wonder if his nervous breakdown had been brewing since the time he had nearly died of rheumatic fever as a boy. Had he really been hyperventilating all that time? Had he been on a high since he was sixteen? The more he thought about it the more he felt he had. The crisis of his wife's death and the tremendous burden of Sherlock Holmes, which he hated, had finally broken him.

In his mind he began to try to rationalise his life. A part of him believed that the inner pressure he felt was to do most of all with not believing ever that he was an actor. He was born the son of a famous soldier, and his mother was a wonderful Irish Quaker. But he just couldn't see how the equation added up to him being a star. It had taken him a long, long time to believe in his ability. Now he doubted it again. And why shouldn't he? After all, he had never won an award for his portrayal of the great Victorian detective. Even Edward Hardwicke was disappointed for him.

Jeremy remembered being tongue-tied as a boy, struggling to pronounce his Rs and Ss. How, then, did he ever believe that the spoken word could be his life's work? He must have buried that fear deep within him too.

The next few weeks crawled by at a snail's pace. Every morning his lungs felt as if they would burst, his legs could hardly support his weight, and he despaired at the bags under the eyes on his bloated face. At least, he thought, he was no longer the pretty boy. At least he had character in his face now. By the fourth week he was so exhausted that one morning he stayed in his hotel room and cried. But there was little enough energy for that. He didn't want to get dressed any more and his legs hurt constantly. He lay in his bed staring at the dressing table. He was reluctant to be with people now because he felt his darkness was an intolerable burden on them. In a way he was glad that Linda had returned to London. She had moved in with him now and gone back to the flat to arrange things for his homecoming at the weekend. He began to wonder if he would die. Or did he want to die? No, not before Robert.

What then? He remembered the words Bunny used to say to him. When her grandmother was once asked: 'Would you like to repeat your life?' she replied: 'Yes, if all the splendid people I have known could do the same.'

Mary Ellis was visibly upset as she watched Jeremy being carried on to the set in a collapsible wheelchair. Her eyes were filled with tears. At 93 she was still fit and able and yet poor Jeremy was so ill.

The situation was desperate. Granada didn't know what to do for the best. In his better moments Jeremy admitted that he needed to come off drugs to save his career. He knew he wasn't playing the part well. The sparkle had died and he felt he was dying too.

His treasured red 'bible' of Holmes mannerisms and habits

was falling to bits. The TV company offered to have it re-printed and rebound for him, but he wouldn't change it or let anyone touch it.

It was September 1993 and they were filming *The Three Gables*. Holmes and Watson were investigating a strange attempt to purchase the house and possessions of pensioner Mary Maberley, played by the legendary American actress and singer Mary. But Holmes was more interested in the recent death of her beloved grandson, concluding that the culprits were thugs hired by the victim's former lover, a notorious Spanish society beauty now betrothed to a young duke.

As always, it was a talented cast. Peter Wyngarde, famous for his role as the flamboyant Jason King in the cult TV series *Department S*, appeared as a stylish Langdale Pike, and Edward Hardwicke's own daughter Emma played Dora.

Mary was not prepared for what she was seeing. The stately actress from New York City had enjoyed a star-studded career. She had sung at the Metropolitan Opera House, been the original Rose Marie on stage, starred in concerts for troops in the Second World War, helped out in hospitals for the wounded and worked alongside the greats of Hollywood. And now this – the Sherlock Holmes America had taken its hat off to.

Tony Eyres and Peter Kersey, Jeremy's drivers and keepers, brought him onto the set. There was an oxygen mask, he needed it now. His weight had shot up to sixteen stone and he had lost all feeling in his feet. Mary felt his face; it was white hot. 'So it has come to this,' he said. 'But, darlings, the show must go on, as they say.'

His professionalism never failed him. He still turned up for early morning make-up and thought of new lines and movements to make an episode work even better. One of the last moments between Jeremy and Rosalie Williams, alias Mrs Hudson, came in *The Cardboard Box*. Mrs Hudson, aspidistra in hand, was preparing the house for Christmas.

'How dare you move my aspidistra!' declared Holmes. Mrs H turned and exclaimed 'I do dare!' before marching off, the only person, man or woman, to put the great detective in his place.

During the final days of shooting it was obvious to everyone that Jeremy couldn't take much more. June insisted that he went to hospital but at first he refused. In the end she managed to persuade him.

'Look, Jeremy, everyone here depends on you. You are Sherlock Holmes, you are the series. All these people here have jobs, they are dependent on you.'

This seemed to convince him and she took him to the local BUPA hospital. Jeremy admitted that he could notice the difference in himself. Everything that once was sparkling now was flat. He felt that his friends and fellow actors found him dull, boring, inadequate and thick-brained. He tried to joke with the cameraman but somehow it didn't work any more. He didn't blame them for being unresponsive because he was unlit, bloodless and drab. He was boring himself to death, so they must surely be bored too. At the hospital the doctors wanted to admit him on the spot but he refused. After tests and X-rays they told him he was suffering from manic depression and emphysema. They showed him one of the X-rays. His lungs looked like lace.

'I'm scared, damn scared,' he told June as he returned to his beloved Midland Hotel.

Life can be cruel sometimes. The newspaper critics kept panning him, little realising the despair deep inside the actor. One critic had written: 'Then there is the mystery of Holmes's glossy lips. Has Britain's most celebrated 'tec opened an account with Max Factor?' The truth was that the TV make-up girls had been struggling to make Jeremy look healthy. The end of Holmes was in sight.

At his 58th birthday party Jeremy suddenly picked up a glass and announced to the packed room of TV executives, stars and production staff: 'I'm sorry, everyone. I'm afraid I am not going to make it . . . please get me to hospital fast.' They did.

A few days after the party everyone learned that Jeremy had suffered heart failure. Over the following few weeks a doctor traced all his problems back to the rheumatic fever he had suffered as a child, which had left him with a weak heart valve. With Jeremy in hospital the fifth episode of the series had to be rewritten so that Charles Gray could take over as Holmes's brother. Edward had other commitments and couldn't appear. The case, which began with the discovery of a dead body and no apparent clue except a pair of gold pince-nez glasses clutched in the corpse's hand, featured Frank Finlay as Professor Coram, and stretched as far as the war-torn city of St Petersburg.

As Jeremy lay in his hospital bed he was already musing on who would one day take over the mantle of Holmes. 'My hunch is Daniel Day-Lewis,' he told Jeremy Paul.

March 1994 was probably the last turning point for Jeremy. There would be no more Sherlock Holmes episodes. He simply couldn't do it any more. What his tired body was going through was captured in Linda's diary. Her words described the pain they both felt. One evening she sat alone at his desk in the flat in Clapham and wrote:

'Today, Wednesday, March 16, has been the worst day of my entire life. I had to take Jeremy to the Chelsea and Westminster Hospital because he was showing signs of a severe manic depressive episode. It was an agonising decision for me to make knowing Jeremy's despair and utter dislike of hospitals.

'As we drove together in the car, I hoped and prayed that we would both wake from a terrifying dream. But it wasn't to be and when we arrived at the hospital and got out of the car we both stopped before the doorway. Jeremy took a few deep breaths of air and then hugged me. I held him so tight and wished we didn't have to live that moment. As he turned to enter the hospital my insides screamed with pain for him. Experience told him the treatment he faced wouldn't be pleasant and yet he walked in with his head held high. I realised then that Jeremy was the bravest person I have ever met and my love for this courageous man deepened.'

The next day Linda returned to the hospital with a few things for Jeremy. She was apprehensive. She knew that because of his manic depressive disorder she might not be well received. He might accuse her of putting him in hospital or just turn nasty for no apparent reason. She was relieved, however, when Jeremy greeted her with a hug. She was even more touched to find that he had a photograph of her on his bedside cabinet.

That night Linda wrote: 'I stayed with Jeremy for a few hours until he was told that he would have to undergo an ECG test to check the condition of his heart. Only then could the doctors decide on what level of medication to give him. As there was a staff shortage, a sister asked if I could accompany Jeremy and another nurse to the heart unit. It was supposed to have taken five minutes to get there, but Jeremy was his usual talkative self and decided to chat to everyone on the way. The journey took a full 30 minutes. At one point, the nurse seemed to get agitated about this, but as Jeremy appeared to be enjoying himself, I was more than happy to let him take as long as he liked and besides, he was doing a lot of good. He brought a lot of joy to the faces of other patients, especially a Down's Syndrome child, whom he paid particular attention to. On our return he showed enormous compassion and understanding to a fellow patient named Irene, who had become distressed. All this touched me deeply and I felt privileged to see human kindness at its very best . . .'

On Friday, 18 March 1994 she wrote:

'Woke early from a difficult night's sleep. Dreams had become nightmares as my concern for Jeremy increased. I dressed quickly and returned to the hospital to see how he was. He seemed subdued, which wasn't surprising after all he had been through. I spoke to the nurse and she told me that they had started Jeremy on medication, but on a very small dose due to his heart problems. I was glad the dosage was low as his stay in the Charter Clinic in Chelsea in 1992 had resulted in a high dosage of drugs causing terrible side effects. At one point I even thought Jeremy was suffering from Parkinson's Disease, but I was informed that the anti-psychotic drug he was taking was causing Parkinsonism – symptoms similar to the disease.'

The following Sunday Linda arrived at the hospital to find Jeremy lying on his bed asleep. For the first time in weeks, his face showed no signs of strain and the deep furrow in the middle of his forehead had gone. He looked so peaceful that she decided not to wake him and just left a card with some words of hope and a packet of his favourite cigarettes, Silk Cut extra mild. Before leaving she gently touched his hand and prayed to God to guide him through his difficult trial.

The next few days were a great strain for Jeremy as he fought to come to terms with another manic depressive episode. In turn Linda was now finding it difficult to find any kind of justice in Jeremy's lot.

One night she wrote: 'In all honesty, manic depression has tested my beliefs and understanding of life to an extent that I never thought possible. Before I met Jeremy, I thought I had life worked out. That pain and suffering was the result of the need to learn and understand certain aspects of life. Now I am not so sure. Jeremy's suffering has gone beyond all those needs and necessities. Now I am left wondering what possible reason there could be for all this misery.'

After twelve days in care, Jeremy showed signs of improvement. Linda was amazed by his quick recovery considering he was on such a low dose of medication. He finally left hospital on Thursday, 21 April 1994, but although he was feeling much better they both knew there was a long way to go before he would be back to his old self. It would take time to rebuild his confidence and self-esteem to enable him to face the world again. But Linda was sure that with Jeremy's strong will and determination the future would be bright. And it was. She helped him as much as she could and for many months it would be a happy and blissful time. But first he had to make a decision.

The room went quiet. Jeremy cleared his throat. 'Dear hearts, I have had several months off during which I have had treatment for my brain and heart and I feel that I cannot play Holmes any more,' he said.

No one said a word. They just looked at him, loving, hating, understanding, not understanding, caring, not caring.

It was the tenth anniversary party of the series and the man who had become the TV Sherlock Holmes was finally hanging up his black frock-coat and putting his long-stemmed pipe back on the shelf for the last time. Everyone had dressed up in Victorian costume for the event but somehow a lot of the fun had gone out of it now.

'Holmes is the hardest part I have ever played – harder than Hamlet or Macbeth,' he continued. 'You see, everyone, Holmes has become the dark side of the moon for me. He is moody and solitary and underneath I am really sociable and gregarious. It has all got too dangerous. I should just have played Bambi right from the start.'

Late in August 1994 Robert Stephens was admitted to the Royal Free Hospital in Hampstead, London. Because of a recurring foot infection and exhaustion he had missed his last performances at the Barbican Theatre where he was playing King Lear to huge acclaim. He was given a blood transfusion and began to feel better. But there was bad news. The doctors told him that unless he had a liver and kidney transplant he would be dead within three months. There was no choice.

One Sunday night a new liver and kidney were flown to London by helicopter and the operation was carried out the next day. They left Robert's old kidneys in his body and sent him off to convalesce at an old actor's home in Northwood, about 20 miles from London. He was under doctor's orders not to smoke or drink. But giving up his beloved Camels would have given him the hump, he said, and so he smoked on. Giving up drinking was hard and he would go through periods of irritability.

'If you are in a play you go out drinking afterwards and, before you know, it's four a.m. If you do it every day for ten years you don't know you're doing it any more!'

These were busy times for Tarn, checking on Jeremy and then driving over to see how Robert was. She had always seemed to be there, right from the time they first needed their jeans washing. She felt that they had all come through life like the threesome in *Butch Cassidy and the Sundance Kid.*

Jeremy believed that things would improve by being with Linda, and they were. They had long walks across Clapham Common, dinner in a favourite little restaurant. Gradually the exhaustion, wariness and black fear began to lift. He started to enjoy television and reading again. He laughed a lot and wrote to friends. He loved life and life seemed to love him. He still cried, though, and nothing moved him more than Bette Midler singing 'Wind Beneath My Wings' from the film *Beaches*. The words reminded him of Joan, who was always content to be the backroom girl behind his fame as Holmes. He bought a cassette of the song and played it over and over again.

The extremes of his moods were not as pronounced now as they had been, but it was clear that a low-grade, fitful instability had become an integral part of his life. It seemed to him that he was constantly recovering from or delving into new moods and new experiences behind which lay a nagging fear that the manic cycle could be starting again. He was sick of analysing himself. He needed to work. One morning he rushed home from a walk across the common, his mind racing with a new inspiration. He had been thinking of animals, how much he loved them . . . dogs, cats, horses, lions, tigers. And then it had suddenly come to him. He might not be well enough to act, but he could still talk. He picked up the telephone and rang the Walt Disney studios in America, telling them he wanted to be one of the voices in their next animal film. Minutes later he excitedly rang June Wyndham Davies. 'I've told them I would like to be a deer or an elephant,' he said.

Jeremy couldn't believe his eyes. Gary Bond was like a skeleton. The slim, supple body of the good-looking young man who had won his heart with his infectious giggle in the early 1970s was racked with the ravages of AIDS. Gary, 55 now, smiled at him from his hospital bed and Jeremy put the flowers he had bought in the vase on the table. They talked for hours about Gary's career . . . his jokes with Michael Caine and Stanley Baker on the set of *Zulu*, his time at Worthing Repertory where he was spotted and asked to play the part of Pip, the public-school recruit on National Service in Arnold Wesker's *Chips with Everything* at the Royal Court. How he strutted and sang as Che Guevara after David Essex and how he too had appeared in TV's *Hart to Hart* with Stefanie Powers.

Then Gary grew tired and Jeremy sat quietly singing to him until he fell into a deep sleep. For a while Jeremy sat in silence, remembering the time they had spent together. Gary had always been much loved by his colleagues. His infectious laughter won over the most difficult of directors or writers. He was, and always had been, entirely without envy, one of the many reasons his friendships stood the test of time. He seemed always to delight in the success of others – much like Jeremy.

As he left Ealing Hospital, Jeremy caught a glimpse of Gary's partner, American artist E. J. Taylor, coming through the glass doors. He didn't say anything; there was nothing left to say. It was fitting, thought Jeremy, that Gary's final theatrical performance should have been as the worldly-wise philanderer George Dillingham in the brilliant new production of Andrew Lloyd Webber's *Aspects of Love* at the Prince of Wales in London's West End. Gary's career in the musical theatre had somehow been inextricably linked with the composer's work.

By October things had taken a turn for the worse. Gary had died and Linda wrote in her diary:

'I am concerned about Jeremy. I have a feeling that another manic depressive episode might be starting again. I don't know why I feel this way. Maybe it is intuition or a subconscious memory from a previous episode of Jeremy's illness setting off warning bells in my head. But whatever it is, I will keep a close eye on him without making it obvious that I am worried. It is times like this that my life's force, my energy, drains from every recess of my body and I hear myself screaming out the words – No, no, please not again! He has been through so much already, please God don't let him suffer any more.'

Linda wasn't sure how much more he could take. She had seen him pick himself up and face the illness with more courage than anyone could possibly imagine time and again. But how much more courage had he left?

Monday, 31 October 1994: 'A sleepless night for both of us. Nothing new for Jeremy, but my concern for him kept me fully awake as I worried about how he was feeling. Eventually I decided I couldn't lay in bed any more and joined him downstairs in the living room. He was pleased to see me and spoke endlessly about all manner of things. I didn't mind one bit as I always love to listen to the things he has to say and besides it gave me the opportunity to see whether there were any further signs of the illness. After a short time, Jeremy seemed to be OK. However, I just didn't think that we were out of the woods yet as his illness could show itself in fits and starts in the early days of an attack.'

Tuesday, 1 November 1994: 'Today Jeremy's thoughts seem to be racing, which worries me greatly. But then again, I could be over-reacting. I might be so sensitive to the symptoms and signs of this illness that my judgement is erroneous. It could be a simple case of stress causing these symptoms. After all, Jeremy has done a few voice-overs lately and visited the hospital for his heart condition. But on the other hand . . . oh damn! This senseless illness and its complexity. I hate it with all my heart. No matter how strong and determined one is, this condition can shatter the nerves of the most resolute carer and cause emotional turmoil. Some days I become so distressed that the only way I can contain my fears and concerns is to sneak off to the bathroom, and cry my eyes out. Sometimes I have cried so long and so hard that the tears have dried up and I have become an emotional zombie. Then, from utter despair at Jeremy's predicament, I pick myself up off the bathroom floor, wash away the signs of my concerns and go and see how he is.'

Wednesday, 2 November 1994: 'In the evening Jeremy told me that he was concerned about how he was feeling. 'Oh Lindy,' he said. 'I'm afraid that something is wrong. I feel agitated and extremely stressed and I think things are getting out of control.' I put my arms around him and hugged him like never before. As we stood, locked in the embrace, we both cried. I with concern and relief that he was able to recognise certain symptoms of the illness in himself, which is something he previously had difficulty doing, and he because of his fear that the illness would get worse and he would end up back in hospital.

'To dispel our fears Jeremy decided to telephone his doctor. He hoped that by acting now he would avoid going back into care. Knowing of Jeremy's dislike of hospitals, I told him that

I would leave my job and take care of him at home rather than see him back in the Chelsea. Jeremy was not too keen on the idea as I had already given up two jobs to care for him. But I was adamant that he shouldn't suffer any more than necessary. In the end we left our options open until the medical appointment.'

The next day was Jeremy's birthday and Linda had prayed all night that he would have a good day. His last two birthdays had seen him so ill. In 1992 he had spent the day in Charters Nightingale being treated for manic depression and in 1993 he was in hospital for heart failure.

Linda wrote: 'Thursday, November 3, 1994. Jeremy managed to contact his doctor first thing this morning. His decision was to do nothing for 48 hours to see if Jeremy improved. As it turned out, he was very relaxed and we had a wonderful day.'

The following weeks leading up to Christmas 1994 proved a difficult time for Jeremy and Linda as the manic depression nearly took hold. Eventually Jeremy pulled through without hospitalisation.

'To me Basil Rathbone is You Know Who.'

It was early in 1995 and Jeremy was telling radio and TV interviewers in America that Sherlock Holmes's crown belonged to the former Hollywood actor.

They listened as he told them he didn't feel he was ideally cast in the role but that SH had been good to him. By now he no longer referred to the great detective directly.

You Know Who and SH and *him* were set in stone in the repertory of his stage vocabulary in the same way that Shakespearian actors called Macbeth 'The Scottish Play'.

American fans of the Sherlock Holmes series being networked across the continent were riveted. They loved every word.

'Some actors fear if they play Sherlock Holmes for a very long run the character will steal their soul, leave no corner for the original inhabitant – and when the role ends, leave them unable to act without a pipe and a deerstalker cap,' Jeremy told them.

'Some actors are becomers – they try to become their characters. When it works, the actor is like a sponge, squeezing himself dry to remove his own personality then absorbing the character's like a liquid.'

Jeremy had been on a ten-city US tour. He was toasted at the British Embassy where he smoked at least 200 cigarettes. His breathing was bad and sometimes his voice grew thin. The drugs he was taking for manic depression seemed to be having an adverse affect on his heart condition. But he struggled on.

Wherever he went the Americans would ask him about Holmes, treat him as Holmes. He didn't disappoint them.

'Did you know *he* only read criminal news and personal ads in the daily newspapers?' Jeremy would ask them. Before they could answer he would press on with a thespian wave of his hand.

'And did you know that You Know Who's favourite author was Edgar Allan Poe? And when *he* wasn't reading, he would sit silently and stare at the fire with a peculiar concentration.' Jeremy would then furrow his brow and narrow his eyes.

When he got into his flow there was no stopping him. He and Holmes would become one. He knew by heart every nuance, mannerism and habit of the dark detective.

'*He* habitually wore patent leather bedroom slippers or rubber-soled tennis shoes, an Ulster overcoat and a top hat. The deerstalker cap that so many admirers took to be his trademark was worn only in the country, dear hearts.'

The list would go on and on, and no one could get a word in edgeways. Holmes hated to get up early and almost never did. *He* preferred German music to Italian, French or English composers. *He* was more than six feet tall and seemed taller because he was so lean. *He* was very strong but carried a British Army revolver when he felt it necessary. *He* smoked a straight pipe, not the curved calabash people had seen him with in the movies. *He* drank an occasional beer, but favoured claret or brandy. His ancestors were country squires and his grandmother was the sister of Vernet, the French painter. *He* attended college for only two years – where and when were never recorded. Jeremy was a walking, talking tribute to the canon.

But by the end of the spring Jeremy's physical health was deteriorating fast. Doctors put him on another course of heart pills in the hope that they would stabilise his condition. It was apparent now to everyone that his acting career was over forever.

One afternoon Jeremy went to see Robert Stephens in London's Royal Free Hospital. It was good to see his old friend and Jeremy thought he looked in better shape than he did. His old chum smoked and talked and answered his mobile telephone.

Robert had undergone a routine biopsy operation the day before to see how his new liver was getting on – and everything appeared to be fine. Jeremy refused a glass of champagne from the bottle under the bed, opting for weak tea after rummaging around to find a polystyrene cup free of cigarette butts.

They talked about old times and sang a song together. Jeremy left feeling that his old friend would pull through.

11 A Theatre in Heaven

O that I had wings like a dove: for then would I flee away and be at rest

Psalm 55

IT WAS A BLISTERING HOT July day when Myra Fulford arrived at Jeremy's flat in Clapham. The doors were open to let in the cool air from the staircase. Jeremy was sitting alone in the chair with his shirt open to the waist, exposing his chest, his face red with the heat of the day which was obviously distressing him.

'Darling, I'm so delighted to see you,' he said, easing himself up.

Myra could tell he was a little tired, and given the sweltering-hot weather perhaps it wasn't the best moment to meet. She quickly went into raptures about his home which appeared pristine. Every ornament looked perfectly set out and the tables gleamed as if they had been energetically polished.

'Jeremy, what a wonderful view,' she said, looking out at the common peppered with sunbathers.

'Yes, this is my window to the world,' he said, 'and this, darling, this is my lawn.' He pointed to the expanse of bright green carpet that covered the floor. 'I don't have a garden you see, so I make do with this.'

'It's wonderful, and everything is so colourful,' said Myra.

He led her upstairs to the roof and she stood for a moment in silence, taking in the spectacular skyline.

They returned downstairs and Jeremy crossed to a side table where he poured them both a large glass of orange juice, throwing in a handful of ice cubes.

'I know it seems impertinent, but your home spells success and power,' Myra said.

It seemed for a moment that he had not heard her, but then he turned towards her, smiling. 'Neither, really. It's just my little womb. I go out and I am born . . . and then I return to it and die from the world for a bit, take sanctuary.' He handed her the glass and walked around, talking and waving his arm about in the air as if he were on stage. For a while Myra was spellbound by his personality, but she quickly began to realise that he was up . . . he was definitely on a high.

Myra was president of the Manic Depressive Fellowship, a voluntary organisation set up to help sufferers and carers. It ran self-help groups throughout Britain and educated public and professionals alike about the illness. Although she had never suffered from manic depression herself, she knew all the nuances of the condition and many of her colleagues were victims. She had read a newspaper article about Jeremy in which he talked freely about his battle against his illness and how he came to meet Linda, who had poved to be such a good friend. Touched by his words, Myra had written to him praising him for being so courageous and asking if he could help in her mission to obtain greater public awareness of the debilitating condition.

The Fellowship had applied for a spot on the Radio 4 programme *The Week's Good Cause*. It was a marvellous opportunity for them to put their case and raise money for much-needed funds. They desperately wanted the public to understand the true ghastliness of acute depression and needed someone who could put those feelings across, someone the pubic would listen to – a celebrity.

'Darling, I would be delighted to do it,' Jeremy told her over the phone.

And so she found herself sitting opposite Sherlock Holmes on that hot summer's day.

They talked for about two hours in the drawing room of his Clapham flat, but every time she took out a pencil and pad to try to write a script for the radio programme with him he waved it away.

'Dear heart, put that notebook away,' he said.

Myra kept trying to focus on the Radio 4 programme but Jeremy began to flit from one subject to another . . . his family, his early days with Robert Stephens and Laurence Olivier, his sad times in the Maudsley Hospital when he was frightened to show his face to the world, and his 'blessed' heart trouble.

'These are my real friends,' he suddenly said, holding up a tattered address book containing the names and telephone numbers of patients he had met in the Charters Clinic. He explained how he rang them in the early hours to cheer them up. They had all become so close. They understood each other.

They talked about Patrick and how his family had to cope with his illness and pick up the pieces.

'Darling, I'm bereft. Patrick has moved so far away from me,' he said, revealing that his brother had moved down to the West Country. 'I feel deserted.'

'I'm sure you're not,' Myra said sympathetically.

'Ah, you see, then, darling, I'm not right am I?'

He turned away from her and for one awful moment she was afraid that her appeal had failed. But it was only to set his glass down on the table before facing her again and telling her about his mood swings in the early days. Slowly the subject turned to life and death and God, then back to the Radio 4 script.

'You see, Jeremy, we can raise a lot of financial help through the appeal,' Myra went on doggedly.

'Oh no, darling, I don't want to ask for money. Far too tacky. What I'll be saying is take your medicine and be good.'

'But, Jeremy, we are not worried about medication. The charity is a broad church and . . .'

The word church seemed to trigger something in his mind.

'I don't want to talk about God again!'

'Nor do I, what I meant was . . .'

'The thing is, he has been in here already.'

'In here?'

Jeremy's look reminded her of a bird of prey, wild with barely controllable bursts of energy.

'Yes, he came in through the small window up there in the roof. Zeus did too, darling. They both sat where you are sitting. But they wouldn't listen to any arguments.'

Myra sat quietly, listening.

'And dearest Father Time, he came to see me too. I was lying on the roof. It was terribly hot and muggy and suddenly there was a flash of lightning and he appeared, standing before me. We talked about life and the future and the afterlife and so on. I have become extremely knowledgeable about those sorts of things you know, thanks to Them.'

After a while, Myra managed to bring Jeremy back to the subject of the script.

'So, I will write it and double-space it for you, then you can amend my words if you want to.'

'Don't worry about that, darling. It will be wonderful. Now, on to the next job for you! Goodbye.' He suddenly stood up and Myra saw herself out.

She crossed the road and walked by the common, the trees standing like black paper cut-outs, flat against the cooling sky. The steady stream of cars flowing past her pierced her thoughts. What a lovely, interesting, generous and terribly tormented man, she said to herself. She must help him if she could, and she prayed he would be strong enough to help others. He was a symbol for all sufferers, living proof that people could still be successful and lead full lives, within the scourge of manic depression. He had been wonderfully controlled, even though he must have been on a manic high. Somehow he had discovered the knack of coming through it, a way of overriding it. If victims could see that a well-known actor like Jeremy was suffering just like them it would give them hope. He had to make that broadcast, he just had to.

'I don't think I can do it, Tarn.'

'Yes you can, you must.'

Jeremy's voice was terribly thin. He had finally written the short address for the Radio 4 programme but he was having second thoughts about doing it.

Tarn put the phone down praying that Jeremy would go through with it.

At 10 a.m. on Monday, 3 August 1995, she switched on the radio and sat quietly listening.

'I . . .' Jeremy's voice faltered for a moment. '. . . started my acting career in repertory and have over the years appeared in many plays in London and New York and at the National

Theatre under the banner of Laurence Olivier. Now, why am I telling you this in *The Week's Good Cause* slot?'

His voice was slow and Tarn could feel him willing himself on. It was obvious that the lithium was affecting him. He was emphasising his words here and there as if he were on stage.

'Because this week's charity is the Manic Depression Fellowship . . . and I myself have been diagnosed as manic depressive, so I know what I am talking about, and I need to remind you that I am a successful actor before admitting to having a severe mental illness. Manic depression is a severe mental illness which causes excessive mood changes with swings from extreme depression to great elation and hyperactivity. These swings are quite different to the range of moods from Monday-morning lows to being on top of the world, which most people understand and experience. In mania people have tremendous activity and energy levels, won't be able to sleep because of the rapid flow of their ideas; will spend money irrationally; will have hallucinations and lose touch with reality. I personally have done some extremely embarrassing and destructive things when I've been high. When clinically depressed one has panic attacks, no energy and suicidal thoughts. One in seven people with untreated manic depression will commit suicide. And one in a hundred of the population have this illness. It can put a real strain on family and friends and employers and can lead to isolation, unemployment, loss of home and bankruptcy. When I was admitted to the Maudsley Hospital in 1986, I . . . I mean I was so confused I couldn't relate to anything or anyone around me. All I could do was lay face down with my fists clenched to my cheeks. I believe I have been coping with these severe mood swings for many more years than I like to think. But being a member of a profession where being a little mad helps, my moods were tolerated far more readily than if I worked in a bank or a school. And it is my success that gave me the courage to admit publicly that I had this illness, as an encouragement to others. It has not stopped me from being employed and leading a fulfilled and successful life.'

Jeremy's voice was growing more tired and shaky. But Tarn and thousands of other radio listeners were moved.

'It is an illness which can be treated and managed,' he went on. 'It comes and goes and between the bouts of illness people are well. If any of this sounds familiar make an appointment with your GP and contact the Manic Depression Fellowship. It's the national self-help organisation for people with manic depression. It is a remarkable organisation because it is largely run by people with manic depression, so they really know how to be of help. There are one hundred and sixteen self-help groups in the United Kingdom. They can offer support, information, literature and the opportunity to meet other people in a similar situation.

'Thank you.'

That day the telephone did not stop ringing at Jeremy's home. Stars, friends and family had been moved to tears by the broadcast. The next morning the former Sherlock Holmes series team at Granada held a collection for the charity. Everyone was pleased that at last Jeremy had begun to talk openly about his problem.

Jeremy and Linda were by now well aware of the heartbreaking statistics of manic depression. They knew that the average length of time before victims sought help was eighteen months. Forty per cent of victims received help within the first six months of the illness; 73 per cent within five years and 27 per cent over five years. Jeremy had been in the latter category. Some 89 per cent of sufferers had been admitted to a psychiatric hospital and 50 per cent of those under a section of the Mental Health Act. Fourteen per cent had been admitted once; 44 per cent between two and four times; and 41.5 per cent five times or more. The majority of victims took medication – most commonly lithium. One of the most depressing aspects of the illness was the resultant quality of life for those who, through no fault of their own, had suffered. Seventy-one per cent reported that their self-esteem and confidence were negative as a result of the illness. Fifty-one per cent reported that their family relationships were destroyed following treatment and 79 per cent found that their work prospects were hopeless.

Another tragic aspect was that 15 per cent of people with manic depression took their own lives. There were particular times when the risk for a sufferer was higher, including when someone was emerging from a depression and was a little more active. At that point they realised that their loss of control might have damaged their life – and maybe also the life of others close to them. This made them feel desperate, as Jeremy had felt after his first breakdown. It all made depressing reading.

It had been a long hot summer and Jeremy was finding it more and more difficult to breathe.

'I'm running out of puff, darling,' he told Jeremy Paul on the phone one evening.

'No you're not, old man, you sound fine to me.'

After their five-minute conversation Paul put down the receiver and sat wondering and worrying about his old friend. At last he went upstairs and got ready for bed but something was nagging him. He collected a spare duvet and a pillow and came downstairs again. Tonight he would sleep, if he managed to sleep at all, on the sofa, next to the phone. He was determined that if Jeremy rang again he would be on hand to talk to him without waking his wife.

Alone in his Clapham drawing room Jeremy knew somehow that he was near death. His lungs felt heavy now, just as they had after he had finally won the near-fatal diving contest at Eton all those years ago. It was as if he were drowning in the murky Thames again. Had he really been a good actor, a good father, a decent human being? He was riddled with self-doubt. He dozed off for a while and woke with an awful premonition. Holmes or God seemed to be beckoning him.

Then the pain registered. Jeremy had a splitting headache and his neck was stiff from lying awkwardly on the sofa, so he sat up gingerly. The day outside was grey as the sun fought its way through a thick mist on the common, and he wondered how long he had been asleep. He was still half-possessed by an atmosphere of menace and he let out a groan. How was it possible to sleep and yet feel he had had so little rest?

On the evening of 11 September 1995, Linda was at her lowest ebb. She sat alone downstairs as Jeremy slept and wrote in her diary:

'Today I took time off work to go with Jeremy to the hospital. It was raining . . . raining in the street and raining in our hearts. We were both concerned about his heart condition. His health has been slowly deteriorating over the last few months, but we put it down to the heat. It has been a record-breaking summer of high temperatures and Jeremy is never comfortable in hot weather. He simply adores the cold, frosty days of winter. Perhaps that suits his mind.

'Earlier this morning, Jeremy insisted that he should go alone to the hospital because I have already taken too many days off work and he was concerned that I would be fired. But I was determined to go with him. I needed to know how serious his condition had become. Ever since Jeremy was diagnosed as having heart failure, I have had to battle to get information from doctors about his condition. I need and want to talk to the medical experts alone because I do not want to worry him. He has enough worries already. To my horror and abhorrence, I have always been refused access to his medical details because I am not a relative. The only information I ever get is what Jeremy tells me and what I have read already. That is very little because doctors do not appear to be keen to give Jeremy the full facts about his illness. They seem concerned that the stress of knowing more facts will cause another manic depressive episode and there is hardly any information about cardiomyopathy in the medical books that I can find. But now, with Jeremy's failing health, I desperately need all the details, no matter how frightening they are.

'We arrived at the hospital today to find that Jeremy's heart specialist was on holiday. We were crestfallen. But we were offered the chance to speak to another doctor and although we felt this would not really be beneficial because he would not have the full facts of Jeremy's case, we agreed to see him in our despair. Jeremy was checked over by the doctor who felt that under the circumstances, he was no worse than he should be. This was not a comfort to Jeremy and me and we left feeling as despondent as we did when we came in.

'As I drove back, I sensed Jeremy's distress and tried to lift him by suggesting that we seek another opinion. Jeremy readily agreed and we decided to telephone his GP the next day.

'When we got home, Jeremy talked about his fears and concerns and even apologised for making it difficult for me to care for him by always refusing to see a doctor until the time came when he was so unwell that he had no alternative. I told him not to be so silly as I fully understood his dislike of hospitals. Each time he had been in hospital with either heart failure or manic depression, he had found the symptoms and treatment difficult to cope with. I know that if I was in his position I would probably feel the same way.'

In the evening, after dinner, Jeremy seemed relaxed and soon drifted off to sleep on the bed. Linda quickly followed. They hadn't had a good night's sleep for weeks.

It was after midnight and Linda was still upstairs. Jeremy quietly picked up the receiver, taking care not to wake her, and dialled a number.

June Wyndham Davies was asleep too when the telephone rang. She buried her head in the pillow, hoping the noise would go away, but it didn't. Finally she relented and picked it up.

'Yes,' she said sleepily.

'Darling, sorry to bother you, just wondered how you were?'

'Fine, Jeremy, how are you?'

'Not too good, dearest, feel terribly unwell. I'm frightened to lie down. If I do I think I will drown. I can feel the water swishing around inside of me.'

'Jeremy, I'm sure you'll be fine. You really must get some sleep.'

At 3 a.m. Linda was woken by the sound of Jeremy's voice. He was calling her from the landing.

'Lindy, I need to talk to you,' he said urgently. She grabbed her dressing gown and went to his side.

'What is it, sweetheart?' she asked apprehensively, alarmed by the worried look on his face.

'I just want you to know that I care about you more than anything in the world and that you mean so much to me,' he said, his voice breaking with emotion.

She put her arms around him and told him how much he meant to her, that it had been a privilege to share these last years with him.

They hugged each other for a long time, and suddenly she was overcome by the strangest of feelings. She didn't want to let go of him. For some reason she wanted to keep the moment forever, as if it were their last together. She wondered whether it was possible to live all one's life as intensely as this brief moment.

Eventually they parted and Jeremy insisted that she went back to bed.

'I'm sorry I woke you,' he said. 'You really must get some sleep now, you've got to go to work soon.'

Her first thought was to tell him that she wanted to stay by his side and that she had no intention of going anywhere in the morning, except with him. But something in his voice and the way he looked at her told her that he really wanted her to do as he said. There was a deep, pleading look in his eyes, and she knew there was no point in arguing with him – and anyway she didn't want to cause him any more stress by disagreeing. He had enough to cope with. With great reluctance she kissed him on the cheek and went back to bed. For a while she lay awake, staring at the ceiling, thinking and worrying, before slowly drifting into sleep.

Downstairs Jeremy fell asleep too. This time forever. He died peacefully of heart failure.

Linda woke to find the duvet twisted round her awkwardly. Disentangling herself, she got up and went to the window, feeling a little dizzy. She hadn't had much sleep and through the fog enshrouding her she began to recall the conversation she and Jeremy had had earlier that morning. There was a pale glow in the sky, but thick cloud prevented her from seeing whether the moon had been full or not. Shivering, she threw on her dressing gown and went downstairs, looking at her watch. It was just 6 a.m. when she found him. It was the moment her world came to an end.

At his funeral service, Linda gave him a single yellow rose with a card. On it she had written a quotation from a book by Richard Bach. It read: 'Fly free and happy beyond birthdays and across forever, and we'll meet now and then when we wish, in the midst of the one celebration that can never end – My love forever, Lindy.'

Linda's own words in her diary summed up her feelings for Jeremy and the torture he suffered.

'When I found Jeremy had passed away downstairs, it was as if a bomb had exploded in my head. I screamed: "Why didn't you let me stay with you!" But then as I looked down at him I realised it was what he wanted more than anything. He didn't want me to suffer the anguish of being there at the very moment he passed away. He had given me his final gift. He had allowed me to remember him as he always was, brave and magical to the end.

'I miss him so very much now he has gone from this life. I have gone through all the emotions that one goes through when the person you love more than anything passes. But Jeremy and I always believed in something more than life on Earth. We knew that greater challenges and adventures laid beyond and that time would bring us back together again. For we had all the proof we needed. The way our lives came together was born of numerous coincidences and fate. Yet neither of us believed in coincidences. We believed in "Meant-to-Bes". We came together because we had a lot to learn from one another and that learning still goes on. I have had a number of things happen to me that tell me Jeremy is still with me. So now instead of being saddened by our goodbye, I look forward to our next hello!'

One month after Jeremy died, his lifelong friend Robert Stephens passed away too. Jeremy had always told Linda he had wanted to get to heaven first – to be able to welcome the people he loved. He would not have been able to bear it if Robert had died before him.

Robert's end came peacefully at the Royal Free Hospital, where he had been a patient for a month. Although he was on dialysis after his body rejected his kidney transplant, he eagerly gave interviews to women journalists about his newly published memoirs, *Knight Errant*. One of them wrote: 'Perhaps the flirting faculty is the last to atrophy!'

To 64-year-old Robert's glee the book brought him a new,

deathbed fame by breaching the media code that only women were permitted to 'kiss and tell' about their old affairs. Among partners he named were Lady Antonia Fraser ('the bubble in the squelch and squeak of daily life') and actresses Vanessa Redgrave and Tammy Grimes.

'If they dish it out, these bloody women, they've got to learn to take it,' he said.

In his final days, Robert, who received a knighthood and was praised as the finest Falstaff and King Lear of his time, was treated with morphine only. He had married again. His wife, actress Patricia Quinn, said after his death: 'The relief was extraordinarily wonderful.'

Among his last visitors was another friend, Prince Charles, who told him: 'It would be so nice if I had a friend like Falstaff.'

Adrian Noble, who directed Robert as head of the Royal Shakespeare Company, said in tribute: 'When he was on form he burnt brighter than almost any other actor. He lit up the stage with extraordinary physical and vocal energy which belied his weak frame and a body racked by illness and abuse.

'He could speak poetry as if he was creating it. I will remember him as a great raconteur, a great embellisher of the truth, a dedicated smoker, a fearsome drinker, a wicked silver wit, a great actor – and a cat with ten lives.'

The acting world had lost two of its most talented sons.

Some months after Jeremy's funeral, to which it had been decided not to invite all his grieving friends and colleagues, a memorial service was held in London to celebrate his life. As the haunting strains of his favourite Eton song, 'Oh For The Wings Of A Dove', echoed through St Martin's Church in The Aldwych, friends remembered the actor who was always more interested in them than he was in himself.

One man who summed up the warmth, friendship and fun of the troubled actor was his Dr Watson, Edward Hardwicke, who read his own moving tribute.

'In October 1993, during the filming of the last series of Sherlock Holmes, an article appeared in the *Independent* newspaper,' he said. 'It was headlined: "Underrated – the case of

Jeremy Brett's Sherlock Holmes". Among other things in the story, Kevin Jackson wrote . . . "Brett's true brilliance is overlooked not because no one says that he is splendid, but because everybody does. He offers a combination of fidelity and audacity. Everything he does can ultimately be justified by chapter and line from Conan Doyle's stories, but he has taken liberties with the myth so confidently that he has, over the last decade, taken possession of it and displaced the literary Holmes!" '

Edward paused for a moment before going on with his own thoughts. 'For me, that is the hallmark of great acting – to take an author's words and push them another mile down the creative road, illuminating the text in a way that even the author could not visualise. But that is to judge Jeremy as an actor, and thankfully, we are all able to do that, with the wonderful legacy of work he has left us. Today, however, we are here to celebrate Jeremy's whole life.

'I first met him three decades ago when we were both members of the National Theatre Company at the Old Vic. He was in such memorable productions as *The Merchant of Venice*, *As You Like It* and *Hedda Gabler*. I never managed to work with him in those days. I had to wait until I had the great good fortune to take over from David Burke as Dr Watson and join the already successful team making *Sherlock Holmes*. It was an exciting if nerve-racking time for me. But it was made easier by Jeremy's support, generosity and humour. Only once did he even attempt to impose on me an idea of his own. On the very first day of rehearsal, he looked at me critically and said: "Dear heart, I think you need more hair and I think you should wear lifts."

'That was the moment I knew I was playing the Ernie Wise part – short, fat, hairy legs and you can't see the join. The toupee lasted eight years and became affectionately known to Jeremy as Roland – Roland Rat.

'The lifts, however, only lasted a day. It was impossible to keep up with Jeremy's Holmes – one gloved hand behind his back, the other holding his silver-topped cane over his shoulder, coat tails flying as he paced ahead with his immense and rapid stride.

'Over the next eight years we became great friends. He was a joy to work with, always daring, positive and generous to his fellow actors. He was a perfectionist in an age of small-screen minimalism. He brought a whiff of Edwardian acting to film and made it work miraculously. He taught himself to think positively. He was an optimist, wonderful for me – a natural pessimist.

'Before we did Jeremy Paul's stage play *The Secret of Sherlock Holmes*, almost before Jeremy Paul had written it, Jeremy B announced positively: "Edward, we are going to do this performance!" And so we did – at the Wyndham Theatre where it ran for a year. His positive thinking and optimism helped carry him through the later series, when his health began to deteriorate and the strain on him was immense.

'The Sherlock Holmes team became a family and Jeremy led it splendidly. I remember he used to carry a little Instamatic camera in the pocket of his costume. Unnoticed he would snap away at actors and crew. Then, a few days later, nothing said, a photograph would appear pinned up around the back of the set. Done with humour and affection, it was a great way of bringing everyone together. Very simple, and very clever. The crew and casts loved him and would do anything for him.

'Jeremy often said that there were few larger-than-life personalities around these days. Jeremy gave the lie to that. He was certainly larger than life, and could be a true eccentric.

'He developed a Jeremy uniform – white cotton trousers and navy or dark green sweaters – always cashmere – and a scarf. Whether entertaining cast and crew, which he frequently did, to dinner at Coco's, a wonderful Italian restaurant in Manchester, or champagne for everyone in the cocktail lounge of the Britannia Hotel or the Midland, he was in the same outfit. It took me a long time to work out why anyone so flamboyant as he was seemed to be so restricted in his dress. Then it suddenly dawned on me. A needless complication had been removed from his life. Whatever the occasion, no one ever expected to see Jeremy in any other clothes – brilliant.

'This did have its funny side, however.

'One morning, as I approached the entrance to the Granada

studios, Jeremy arrived in a cab. As he leant forward on the pavement to pay the driver, the waistband of his well-worn, much-laundered white trousers parted company with the legs which fell in a heap on the kerb. Giggling, Jeremy pulled them back up and struggled to the safety of the wardrobe, where his laughter could be heard as far away as Liverpool. His laugh was always infectious. When I think of Jeremy, I think of his laughing . . . that will always be my lasting memory of him. I cannot pay him a greater compliment.

'Among the many, many letters of tribute that have arrived from all over the world, one in particular from America appealed to me. It starts with a wonderful tribute to Jeremy's performance as Holmes and then says: "Do you believe in an afterlife? I do and I'll bet that wherever Jeremy is right now he is buying everyone champagne."

'I don't know the exact quote, but someone once said: "No one is truly gone as long as they are remembered." My dear late friend will be remembered and greatly missed. Here's to you, Jeremy!'

Jeremy Brett always liked to have the last word, and it is fitting that he should have the last word at the end of his life story.

Several months after the memorial service, attended by celebrities such as Patricia Hodge and Alistair Cooke, the Northern Musgroves Sherlock Holmes Society, headed by co-presidents David Stuart Davies and Kathryn White, met for a luncheon at the Café Royal to celebrate Jeremy's life.

David introduced the proceedings by playing a tape recording of a telephone inteview with Jeremy a few months before his death. It was a haunting, moving talk with an actor who at that time was deeply missing people and his work. He was having trouble with his breathing but still managed to roar with his own brand of throaty, infectious laughter. His own words, perhaps, sum up the life of the man who became Sherlock Holmes.

David spoke of Conan Doyle, who was born in Edinburgh, and the statue of Sherlock Holmes the city had recently erected in his memory.

'If you have a chance go and see it,' said Jeremy. 'I was asked to pose for it and the reason I chose not to was because of the position he was in. He was looking down – very depressed, mourning as it were for Conan Doyle. I said: "Oh no, I can't. This isn't SH. I don't see *him* like that. I see *him* looking up, blazing-eyed, body tense, on the balls of his feet, pointing at some fascinating place across the street; at the castle or somewhere. *He*'s alive! You don't want a statue that is going to depress people. You want something uplifting, and also when you are leaning forward the drips and the rain run down your nose, they run off your cap and the birds shit on your shoulders. I regret it now to a degree because I've finished the series. But nevertheless that's the reason. It wasn't what I saw SH as. I whispered all this to Dame Jean Conan Doyle and she said: "Oh, of course, it should have been a statue of my father in any case." I believe she was right. Well at least it's there, that's something.'

'Our members will be concerned to know how you are feeling, Jeremy,' said David.

'Well, the ticker is a little weary but what a way to go with Sherlock. I had a crack at him. I did please some and I didn't please others and that must be remembered. There's another Sherlock coming along at any minute, like a young, lively Douglas Wilmer. I've never seen him – I've never had a chance to see all my own performances. Let's wait for this next generation with a likely lad.'

'If you could wave the wand and do one more story?'

'Oh, I would do *The Hound of the Baskervilles* again. I think we can do much better than we did.'

'We wish you well, Jeremy, for the future.'

'Bless you. Don't worry about me, I'm fine. I'll dance round the next corner as a leprechaun, you'll see.'

'And God bless you for our Sherlock Holmes.'

'Bless your darling hearts. Much love, keep warm and dry and if you see *him* whisking round the corner – you know who, SH – then wave, because that's all you'll see of him. Bless his darling heart, isn't he wonderful, streets ahead of us – still.'

If God has a theatre in heaven, Jeremy Brett will have auditioned by now.

Index